# Inside ADW and IEF

## The Promise and Reality of CASE

John A. Stone

McGraw-Hill, Inc.

New York St. Louis San Francisco Auckland
Blue Ridge Summit, Pa. Bogotá Caracas
Hamburg Lisbon London Madrid Mexico
Milan Montreal New Delhi Paris San Juan
São Paulo Singapore Sydney Tokyo Toronto

FIRST EDITION
FIRST PRINTING



Information contained in this work has been obtained by McGraw-Hill, Inc., from sources believed to be reliable. However, neither McGraw-Hill nor its authors guarantees the accuracy or completeness of any information published herein and neither McGraw-Hill nor its authors shall be responsible for any errors, omissions, or damages arising out of use of this information. This work is published with the understanding that McGraw-Hill and its authors are supplying information but are not attempting to render engineering or other professional services. If such services are required, the assistance of an appropriate professional should be sought.

**Library of Congress Cataloging-in-Publication Data**

Stone, John A.
Inside ADW and IEF : the promise and reality of CASE ./ John A
Stone.
p. cm.
Includes index.
ISBN 0-07-061716-3
1. Computer-aided software engineering. I. Title.
QA76.758.S76 1992
005.1-dc20 92-23354
CIP

For information about other McGraw-Hill materials, call 1-800-2-MCGRAW in the U.S. In other countries call your nearest McGraw-Hill office.

Acquisitions Editor: Jeanne Glasser
Editor: Sally Anne Glover
Direction of Production: Katherine G. Brown

# Contents

## Part 3 Strategies & Techniques for Success with CASE

*To My Parents,*
*Morton and Dorothy Stone.*

# Acknowledgments

During the three years that it took to write this book, I was greatly assisted by many people, and I want to take this opportunity to thank them. John Sifonis, my business partner in Siberg Associates, deserves special thanks for his ideas, experiences, suggestions, and encouragement, as does my other partner, Beverly Goldberg. Thanks to Jeanne Glasser and her staff at McGraw-Hill, and to Roger Pressman for their ideas and suggestions. Thanks also to Paul Patton and Marcia Sherwin of KnowledgeWare, and to John Grant and Jane Bixler of Texas Instruments for product information and illustrations. Thanks to Roni Pessin for her reviews and editorial comments, to Tom Gunn and Mike Shields for their encouragement, and to Don Saulic, Mary Weddig, Diane Orndorff and Tom Bogan at Budget Rent a Car for doing it right.

Finally, special thanks to my parents for their encouragement, and to Alice Nakhimovsky, my sister. Without her ideas, advice, and editorial comments, this book would not have come into existence. And most of all, thanks to Barbara Schaefer, my wife, for her advice, editing, encouragement, patience, and perseverance that went way beyond what any husband has a right to expect, and without which I would not have been able to complete this project.

# Acknowledgements

# Foreword

Over the last four decades, no phenomena has been as consistently significant as the evolution and diffusion of information technology (IT). As a result of the pervasive spread of IT, a totally new set of managerial challenges has been identified. Both managers of the IT function and general managers of the enterprise have been involved in the creation of new departments, massive recruiting of staff, major investments in hardware and software, and the installation of systems that have profoundly affected both how the firm operates and how it competes. Facing these challenges is further complicated by the frequent change in what's considered acceptable management practice. Virtually all the major, currently accepted frameworks for managing in this field have been developed since 1981, although many existing applications were developed before that time. This special burden of meeting day-to-day operating challenges while assimilating new technology and practice is most evident in planning, application development, and application maintenance. Applications, "where the rubber meets the road" for IT functions and organizations, have proven to be the key focal point for successful investment in this area.

No other set of tools or management practices have affected or will affect applications more than the introduction of CASE (Computer Assisted Software Engineering) tools. Mastery of the concepts, insights, and techniques contained in this pragmatic book is imperative for successful exploitation of IT resources in large firms. I can think of no greater point of leverage for today's manager.

John Stone's substantial experience with large, complex projects is evident in this insightful and practical book. He identifies the land mines and helps you avoid them!

James I. Cash
Professor of Business Administration
Harvard University
Graduate School of Business Administration

# Foreword

# Introduction

ADW and IEF are CASE technologies that are capable of revolutionizing the way large-scale information systems are planned, developed, and maintained. These technologies can also provide substantial and much-needed gains in productivity and quality. But, ADW and IEF are misunderstood, mismanaged, and misused to the extent that it can be difficult to find companies that have reaped the substantial benefits these products can provide. For those seeking to harness CASE's benefits for their organizations, and for those who have tried CASE and need to understand what went wrong, the multitude of publications, rumors, anecdotes, and finely crafted marketing hype are of little help.

My objectives in writing the book were therefore to:

- Provide a realistic perspective on ADW- and IEF-based CASE, clearly articulating what it does and how it works.
- Identify and explore the critical success factors (CSFs) that are required to derive substantial benefit from CASE.
- Treat the subject from a hard-nosed, business point of veiw, emphasizing the investments, prombles,changes, and risks associated with CASE.
- Give practical advice on how to successfully implement and use CASE in a real, corporate environment.

To help readers get the most out of this book, I have organized it into three parts—each addressing ADW- and IEF-based CASE from a different perspective. Part 1 identifies and explores the CSFs that must be achieved to derive substantial benefit from ADW and IEF. The chapters in this section deal with the myriad of business, cultural, and technical problems and issues that must be overcome to achieve each CSF. Part 2 addresses what ADW- and IEF-based CASE does and how it works when applied to the planning, analysis, design, and construction of information systems. As ADW and IEF represent *integrated* CASE, I also address the ways in which CASE-based planning, analysis, design, and construction interact, and the significance and risks associated with each interaction. The final part presents strategies and techniques for introducing, managing, and effectively using CASE.

This book is primarily for information technology professionals—programmers and analysts through top management, and for support personnel such as data administrators, database administrators, and system architects. As CASE-based development projects often involve substantial user participation, business users might be interested in the book, depending on their level of frustration and fascination with information technologies. Corporate management might also be interested in this book because of the strategic importance that information plays in today's fast-moving, global economic environment, and because of the possibilities and risks associated with using CASE to garner competitive advantage.

The issues, suggestions, and ideas expressed in this book are the product of my experiences, good and bad, with these technologies. Although there are many ways to use ADW and IEF, I have based much of this book's content on an information-engineering, integrated CASE approach, which, in my experience, uses these CASE tools most effectively and provides maximum benefit. I have tried to present a realistic, balanced view of information-engineering-based integrated CASE using ADW and IEF, a view that's neither optimistic nor pessimistic, a view that includes the major issues and problems that, in my experience, users of these tools are likely to encounter. I also include strategies and solutions for dealing with problems.

Part

# 1

# Critical Success Factors for CASE

# Chapter 1

# Information Systems Development

Carol was pleased, really pleased. Her team had completed seventy-four programs in the past month, twenty-six last week, and the final six just yesterday. Not only was the first, and most crucial, part of the new customer information system complete, but in just one day, her team had regenerated the completed system into all three hardware environments, with three different databases and two different languages. And each one worked! Carol had been a doubter, fighting tooth and nail the introduction of CASE on her important project, but now there was no question about it. Once her team finally got it, CASE really boosted their productivity, way beyond her expectations. She had run the numbers for the third time, checked them with each of her team leaders, and for the third time they delivered the same unmistakable message: the entire project, which had been running up to eighteen months behind schedule, would be delivered three months early, and $250,000 under budget!

Carol cast her mind back to the beginning of the project—the wholly inadequate training, the terrible fights with Data Administration over methodology and modeling, the analysis that everyone thought would never end, and the users who stormed out of the model confirmation meeting, refusing to participate in the development of their own system. Thankfully, that was all behind her now. The crucial customer information system would be a success, and she could certainly expect a good bonus, possibly a promotion as well. Though it was only 2:00 in the afternoon and there were lots of things to take care of, Carol gently closed the door to her office, sat down behind her well-organized desk, and leaned back in her chair to gloat.

It was just after 2:00 p.m. when Bill, Carol's supervisor, got the call. There could only be one reason why Bill's boss and his boss's boss, the C.I.O., who Bill saw only four times a year, would both need to see him. Bill wasn't surprised; in fact, he had been expecting it for some time. The customer information system, the project that he and Carol had chosen to spotlight CASE, was a complete failure, and the failure was his! As he struggled to his feet, Bill wondered how much time they would give him. These were recessionary times, and it would be difficult to replace his position as Director or his $125,000 salary.

Bill's thoughts once again turned to his failed project. There was no question about it, the Director of Data Administration got him: CASE had no future at this company and neither did Bill. Maybe he shouldn't have supported Carol in her fight with Michael, Bill's peer and head of Data Administration, over what she had come to call "Michael's manual methodology." Maybe he should have doubled the CASE tool vendor's estimates. Maybe he should never have thought of CASE in the first place!

Michael was glad it was over; this "CASE" business was a close call and might have cost him his job! Ten years of personally nurturing his structured development methodology and his data administration organization, indeed his data modeling expertise, could have come to a total waste. But the customer information system project's interminable analysis and disenfranchised users were his lucky breaks. It was good that he was able to collar the project's skeptical business sponsor and sit down with his boss off- line, to . . .

Carol, Bill, and Michael, our unfortunate information system professionals, are fictional, as are their users and their CASE-based customer information system project. Their situations, however, are all too real and are played out over and over in our leading companies as they struggle with acquiring and learning to use CASE. The objectives of this book are to analyze what CASE does, examine what goes wrong, and provide a set of practical strategies and techniques for achieving the full potential of CASE so that these kinds of ludicrous situations can be avoided.

## The Current State of Information Systems Development

In spite of the uncertainty and chaos that often accompany the introduction of CASE, the origins of corporate interest in CASE are understandable. Most companies engaged in large-scale information systems development find the process far too expensive, time-consuming and uncertain. Faced with continuous and increasing pressure to produce systems on time and within budget, application development projects often deliver systems with only a fraction of their needed functionality. The "delivered" systems are then brought into conformity with their users' needs. In many cases, extensive rewriting takes place over a period of months—even years—without management even being aware of it.[1]

The systems themselves have trouble keeping up as the enterprises they serve change to meet the new demands of an increasingly dynamic business environment. The result is a continuous series of costly retrofits, which information systems people call "maintenance." The cost of maintaining systems, when examined from a budgetary perspective, is often large compared to the cost of developing new systems that support the company in new and innovative ways. Companies typically spend between 70% and 80% of their total software dollars on maintenance.[2]

But the problems don't end here. Even when fully delivered and retrofitted, systems still often fail to do everything that the enterprise they serve really needs. Systems don't always take into account the goals and strategies of the business, the environment in which the system must operate, and how these factors are likely to change over time.[3]

Most key business functions, such as finance, marketing, manufacturing, and distribution, aim toward a significant and positive impact on the success of the business. Information system functions, however, are rarely that contribution oriented. Often accounted for as a service organization and cost center, information system functions tend to follow whatever the enterprise happens to be doing. This is odd, and unfortunate, because information systems technology is developing at a faster rate than almost any other corporate recourse,[4] and businesses that can't leverage these developments for competitive advantage run the risk of losing out to competitors who can.[5]

Compounding these problems is the fact that communication between information systems and business professionals is often poor, and in some cases, close to nonexistent. Systems people have trouble understanding their enterprise, what it needs, the underlying business reasons behind its needs, and how those needs can best be served. Businesspeople have trouble understanding information systems technologies and their potential in terms of a

---

[1]R. Jones, "Time To Change The Culture Of Information System Departments." *Information And Software Technology*, March 1989, Volume 31.

[2]Roger Pressman, *Software Engineering: A Practitioner's Approach*, Third Edition, McGraw-Hill, 1992, Sections 1-4. See also Jerry Huchzermeyer, "What Can We Expect From Re-Engineering," *CEC Rapid Exchange*, Winter, 1991.

[3]Chris F. Kamerer, Glenn L. Sosa, "Systems Development Risks In Strategic Information Systems" Massachusetts Institute Of Technology CISR Working Paper No. 206, May 1990.

[4]"CIOs Not Up To Snuff As Active Business Leaders," *Computerworld*, March 16, 1992.

[5]Michael E. Porter, and Victor E. Millar, "Michael Porter On Competition And Strategy," *Harvard Business Review* paperback No. 90079, 1991, Pages 33-44.

business resource that can be used to help the enterprise achieve its objectives. Even after specific systems have been defined and funded, businesspeople have trouble visualizing what the systems will look like or how they will work until after they have been developed, delivered, and put into production.

## Information Systems and CASE

There is considerable potential for computer aided software engineering (CASE) to help develop information systems that are higher quality, more relevant, and less expensive. This potential is also achievable. Code generators and fourth-generation languages can boost productivity by allowing programmers to enter and debug code at a higher level than previously possible.

CASE-based analysis and logical modeling can help analysts learn what their users really need, along with the reasons behind their needs. The organization that these models bring can help make systems more flexible and less expensive to maintain. Enterprise data and activity modeling can provide a viable framework for integrating systems and managing the enterprise's information asset. Prototyping can help users and information systems personnel develop a common understanding of what the system will look like and how it will work. Finally, CASE-based strategic planning can help ensure that business and information systems goals and objectives are in alignment, and that the business plan is adequately supported by the company's information systems.

There are many instances in which CASE has helped a business to realize each of these potentials. Yet, when applied generally to a broad range of companies and their large-scale information systems, CASE has not been universally successful. The productivity gains promised by CASE sometimes turn out to be nonexistent. Many systems get mired in analysis and never even make it to implementation. Those systems that do make it to the implementation stage sometimes end up taking more time and more resources to develop than their conventionally developed counterparts.[6]

The disappointment accompanying the deployment of CASE is often grounded in genuine cultural and managerial difficulties. Indeed, many CASE-based methodologies turn out to be counterintuitive. CASE-based methodologies, and the CASE tools that support them, do things in a new and different way. They produce diagrams that are difficult to interpret, and the projects on which CASE is used sometimes produce unexpected signals that user and information systems management are at a loss to interpret. The unfortunate result is that CASE is all too often accompanied by a combination of confusion and mayhem not unlike that experienced by Carol, Bill, and Michael.

---

[6]Robert Moran, "The Case Against CASE," *Information Week*, February 17, 1992.

Why should this be? Why should the industry, which so successfully developed CAD/CAM for the design and manufacture of everything from cars to clothing, have so much trouble applying similar technologies to its own design and manufacturing processes? How can we fix these problems? How can we make CASE work? Before we can seek meaningful answers to these questions, we must first have a common understanding and definition of CASE.

## What Is CASE?

There has been a lot of confusion about the definition of CASE. Much of this confusion has been due to the many different kinds of application development tools, techniques, methodologies, and repositories currently in use, and the speed with which the CASE market and the products that serve it are developing. There is currently a vast and bewildering array of tools, methodologies, and techniques that might include CASE. (See Fig. 1.1.)

What purports to be CASE is evolving at a dizzying pace, and because CASE addresses such a wide spectrum of application development in so many different ways, any definition of CASE must be, to an extent, both temporal and arbitrary. The confusion, however, is real, and if this book is to be useful to those who want to reap real benefits from CASE, the problem of developing a workable definition for CASE must be addressed.

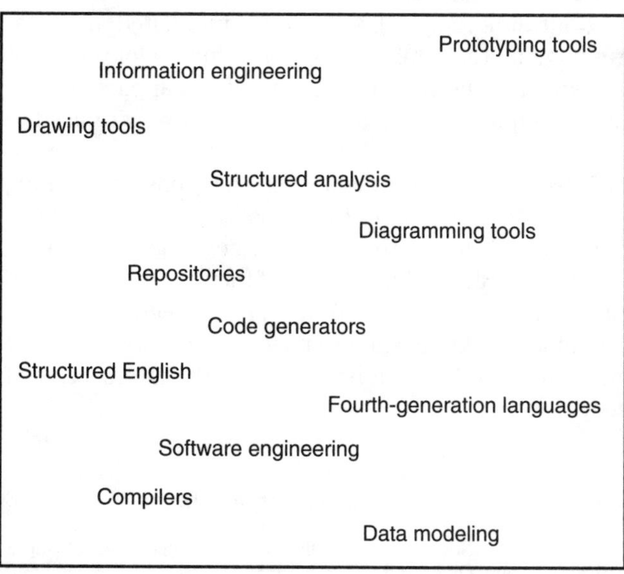


**Fig. 1.1** Tools, methodologies, and techniques that might be CASE.

## A definition of CASE

We can begin to cut through the confusion by defining CASE to include tools, techniques, and methodologies that add significant value by increasing the productivity of the application development process and increasing the quality of the resulting applications. In terms of application development, this definition of CASE covers the entire spectrum of forward and reverse engineering of computer applications, from planning through maintenance. In terms of tools, techniques, and methodologies, the definition becomes somewhat narrower. It excludes drawing, diagramming, and prototyping tools, for example, since they don't contribute directly to application development productivity, although they can enhance the quality of the applications that they're used to develop. Fourth-generation languages (4GLs), code generators, and compilers don't qualify either, since they contribute to productivity but not necessarily to quality. A high-level version of COBOL, for example, may well increase productivity over standard COBOL by decreasing the number of instructions that programmers have to write. But the high-level version of COBOL will not increase the quality of the applications that it is used to build unless it is integrated with analysis tools and techniques, through which quality can be addressed.[7]

Our definition of CASE, although certainly better than no definition, is still too broad to be really useful, since most of the products in the vast array of CASE candidates would still fit. For example, data modeling, in the form of entity relationship diagrams drawn by hand on huge sheets of brown paper, would still quality as CASE, even though nothing about their production or use could be considered "computer aided." We can solve this problem by narrowing our definition of CASE to be: automated and integrated software development tools, techniques, and methodologies that add significant value by increasing the productivity of the application development process and the quality of the applications that they're used to develop.

In terms of this definition, our hand-drawn entity relationship diagram, like our high-level COBOL compiler, would not qualify as CASE. Indeed, neither would any of the other fragmented tools, methodologies, and techniques listed in our array of CASE candidates. But, if they're automated, using workstations along with servers or mainframes, and integrated so that the products of one become checks on, and inputs for, the others, then they would be CASE. Thus defined, CASE can be viewed as the intersection of three component technologies:

---

[7]If the level of a language were sufficient to qualify it as CASE, then the definition of CASE would be arbitrary indeed. After how many extensions, for example, would a COBOL compiler become a CASE tool? Might a standard ANSI COBOL compiler be CASE, since it accepts input at a much higher level than, and certainly boosts productivity over, an assembler? What about an assembler?

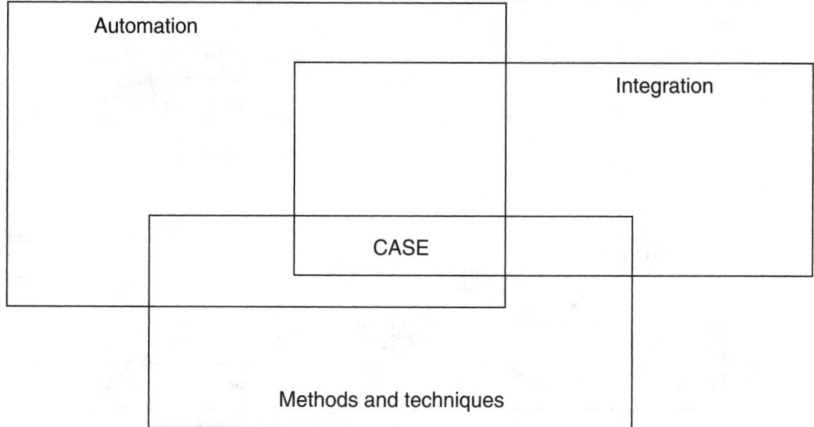


**Fig. 1.2** CASE can be defined as the intersection of automation, integration, methods, and techniques.

- Software engineering techniques and methodologies that add productivity to the application development process and quality to applications.
- Automation of the software engineering methodologies and techniques, in the form of computer-based tools.
- Integration, in the form of common repositories containing information that can be created, read, and used by the tools and techniques. (See Fig. 1.2.)

There are many tools, techniques, and methodologies in use today that qualify as CASE under our definition, and many more will almost certainly appear in the future. To make this book as useful as possible to CASE practitioners, as well as to those who may become CASE practitioners, we will examine CASE primarily in terms of two CASE tools that are both current and ubiquitous: KnowledgeWare's ADW and Texas Instruments' IEF.

### The evolution of CASE

Although CASE represents a new way of approaching software development, the ideas and technologies that comprise CASE are the product of a logical progression spanning four decades. CASE has evolved from software development that was something close to an art form that was poorly understood and was not approached with consistent methods and techniques. Today, software development is becoming an engineering discipline, and in that context, the advent of CASE makes sense. (See Fig. 1.3.)

As the software development process became better understood, structured programming, and eventually, analysis techniques for increasing consistency and quality began to emerge. The advent of the micro-

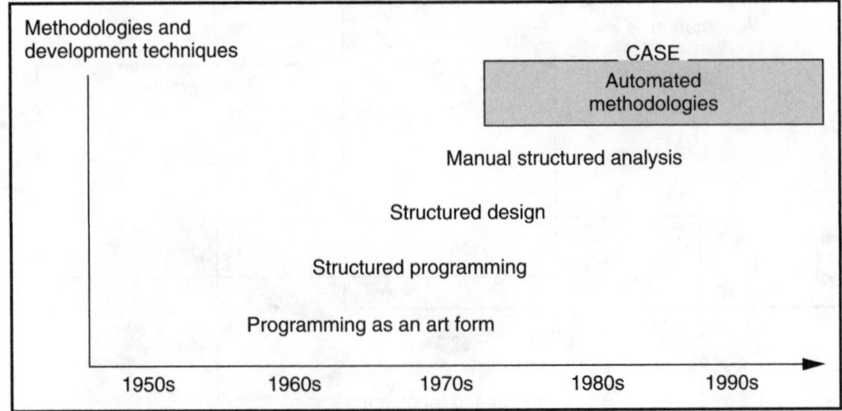


**Fig. 1.3** The evolution of CASE methodologies and techniques.

processor, CAD/CAM, and communications technologies paved the way for CASE tools and techniques. Today, integrated CASE tools, such as ADW and IEF, along with the methodologies and techniques that they support, are beginning to incorporate other emerging technologies such as artificial intelligence, object-oriented design, reverse engineering, and common repositories. (See Fig. 1.4.)

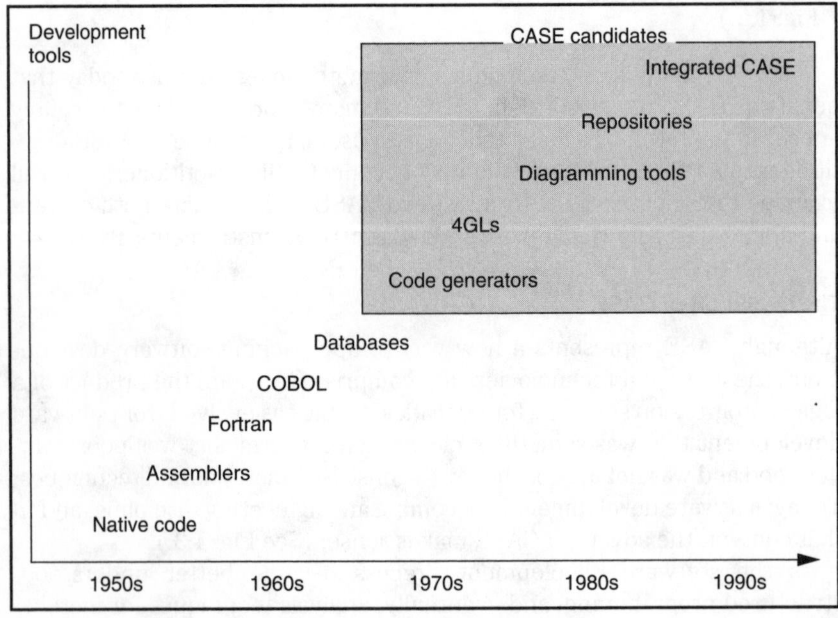


**Fig. 1.4** The evolution of information system development tools.

| Critical Factors For CASE |
|---|
| ■ The right CASE tools |
| ■ A CASE-based methodology |
| ■ A CASE-compatible culture |
| ■ Appropriate, properly applied human resources |
| ■ Appropriate expectations |

**Fig. 1.5** Critical success factors for CASE.

## Critical Success Factors for CASE

Successful application of CASE to large-scale information systems development requires a good deal more than the purchase and deployment of CASE tools such as ADW and IEF, or the implementation of a CASE-based methodology. Adopting CASE for information systems development, even when successful, can be a wrenching experience for a company to go through. It can cause disruptive changes in human resources, management, and culture. These changes may be greater than those that accompanied the evolution from assemblers to high-level languages, or flat files to databases.

The ability to overcome these obstacles can be expressed in terms of critical success factors ("CSFs").[8] There are five definable CSFs that must be in place and properly managed before an enterprise can derive significant benefits from CASE. (See Fig. 1.5.)

The five CSFs might seem straightforward and easy to manage. But, they're not. The CSFs for CASE can be surprisingly subtle and complex, and their achievement can be elusive, even for seasoned managers. Although the achievement of each CSF is the subject of its own chapter in this book, taking a closer look at the CSFs, along with some of the consequences that you can expect if they're not achieved, can provide additional insight into what they are and the importance of their achievement.

### The right CASE tools

Today's CASE tools represent a diverse array of products that all, in some way, address information systems development. Reaping quality and productivity benefits from CASE tools depends on selecting tools that:

- Can function in the intended target technology environment.
- Are a reasonable fit for the organization's information systems and culture.

---

[8] For an in-depth discussion of the application of CSFs, see Nancy S. Foster, and John F. Rockart, "Critical Success Factors: An Annotated Bibliography" Massachusetts Institute Of Technology CISR Working Paper No. 191, June 1989.

- Are fully compatible with the intended systems development methodology.
- Are compatible with each other.

Selecting CASE tools that are a good fit for the kind of systems that you plan to build requires looking at candidate tools from project as well as functional perspectives.

One company, when embarking on an order processing system development project, took great pains to find the right CASE tool for design and construction. The tool they selected was a good fit for each of their requirements. It supported very fast applications development for their Unix database and client/server architecture. This was a prime consideration. The tool also elegantly addressed approximately 85% of their order processing functional requirements, and it came with a C interface for the rest.

The CASE tool worked well, and most of the system was completed within four months. They then got down to coding the remaining portion of the system in C. Eighteen months later, the order processing system had not yet processed its first order. The development team was, in fact, still busily debugging their C code.

What happened? Although the CASE tool was a near perfect fit for over 80% of their required functionality, when viewed from a development project resource perspective, it was useful in building only about 20% of the system. The particular functions that were not addressable with the tool included many of the most difficult functions for programs to write.

The point is that when selecting CASE tools, candidate tools must be evaluated from both functional and project perspectives. When selecting a CASE tool, everyone from the CASE salesperson to the selection committee will be eager to justify their recommendation on the basis of all the things the tools will do. It's far more important to understand the CASE tool's limitations, the boundaries of where and how it's likely to be useful. If you know what the tool will not do for you, from project as well as functional perspectives, you'll be in a good position to assess the true benefits that you're likely to experience.

Compatibility between CASE tools, even when purchased from the same vendor, can be just as problematic. Using the best CASE tool for planning, the best CASE tool for analysis, and the best CASE tool for coding your system, will not always yield the best results. The CASE payoff in quality and productivity will not be realized unless the CASE tools employed throughout the application development life cycle are highly compatible and integrated with each other.

One company, upon embarking on developing a very complex set of information systems, chose what was arguably the best analysis tool along with the best code generator for their purposes. The analysis tool was both detailed and rigorous. It produced a fully normalized and attributed entity relationship data model. Its leaf-level processes contained procedural pseudocode that the tool ensured was fully consistent with its data model. They felt that the extra time and effort required to produce the tool's detailed and rigorous analysis work products was justified because it would mean less rework during code generation and testing. The code generator they selected was widely used and produced consistently good results. Code generator users who were contacted as references were uniformly pleased. The generator was also fully compatible with their DB2, COBOL and IMS/DC environment. Of all the code generators considered, the one they chose was also the most suitable for producing the kinds of business-oriented applications that they had to produce. Compatibility between their code generator and application requirements was virtually assured.

Far less assured was compatibility between their code generator and the work products created by their analysis tool. In fact, they weren't compatible at all. While the analysis CASE tool produced procedural pseudocode, expressed very precisely in terms of their fully normalized logical data model, the code generator required nonprocedural input based on physical DB2 tables.

The code-generator-trained design and construction teams were therefore faced with double translations. They had to translate fully normalized entity types into denormalized DB2 tables, and at the same time, translate procedural process logic to nonprocedural input for the code generator. One by one, the development teams went back to their bewildered users to reproduce the analysis in a form they could deal with. All of their CASE-based analysis, along with the projected gains during code generation and testing, were lost.

Choosing the best CASE tools is certainly a good idea. But if the tools are not integrated with, or at least compatible with, one another, then many of the potential gains resulting from their use can be lost.

### A CASE-Based Methodology

Methodologies for developing information systems have been around for many years and are now generally accepted as part of our large-scale information systems development culture. There's hardly an information technology organization to be found that doesn't employ some sort of methodology for their large-scale systems development.

It's also generally accepted, and true, that CASE can't be successfully deployed without the guidance and discipline that are the most basic by-products of a methodology. The catch is that CASE places additional requirements on information systems development that many traditional methodologies can't support. This situation is aggravated by two things. The first is that while many of the development strategies and techniques built into today's CASE tools resemble those used in traditional structured analysis and design, they often turn out to be quite different. The second, and more insidious, is that many CASE vendors and consultants will not allow requirements for new development strategies and techniques to stand in the way of a sale. This combination can lead to chaotic situations as companies try to implement CASE.

Consider an organization, which after years of conventional systems development using the Warnier-Orr methodology, purchased a new CASE tool. Although the tool's basic design was consistent with the Information Engineering Planning-Analysis-Design-Construction paradigm, it was flexible in terms of methodology. After carefully verifying that the tool could support each of the diagrams and techniques required by Warnier-Orr, they launched their first systems development project using their new CASE tool along with their tried and proven methodology.

Following their methodology, they began analysis by defining the screens and reports that represented the system's "external design." To facilitate this, they chose the tool's screen and report painter. But the tool's screen and report painter, in keeping with Information Engineering, was tied very tightly to a relational database design. The relational design was, in turn, based on a fully attributed entity relationship model. As neither the entity relationship model or relational database design existed yet, the development team was unable to automatically paint their screens by clicking a mouse on previously defined columns or attributes. Instead, they had to paint each screen by hand, entering each field as if the screen painter was a word processor. After completing this initial but very labor-intensive task, they abandoned their CASE tool for the remainder of the project.

The problem illustrated here is not that the CASE tool or the methodology was bad or inadequate, but that if the methodology doesn't support the application development paradigm upon which the tool is based (in this case, Information Engineering) successful use of CASE will generally not be achievable.

### A CASE-compatible culture

Large-scale information systems development always takes place within the context of an enterprise's information systems, user, and management cultures. The adoption of CASE affects each of these corporate cultures to an even greater degree than CAD/CAM affected their manufacturing counterparts. For CASE to be successful, each of these cultures must be prepared to deal with information systems development in a new, and different way.

For information systems developers, the combination of doing a much more business-oriented analysis, specifying, and debugging programs at an alarmingly high level, throwing away the source code, and fearing the loss of their jobs can turn exposure to CASE into a trying experience. CASE-based analysis puts premiums on competencies in business, interpersonal skills, and communication. New skills such as logical data modeling, which may have previously been handled by Data Administration, must be acquired by application development project teams. To remain viable, Data Administration, and in some cases Database Administration, may have to take on new roles, such as model coordination and logical-to-physical translation.

Information systems management must learn to interpret new and sometimes confusing signals from their development projects. Completion of analysis way ahead of schedule, for example, used to be a good sign, something an information systems manager could be proud of. On a CASE-based development project, the same speedy analysis can be a warning sign that significant delays should be anticipated during design and construction.

Business users on CASE-based development projects are apt to find themselves immersed in information systems analysis and development to an unforeseen (and often unwanted) extent. And, as if to add insult to injury, CASE-based analysis often surfaces knotty business issues that the project's users are not prepared or empowered to resolve.

This is exactly what happened when a multinational holding company employed CASE in the analysis phase of their new consolidation and accounting system development project. Their old system rolled up affiliate data based on two hierarchies: Division-Within-Country, and Country-Within-Division. The totals of each hierarchy were checked against one another to ensure that all data were properly collected and correct.

The CASE-based analysis showed that the data in the two hierarchies, although represented differently, were exactly the same. The data resided in the same entity type, and were updated at exactly the same time from the same source. The costly interhierarchy proofing procedures could therefore be eliminated with no loss in integrity. The project's accounting users understood and agreed. They liked the concept and were enthusiastic about the savings that it would yield.

But this kind of insight was not anticipated, and no mechanism existed for gaining the user consensus necessary to do away with the costly proof. The accounting users who participated in the analysis were not responsible for doing the consolidations, and therefore couldn't make the decision. The user department, which was responsible for performing the consolidations, was under a new and cautious management. They had not yet gone through their first consolidation, and they didn't want to rock the boat. The recommended change was not adopted, and the costly but unnecessary proofing procedures were built into their new system.

This anecdote underscores the impact that CASE can have on a user culture that doesn't understand the CASE paradigm for application development, and is therefore not prepared to deal with its by-products. Similarly severe impacts await application development and management cultures that have not been adequately prepared for CASE.

## Appropriate, Properly Applied Human Resources

Even with each of the other CSFs fully achieved, plunging ahead with a CASE-based information systems project that is not properly staffed almost always leads to disaster. Knowledge and experience with CASE tools and methodologies are certainly prerequisites for successful CASE-based systems development. Less obvious, but equally important, is the emphasis that CASE places on competencies such as business knowledge, interpersonal communication, consensus building, and negotiating.

Staffing CASE-based projects with knowledgeable and experienced resources is compounded by two additional problems. The first is that the information systems professionals who populate most systems development organizations tend not to be rich in interpersonal competencies. The second complicating factor is that successful CASE-based development requires these competencies not only in information systems professionals, but in users who participate in CASE-based systems development as well.

Achieving high productivity from 4GLs, for example, requires that the system be designed for high use of the 4GLs' capabilities. To do this, compromises between required functionality and 4GL productivity will have to be continually made all through analysis and design. User and information systems compromises and trade-offs between productivity, projected maintenance costs, screens, menu structure, and user dialogue can't be made unless everyone involved approaches the development project with the skills and competencies previously described. These problems are solvable, provided that they're understood, and that CASE-based development projects take them into account.

### Appropriate expectations

Success with CASE can certainly be measured in terms of changes in system quality and productivity. Both are quantifiable and measurable, as will be shown later in this book. The bad news is that the results of quality and productivity measurements, however impressive and accurate, will always be evaluated against a framework of information systems, user, and management expectations.

It's therefore possible to make a successful and profitable transition to CASE at the project level, only to find that the same success, as perceived by information technology, corporate, or user management, looks a lot like a disaster. It's equally possible, even common, for a CASE-based project to revert back to traditional development half way through, or to be killed outright, simply because the project wasn't progressing as expected. When weighed against the repercussions of a large-scale information systems development project going bad (or even looking like it might be going bad), the promise of higher quality and more productive systems development doesn't always hold up.

Failures to achieve expectations result primarily from information systems, corporate management, and users looking for the return from CASE without an understanding of the investment. CASE can provide quicker, higher-quality and lower-cost systems development. But as with CAD/CAM in manufacturing, the benefits of CASE can be realized only after sufficient time, money, and effort have been invested.

Unachievable expectations for CASE are understandable. They're fueled by a combination of:

- The information systems function being viewed primarily as a cost center, rather than a strategic resource.
- The trend for information systems costs to continue to rise while other corporate costs go down.
- The natural perception that automating anything makes it quicker and cheaper.
- CASE tool, methodology, and consulting vendors who look to cost reductions as a handy and immediate justification for sales.

CASE works. But for CASE to be a success in a real-world corporate environment, the expectations of information technology management, users, corporate management, and project personnel must be both realistic, and properly managed.

### Dependencies among the CSFs

The five CSFs for CASE can't be managed or achieved in isolation. They're highly dependent on one another, as well as on their corporate and information systems environment. Different methodologies, for example, look upon business functions and data from different frames of reference. An information system plan executed under a methodology that emphasizes functions and their alignment to organizational objectives, for example, may not provide a suitable platform for doing analysis under an information-engineering-based methodology that emphasizes data and functions equally.

CASE tools used in different stages of the applications development cycle are also highly interdependent in terms of data and how the data are interpreted by each. Even ADW and IEF, which both support information engineering methodologies, don't do so in the same way.

CASE tools are often designed with specific target hardware and software technologies in mind. Sometimes the dependency is obvious and strong, as with the Synon code generator, and the IBM AS/400. However,

| Critical success factor | Dependencies |
|---|---|
| Methodology | CASE tools<br>Corporate culture<br>System scope and complexity<br>Type of system |
| CASE Tools | Target hardware & software<br>Methodology<br>User flexibility<br>System scope and complexity<br>Type of system |
| Cultural Changes | Methodology<br>CASE tools |
| Human Resources | Methodology<br>CASE tools |
| Expectations | Methodology<br>CASE tools<br>Human resources |

**Fig. 1.6** Critical success factor dependencies.

hardware and software dependencies can be blurred, as CASE tools and methodology vendors struggle to support a continuous stream of new technology architecture environments. The types of systems being developed, along with their scopes and complexities, can also affect methodologies and CASE tool effectiveness.

The dependence between the cultural impact of CASE, including the development of appropriate human resources and the selection of CASE tools and methodologies, can be significant. Selection of a methodology that emphasizes prototyping, such as Information Engineering with RAD, may not be effective if the user culture interferes with getting directly involved with the development of applications. Corporate cultures that emphasize project control and management may do better with a methodology such as LBMS, which has strong project management components.

The ability to meet information systems, user, and management expectations are dependent on methodology, CASE tools, and the ability to develop appropriate human resources. (See Fig. 1.6.)

## Implementing the five CSFs

Achieving the five CSFs for CASE is not a quick and easy process. The magnitude of their impact on information technology and user organizations, when coupled with technical complexities and organizational inertia, make their implementation a slow and sometimes painful process.

CASE tools, along with the methodologies that they support, need to be carefully evaluated for current features and long-term direction. The abilities of information technology and user organizations to adapt to the use of CASE tools must also be taken into account. Dealing with rigor and detail early in the applications development cycle is a good idea. But it won't have much of an impact if user and information technology organizations have trouble dealing with the resultant models. Even after tools and methodologies have been purchased, training has been completed, and everyone has bought into the new process, additional time will be required before the subtleties of CASE are understood and CASE becomes really useful. For most large-scale systems development organizations, this can take up to six months for CASE tools, and a year or more for methodologies.

It's more problematic to estimate the time required for information technology, user, and management organizations to develop an understanding of what is and is not achievable with CASE. Years of traditional systems development, coupled with the hype of a new industry that's hungry for sales, can get in the way. In many companies, realistic expectations for CASE are internalized only after one or more CASE-based projects have been completed. This can take up to two years to achieve.

Developing a CASE-compatible system development culture and sufficient numbers of CASE-knowledgeable human resources can take more time than all of the other CSFs combined. The reason is that the achievement of each of these CSFs depends on moving substantial numbers of people through CASE-based system development projects that are both real and credible. For a large-scale systems development organization, the adoption of CASE can affect hundreds, even thousands, of employees. Two to four years for achievement of cultural and human resource CSFs is therefore not unrealistic.

Because information technology can vary greatly among large companies in terms of development, strategic importance, and use, the actual time required to achieve each CASE CSF can vary greatly from organization to organization. The magnitude of the time spans presented in Fig. 1.7 are representative of what can be expected in a typical large company that is implementing CASE.

| Critical success factor | Time required to implement |
|---|---|
| CASE Tools | 3 to 6 months |
| CASE-based Methodology | 6 to 18 months |
| Expectations | 12 to 24 months |
| Cultural changes | 24 to 48 months |
| Human resources | 24 to 48 months |

**Fig. 1.7** Time spans typically required to achieve each CSF in a Fortune 500 corporation.

| Critical success factor | Difficulty to manage |
|---|---|
| Cultural changes | High |
| Expectations | High |
| Human resources | Medium |
| Methodology | Medium |
| CASE tools | Low |

**Fig. 1.8** Degree of difficulty in managing each CSF.

## Managing the CSFs

Although each of the five CSFs must be in place for an organization to be successful with CASE, they're not all equally difficult to achieve. The biggest challenges are managing expectations and cultural changes in information technology, user, and corporate organizations. (See Fig. 1.8.) This is primarily due to the extent to which applications development can change with the introduction of CASE. Also, the people responsible for rolling out CASE may not have much influence over the different organizations.

The human resource CSF is challenging to manage primarily because it takes lots of time to fully achieve. In addition to orientation and training for all involved, people need to use CASE on real projects before they fully understand how it works. Also, as with the evolution of assembler to COBOL or flat files to databases, not everyone will be able to make the switch.

As we shall see, the five CSFs for CASE are achievable, provided that:

- The requirements and pitfalls associated with each CSF are fully understood.
- Each CSF is specifically managed, along with its information technology, user, and management implications.
- The five CSFs are concurrently managed so that their interdependencies can be taken into account.

Chapter

# 2

# CASE Tools

A sampling of CASE tool advertisements in a recent issue of *CASE Trends* magazine produced the following claims: "Our 75,000 users include all of the 10 top software publishers . . ." "Our revolutionary new CASE system was designed to help eliminate the chaos found in the world of software development." "The product everyone is talking about." "The better way to develop better applications." "The best CASE for your business."[1] The CASE market is hot, and the dizzying array of CASE tool claims and counterclaims can paint a confusing picture for sophisticated CASE users and prospective purchasers of CASE tool products. What exactly are CASE tools? How do they support application development? What trade-offs do different CASE tools represent, and how should CASE tools be purchased? Let's take a closer look.

## Definition of CASE Tools

CASE tools are a class of software products that help automate techniques for information systems development. CASE tools can support each phase of application development, from planning through maintenance. These tools also add value to the application development process through functions such as central repositories for integration and development coordination, highly leveraged languages, rigor, and consistency checks. Some CASE tools include artificial intelligence (AI)-based rules that enforce specific methodologies and techniques. CASE tools can be used on a PC

[1]*CASE Trends*, Volume 3 Number 8, November/December 1991.

workstation, network, or mainframe, with some tools spanning several of these platforms.

Although there are many worthwhile application development tools such as diagramming aids, presentation tools, library managers, estimating tools, data dictionaries and code generators, they're not all CASE tools. To qualify, under our definition of CASE, application development tools must not only add significant value by increasing the productivity of the application development process and the quality of the applications that they're used to develop, but they must also be automated and integrated. Workstation-based diagramming tools, for example, certainly facilitate the drawing of charts, graphs, and pictures, even data flow diagrams, screens and structure charts. But our integration requirement means that CASE tools must add their value through what they do with the information contained in the charts, graphs, and pictures, as well as through the graphics themselves. If an application development tool doesn't add value by processing, checking, or coordinating the information about the graphics its users draw, it may be a fine aid to application development, boosting both productivity and quality, but by our definition, it's not CASE. Application development tools, therefore, can't be considered CASE tools based solely on the hardware platforms they run on, the diagrams, charts and pictures they draw, or their graphical user interface (GUI).

## A Value-Based CASE Tool Taxonomy

There are probably as many ways to classify CASE tools as there are CASE tools themselves. Most books on CASE classify CASE tools by the functions they perform (e.g., planning tools, analysis tools, design tools, 4GLs, code generators, even diagramming tools and data dictionaries, depending on how broadly the author cares to define CASE).[2] This book will take a more focused and more value-based approach. To do this, we will confine our attention to integrated CASE tools such as ADW and IEF, which meet our narrow CASE definition and contribute directly to application development. We will also classify the tools not only by the roles they play in application development, but by their value—the level of integration they provide, the broadness of the techniques and methodologies they support, and the target technologies that they serve. This will help us gain insight into how CASE tools can affect the other CSFs and what the magnitude and breadth of CASE's potential benefits are.

---

[2]For a broader, function-based CASE tool taxonomy, see: Chris Gane, *Computer Aided Software Engineering,* Prentice Hall, 1990, and Roger Pressman, *Software Engineering A Practitioner's Approach,* McGraw-Hill, 1992, Chapter 22.

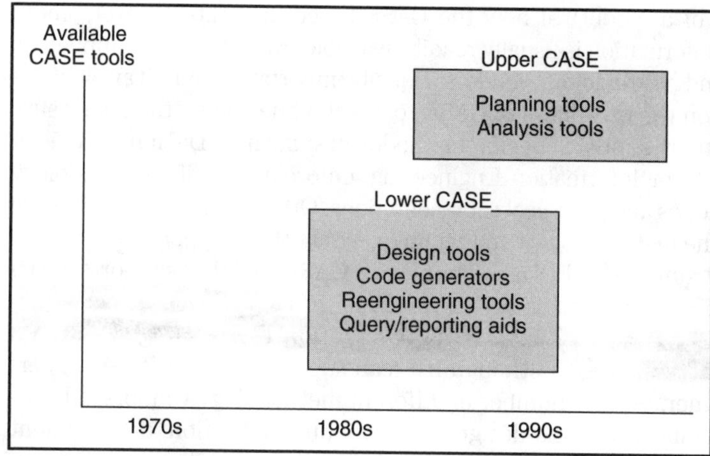


**Fig. 2.1** Lower and Upper CASE tools.

## Roles CASE tools play in application development

CASE tools can be useful during the entire application development cycle, from planning through maintenance. In terms of the roles they play in application development, CASE tools can be classed into one of two general categories known as Upper CASE and Lower CASE. Lower CASE tools were the first to reach the market. They produce physical designs and executable code for specific hardware, telecommunications, and system software technologies. Code generators, 4GLs, and inquiry and reporting systems fall into this category. Although Lower CASE tools produce working systems, sometimes very productively, they don't address the way the systems they produce fit together, how well they support the business areas they serve, or how they fit into the company as a whole.

Upper CASE tools address information systems planning and analysis by supporting business coordination and modeling techniques. They support analysis techniques such as matrix processing, decomposition diagramming, and data modeling that can be used to help ensure integration and business support. Although the models they produce can be very detailed and rigorous, and may even include elaborate prototyping, they don't produce working applications. In fact, Upper CASE business models tend to be "logical models" that are independent of designs and target technologies. (See Fig. 2.1.)

## Classifying CASE tools by techniques and methodologies

Almost all CASE tools support a set of methodologies and techniques that correspond to an internal view or model (sometimes called a "metamodel" since it's a model of a model) of how the CASE-based application development works. This information is usually readily available from literature supplied by CASE tool and methodology vendors. Equally important, but less available, is information on the broadness of CASE tool technique and methodology support. Some tools support specific methodologies such as DeMarco, Gane & Sarson, LBMS, or Information Engineering, enforcing specific methodology rules, techniques and graphical representations. Other tools are more flexible in terms of the methodologies and techniques that they support.

Texas Instruments' IEF is an example of a CASE tool that supports a narrow range of methodologies and techniques. In fact, IEF supports implementations of a single methodology, Information Engineering, through a single set of techniques.[3] Although IEF can support information engineering as implemented by a number of different methodology vendors, all support the planning-analysis-design-construction application development paradigm, all support the same information engineering diagramming and all support the same set of conventions and techniques. The IEF CASE tool takes its information engineering-based consistency checks so seriously that it will prevent its users from proceeding to the next phase of application development unless all IEF consistency check errors associated with the current phase are resolved.

KnowledgeWare's ADW supports similar information engineering methodology interpretations, along with other methodologies, through a moderate range of methodologies and techniques. Although ADW contains some 2,000–3,000 Prologue rules[4] that enforce many Information Engineering concepts, methodology inconsistencies don't prevent ADW users from moving on to the subsequent phases of applications development. ADW can also accept and produce graphical information according to a number of different user-defined conventions.

Excelerator is an example of a tool that is very methodology independent and supports a broad range of methodologies and techniques. Although it loosely tracks how information and diagrams relate to one another, it doesn't provide consistency checks that enforce adherence to specific methodologies or techniques. Popkin Software's System Architect, another good example of a CASE tool that supports a broad range of methodologies and techniques, allows its users to customize its metamodel to support user-defined methodology and technique requirements. (See Fig. 2.2.) As we shall see, differences in broadness of techniques and methodology support can affect not only the potential value of a CASE tool, but also the way the CASE tool affects the company.

---

[3]Dennis Minium, *A Guide To Information Engineering Using The IEF,* Texas Instruments 1990.

[4]Based on an interview with KnowledgeWare, there are some 2,000 to 3,000 Prologue rules in their entire product set.

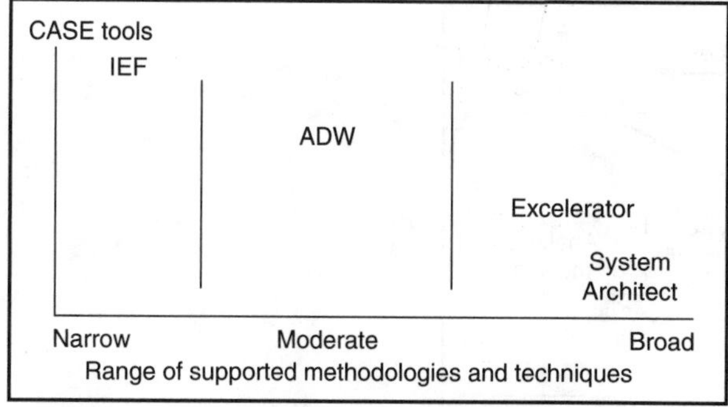


**Fig. 2.2** CASE tools can be classed according to the range of techniques and methodologies they support.

### Classifying CASE tools by integration

The degree of integration and coordination of CASE tool products and the models produced by each phase of CASE-based application development can vary considerably from tool to tool. Some CASE tools are so tightly integrated that changes to data or activity models developed during analysis, for example, will not only affect other analysis models, but design and construction models as well. Other tools are less particular about maintaining consistency among CASE-tool-developed products. To help understand these differences, let's examine CASE tools in terms of:

- Vertical CASE tool integration over different application development phases.
- Horizontal CASE tool integration over CASE tool products within a single application development phase.

**Vertical CASE tool integration.** Vertical CASE tool integration is the integration of CASE tools that serve different phases of application development. *High vertical integration* means that the information produced by planning tools is fully compatible with and used by analysis tools, and that its use requires little manual intervention. The same thing applies to the information produced by analysis tools being used by design tools, and the information produced by design tools being used by code generators during construction.

IEF is a highly vertically integrated CASE tool—the data, activity, and data-to-activity interaction models produced during analysis are all fully used by IEF's design tool. Indeed, IEF is so tightly integrated that the analysis-based Process Action Diagrams (PADs) can be read by the IEF's code generators. ADW is somewhat less vertically integrated. Although ADW's analysis data model can be fully used by the ADW design tool (after using the relational translator), its analysis mini-specs cannot. Mini-specs gener-

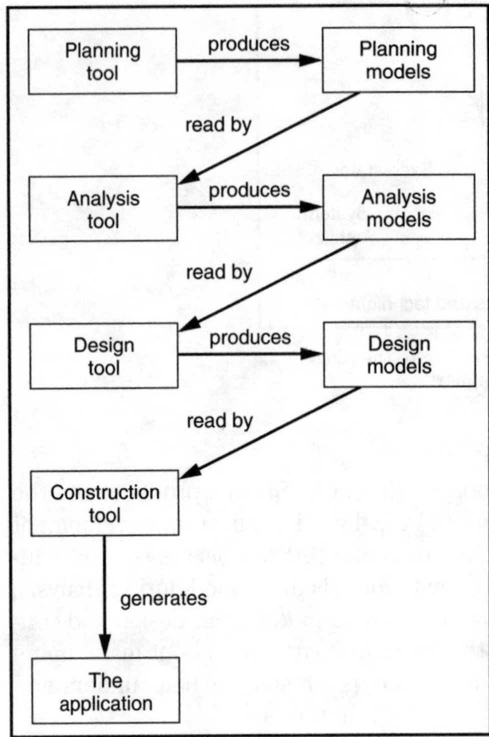


**Fig. 2.3** Vertical CASE tool integration.

ated during analysis can be read by the ADW design tool, but they're used only as comments, not as direct design model input. (See Fig. 2.3.)

**Reverse integration.** The vertical integration described so far dealt with the ability of each phase in the CASE-based application development cycle to take full advantage of information developed during the phases that preceded it. But CASE tools do more than use information produced during earlier phases—they produce new information, and some of that new information can directly affect the models produced during earlier phases. The detailed and rigorous models produced during analysis, for example, may uncover subtle but important data relationships that were not obvious during planning. Design efforts can uncover data and logic requirements that were not apparent during analysis. The target technology environment, in which the generated system will execute, often imposes additional design requirements such as look-up tables, denormalization, and creation of secondary indices. Prototyping of screens, dialogues, and graphics can also uncover new data and logic requirements.

Reverse CASE tool integration deals with ensuring that all models developed during applications development continue to accurately reflect what's learned in subsequent phases. If a new data element is discovered while prototyping a screen using a design tool, reverse integration ensures that the new data element finds its way back into the logical data models maintained by the analysis CASE tool, and all the way back to the enterprise data model maintained by the planning CASE tool as well. (See Fig. 2.4.)

Reverse integration is especially important during maintenance. If changes to design models are not propagated back into analysis, and changes to analysis models are not propagated back into high-level planning models, the planning, analysis, and design models will degenerate into "snapshots" of what the business rules and developing application looked like at a single point in time. The ability of planning and analysis models to add value in terms of system integration, regeneration into new environments, and provision of maintenance insights, will gradually degrade until they're close to worthless. Pressure to deliver new applications, enhancements, and changes on time are more than sufficient in most information systems organizations to ensure that if reverse integration capabilities are not built into the CASE tools being used, reverse integration will not be achieved.

**Horizontal CASE tool integration.** Horizontal integration is the ability of a CASE tool to coordinate models during a single phase of the application development process. High horizontal integration means that the data, activity, and interaction models for each phase are fully coordinated with each other. (See Fig. 2.5.)

ADW and IEF processes, for example, create, read, update, and delete entity types in their analysis data models,[5] and both tools ensure that data

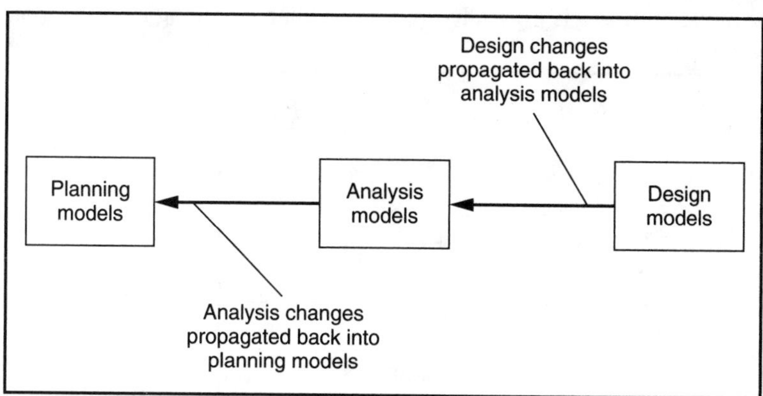


**Fig. 2.4** Reverse CASE tool integration.

[5]Some very strict interpretations of information engineering don't include the modeling of process reads, since reads don't alter the state of the data model. However, many information-engineering-based methodologies do support process reads. Process reads are supported by both ADW and IEF.

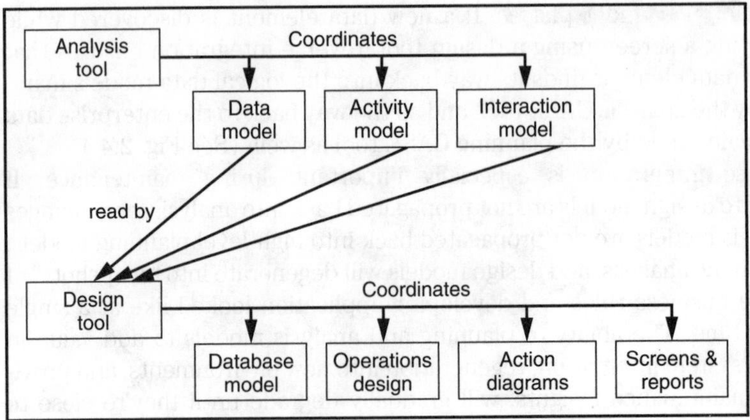


**Fig. 2.5** Horizontal CASE tool integration.

represented in action diagrams and screens are fully consistent with their design model of the database. In terms of the general CASE tool market, both ADW and IEF are very tightly horizontally integrated, although IEF enforces horizontal integration more rigorously than does ADW. (See Fig. 2.6.)

## Classifying CASE tools by target technologies

As with techniques and methodologies, target technology support, in terms of specific hardware platforms, operating systems, and databases, can be obtained from vendor literature. This information, along with methodology and technique support, is critically important when choosing a CASE tool.

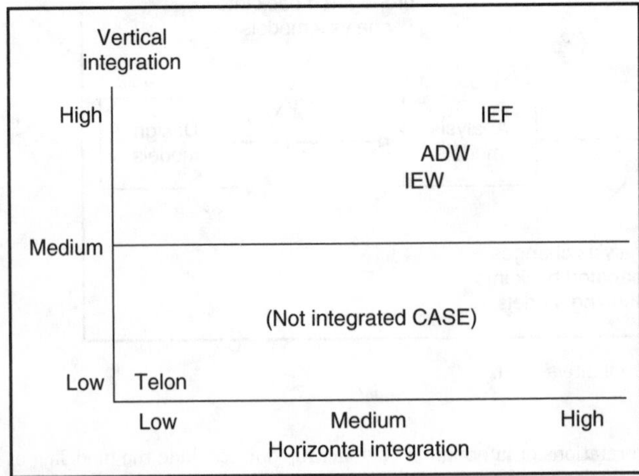


**Fig. 2.6** CASE tools can be classed according to horizontal and vertical integration.

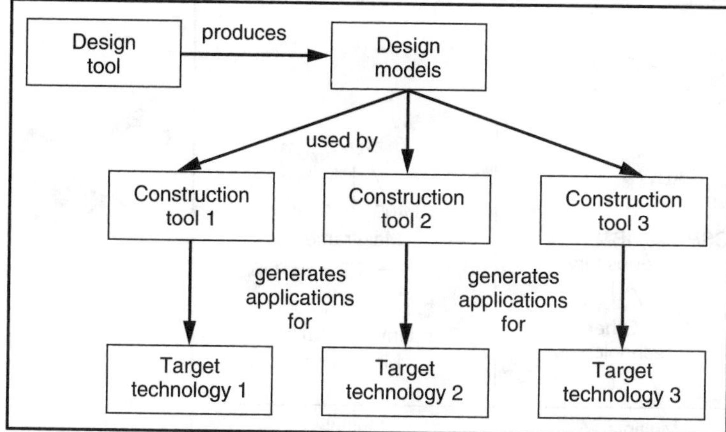


**Fig. 2.7** A single set of design models can be used to generate applications in multiple target technologies.

Less obvious, but potentially important, is CASE tool ability to support multiple target technologies. For integrated CASE tools such as ADW and IEF, multiple target technology support should include the ability to regenerate applications for alternate target technology environments from a single set of analysis and design models, with minimal rework. (See Fig. 2.7.)

For CASE tools such as IEF, a single model can be used to generate an application in multiple languages and technologies simply by choosing a different generation option. ADW supports several target technologies directly, and through the IBM repository. ADW and IEF can also generate applications for additional target technologies via interfaces to a variety of third-party construction tools developed by their vendors and users. This kind of alternate technology support can be problematic, since multiple vendors are involved and different agendas can drive their development and distribution. Such interfaces should not be counted on to be either fully operational or seamless. (See Fig. 2.8.)

Other target technology differences among CASE tools, and CASE tool vendors, include support of an expanding set of target technologies and target technology bias. CASE tool target technology support should therefore be constantly reevaluated.

## How CASE Tools Are Purchased and Used

CASE tools are available as "off-the-shelf" products, and are generally purchased by information technology departments, although the entire company can be affected by their use. CASE tools have a higher market profile than other CASE components such as techniques, methodologies, and training. There are two principal reasons for this. The first is that CASE tools are tangible and easy to acquire. A lot has been written about them,

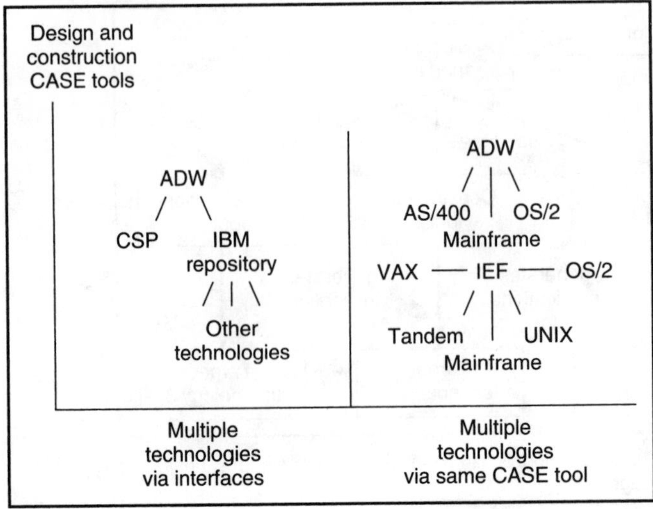


**Fig. 2.8** Alternate approaches for multiple technology support.

and their differences are easy to identify, quantify, and tabulate. The second is that CASE tool vendors maintain large sales forces, show their wares at computer shows and CASE exhibitions, and they maintain high profiles through lectures, articles and public relations.

Today's CASE tools come with sophisticated GUIs, and are consequently easy to learn to manipulate. Although some CASE tool vendors would have you believe that GUI differences among tools are significant in terms of better analysis and application development productivity, my experiences don't bear this out. The combination of emerging GUI standards, ever-faster hardware platforms, and the ease with which today's GUIs can be mastered, all serve to mitigate CASE tool differentiation in this area. Only two to five days are required for most information technology professionals to become proficient "mouse drivers," enter lots of data, and produce impressive-looking diagrams and reports.

It can take far longer to learn to use CASE tools correctly, since deriving value from CASE tools requires that each of the other CASE-related CSFs be in place. Using a powerful CASE tool without achieving the other CSFs is a little like driving a Ferrari from Los Angeles to New York without a license or a road map. Although you know which direction you want to drive in, and the car can cover the 2,500 miles at 200 MPH, it doesn't necessarily follow that you'll really get there in 12.5 hours. To be successful with a CASE tool, the tool must also be understood within the context of a CASE-based methodology. Achieving sufficient understanding can require significant investments in terms of time, training and experience.

Not achieving sufficient understanding almost inevitably leads to a very direct and quick disaster.

This is what happened to Sharon, an experienced and capable systems analyst, when she was first given a copy of the ADW Analysis Workstation without the benefit of training or a CASE-based methodology to guide her. She began her analysis by creating a context data flow diagram of her system since the concept of defining all of the data flows between a system and the outside world was familiar to her. Her second step was to decompose the context diagram down to the next lower level. When she did so, she was horrified to find that her lower level diagram was "so full of context junctions, there was no room for anything else." She didn't know what context junctions were, where they came from, why they were there or what she might do with them. What she did know was that no matter how hard she tried, she couldn't make them go away. As a conscientious and goal-oriented analyst with no apparent way to continue, she gave up on using the CASE tool and completed a successful, but traditional, analysis. To Sharon, the CASE tool was a disaster.

The extra time spent during analysis, dealing with sophisticated CASE tool diagrams and constructs such as resolving ADW-generated context junctions, will pay a team back only to the extent that the team understands what the constructs are and how to use them to speed up development. Without a methodology to guide an application development team in how to do this, the best CASE tool is likely to do little more than slow down the application development process.

## How CASE Tools Fit in with the Other CASE CSFs

CASE tools support CASE-based methodologies through automation of techniques, information coordination, and consistency checks. It's the methodologies, not the CASE tools, that impact the rest of the organization via altered expectations, new human resource requirements, and cultural shifts. (See Fig. 2.9.)

### How the same methodology can be supported via different techniques

Compatibility between CASE tools, methodologies, and techniques is therefore essential if CASE is to be successfully deployed. But the compatibility requirement doesn't imply that CASE tools have to support methodologies in the same way. Indeed, the ways in which CASE tools employ techniques to support methodologies can vary significantly from tool to tool. Both CASE tools shown in Fig. 2.10, for example, support the information engineering methodology requirement that all processes that are children of a

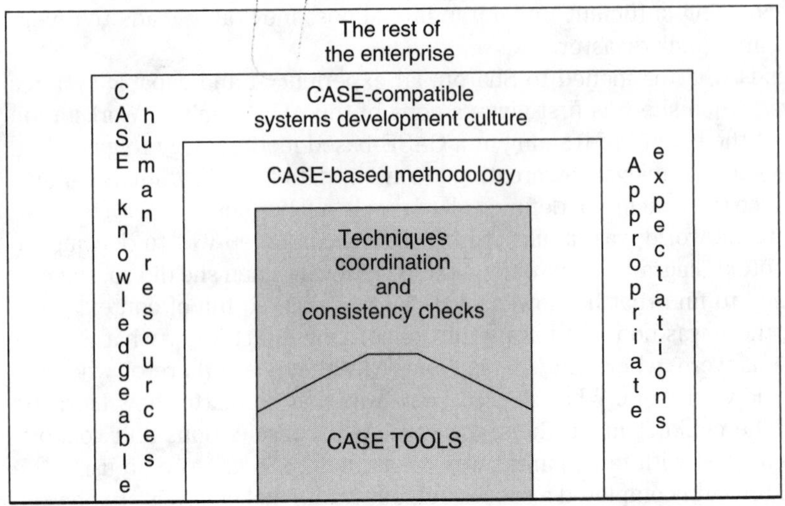


**Fig. 2.9** How CASE tools fit in with the other CASE CSFs.

single process must be dependent on one another. But the two CASE tools support this requirement in very different ways.

IEF, through activity dependency diagrams, requires its users to enter and specifically define dependencies among the children of each process. This is done directly on a diagram. ADW satisfies the same requirement by stipulating that all data flows that enter and/or leave a process must be completely resolved among the process's children.

While both techniques satisfy the same methodology requirement, significant differences nevertheless exist; activity dependency diagrams exhibit equal sensitivities to timing and data dependencies. Timing dependencies among processes tend to show up in data flow diagrams only when the timing issue is associated with a significant piece of data. Data flow diagrams however, by ensuring that 100% of the data that enter and leave a process are completely resolved among a process's children, can uncover subtle dependencies that may not be obvious when diagramming dependencies. (See Figs. 2.11 and 2.12.)

| Methodology requirement | CASE tool | Technique |
|---|---|---|
| Dependency among children of a process | IEF | Process dependency diagramming |
| Dependency among children of a process | ADW | Data flow diagramming |

**Fig. 2.10** ADW and IEF support the same methodology requirement through different techniques.

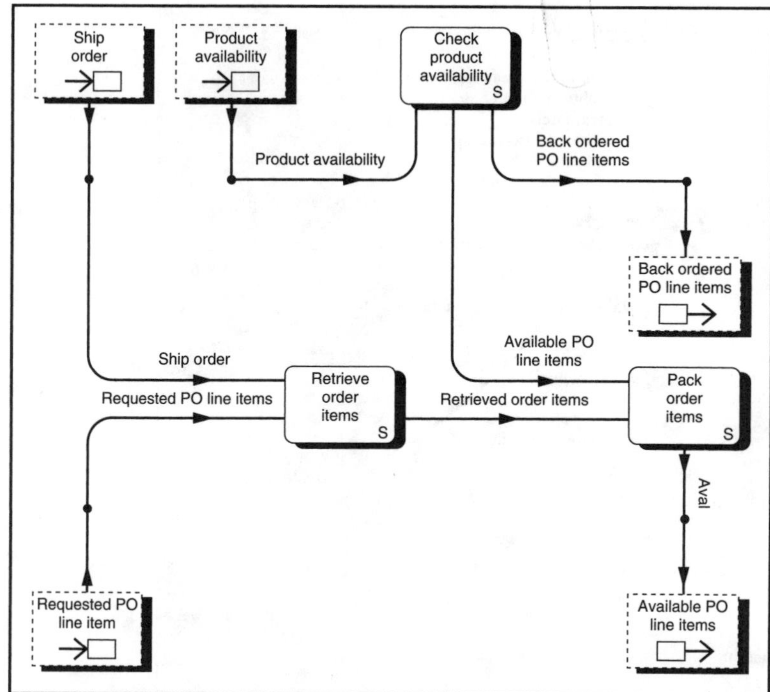


**Fig. 2.11** ADW Data flow diagram.

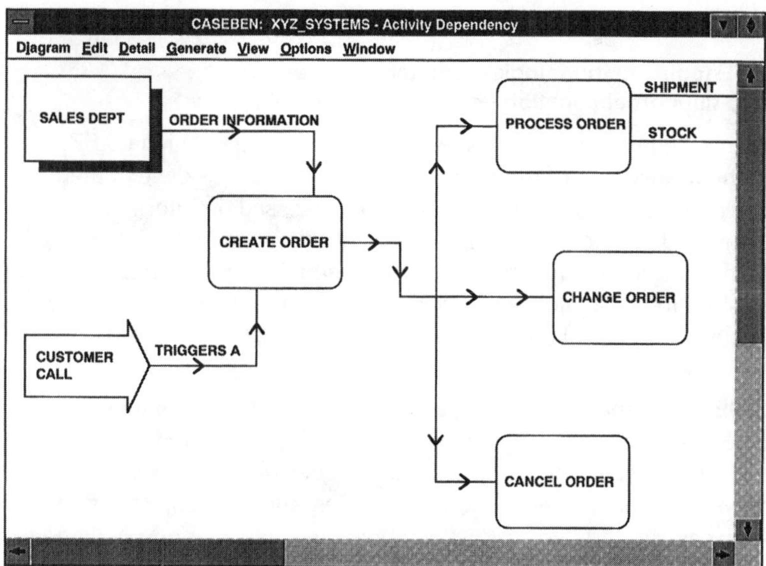


**Fig. 2.12** IEF Dependency diagram.

| Phase & requirement | Methodology support | CASE tool techniques |
|---|---|---|
| Planning | | |
| I/S to business alignment | Exec & operations interviews to obtain alignment parameters | Matrix processing |
| | Creation of association matrices | Affinity analysis |
| Enterprise modeling | Data modeling | Entity relationship diagramming |
| | Functional decomposition | Entity supertyping<br>Decomposition diagramming |
| | Data-to-function alignment | Affinity analysis, C-R-U-D matrices |
| Analysis | | |
| Business modeling | Activity modeling | Functional decomposition |
| | Data modeling | E-R diagramming, Normalization |
| | Consistency checking | Dependency diagramming, Data flow diagramming, Action diagramming |
| | User verification | Prototyping, RAD<br>Matrix processing |
| Design | | |
| System design | System flow | Structure charts |
| | Database design | Database diagrams |
| | Program logic | Action diagramming, Screen painting |
| Construction | Generation and testing of the system | Code generators, 4GLs<br>Inquiry languages<br>Report writers |

**Fig. 2.13** How CASE tools and methodologies interact to support each phase of information-engineering-based applications development.

## How CASE tools, methodologies, and techniques interact to support application development

Methodology requirements, and the techniques through which CASE tools support them, vary for different phases of the applications development cycle. This variance is shown in Fig. 2.13, which is based on information engineering methodology concepts. There are, of course, many methodologies that are information engineering-based, and equally many CASE tools that strive to support these methodologies. Particular methodologies and CASE tools may not support all of the functions listed in Fig. 2.13.

**How CASE tools and methodologies interact to support planning.** Many information systems planning methodologies call for the creation and population of matrices. These show associations between business and information systems management-level properties such as objectives, goals, critical success factors, critical assumptions and information needs. Planning tools typically address this requirement through powerful matrix processors that support combinations of predefined and user-defined two-dimensional matrices. Tool-based matrix processors add value to the planning process by providing:

- An accessible repository for storing and relating business and information techonology management parameters.
- A mechanism for associating the planning parameters with objects in enterprise data and process models.
- Clustered algorithms that are useful in exploring the nature of the relationships.

Planning tools also provide facilities for developing enterprise-level data and activity models. The enterprise-level data model will typically be composed of a small number of very high-level enterprise-wide entity supertypes such as customer, product, cost, agent, distributor, and vendor, along with their relationships. During analysis, entity supertypes, such as customer, can be expected to turn into many entity types such as name, address, demographics and credit information. Enterprise-level functions, such as marketing, sales, engineering and product acquisition are also defined and decomposed using the planning tool.

Having thus developed enterprise-level data and activity models, the matrix processor can add further value to the planning process by associating the high-level entities with functions (to ensure that each model is correct and complete) and associating high-level entities and functions with business parameters such as objectives, critical success factors, and information needs (to help quantify the ways in that each supports the business).

**How CASE tools and methodologies interact to support analysis.** Analysis CASE tools support a variety of techniques, all designed to promote very detailed, rigorous, and time-consuming data, activity, and (data-to-activity) interaction modeling. The idea is that every dollar spent here is worth ten dollars spent in design and a hundred dollars spent after the system has been delivered.

Modeling techniques such as normalization and value-added consistency checks help make the analysis data model granular and help ensure against multiple and inconsistent representations of data in the model. Decomposition diagramming breaks functions down into single-task levels. High value-added CASE tools such as ADW and IEF use data flow and dependency diagramming to help ensure that each entity and process in the model really serves a useful purpose. Rapid application development (RAD)-type prototyping can add more value by providing users with additional insight into what the application might look like and by using that information to enhance and correct the data and activity models. CASE tool supported action diagramming, by checking each entity create, read, update, and delete against the data model, adds additional value by ensuring that the data model fully supports each process's logic requirements.

**How CASE tools and methodologies interact to support design and construction.** Design CASE tools convert the detailed and rigorous analysis models into physical designs that can be implemented in specific target technology environments using construction CASE tools. They can be used to help create and document physical designs through diagramming techniques such as structure charts, database diagrams, dialog flow diagrams and action diagrams. But the added value that CASE tools provide to the design process comes not from their impressive documentation and diagramming features, but from their integration with the analysis-based models and construction tool requirements. It's through tight integration with the rigorous and detailed analysis models that the rules, issues, and logical constructs developed and verified during analysis can be faithfully translated to physical designs, and the substantial investment in CASE-based analysis made to pay off.

Construction CASE tools used by themselves achieve modest productivity gains over hand-coding. These gains are achieved primarily through a combination of their abilities to translate very high-level language constructs into executable (or compilable) lower-level code, and to facilitate the reuse of objects. These productivity gains can be substantially increased if the design and construction tools are vertically integrated tightly enough so that the physical designs produced by the design CASE tool can be used directly as construction tool input. Highest productivity gains are realized when the design CASE tool functions as a translator of detailed and rigorous analysis designs into construction tool and physical database requirements.

## CASE Tool Trade-offs

The potential value that a company can derive from a CASE tool, and the impact that the tool can have on the way information systems are developed and used, are the product of a complex set of tool-related interactions and trade-offs. Let's explore some of the major CASE-tool-related trade-offs and see where ADW and IEF fit.

### Added value for Upper and Lower CASE

Both Upper and Lower CASE tools can affect the productivity and quality of the applications that are developed. They do so in different ways, and their effect on the applications they produce is therefore different. The pro-

| Upper CASE | Lower CASE |
|---|---|
| ■ Stable and accurate models of business requirements | ■ Higher development productivity |
| ■ Better business understanding and support | ■ Quicker initial application delivery |
| ■ More usable initial application deliveries | ■ Lower adaptive maintenance |
| ■ Lower corrective maintenance costs | ■ Target technology independence |

**Fig. 2.14** Principal added value of Upper and Lower CASE.

ductivity gains afforded by Lower CASE are generally realized in the form of quicker initial application deliveries. The insights that Lower CASE tools provide into how complex applications fit together can help lower adaptive maintenance. When they can be used to generate applications for different target technologies from a single set of models, Lower CASE tools can provide a degree of technology independence as well. But since design and construction tools don't provide insight into business requirements or strategic business support, the period of corrective maintenance that typically follows initial application delivery is not addressed.

Upper CASE tools increase application development productivity primarily by providing an accurate and stable business requirements platform, in terms of activity, data, and interaction models that Lower CASE tools can build upon. When Upper and Lower CASE tools are integrated, the Upper CASE-produced models can sometimes be used by construction tools as well. Since Upper CASE tools can be used to gain substantial insight into business issues and user requirements, they can add value in terms of information system usability and relevance. This added value is typically realized in the form of a more usable initial application delivery and in lower corrective maintenance. (See Fig. 2.14.)

### CASE tool value and integration

The extent to which planning, analysis, design, and construction tools are vertically and horizontally integrated has an exponential effect on the value that the CASE tools can provide. The exponential relationship reflects the facts that the value of CASE tools to a company is the product of:

- The productivity and quality gains that each tool can provide.
- The extent to which the tools ensure that the applications produced with the tools fully serve the company and its business areas.

Each of these factors is highly dependent on vertical and horizontal CASE tool integration.

ADW and IEF are highly integrated CASE tools and consequently have the potential to provide substantial added value to companies that use them. Both can be used to fully integrate planning, analysis, design, and construction functions, and although the IEF is the more tightly vertically integrated of the two, both provide mechanisms through which the products of each phase of application development can be used in subsequent phases. (See Fig. 2.15.)

### Trade-offs between flexibility and productivity

The ability of Lower CASE tools to increase application development productivity over that of hand-crafted systems comes, in part, at the expense of flexibility. The flexibility-to-productivity trade-off is part of a trend that started with assemblers that were less flexible and more productive than the machine languages that preceded them. Writing programs in third-generation languages such as COBOL or C can be many times more productive than writing the same programs in assembler language. But, as with the evolution from machine language to assembler language, the added efficiency came at the expense of flexibility. (See Fig. 2.16.)

Although code generators and 4GLs offer substantial gains in productivity over COBOL and C, the added productivity once again comes at the expense of flexibility. Required functionality is achieved, but not necessarily exactly

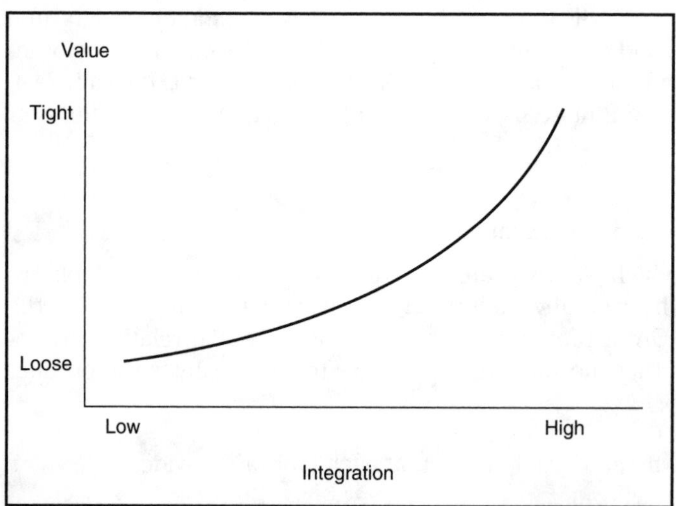


**Fig. 2.15** The exponential relationship between integration and CASE tool value.

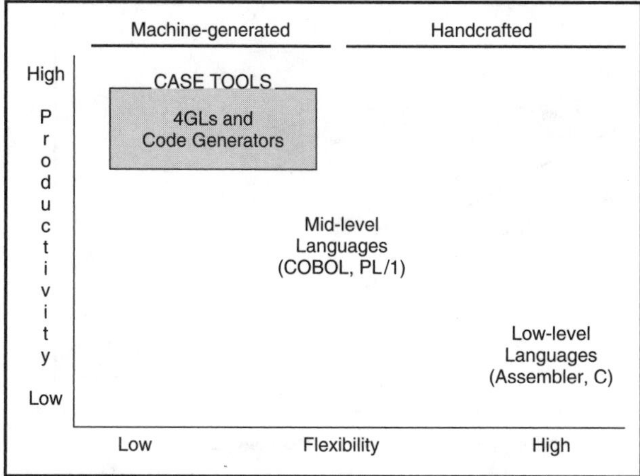


**Fig. 2.16** The inverse relationship between flexibility and productivity.

the way the application's users would like it. Construction CASE tools that make it easy to be very productive, tend to do so within a design paradigm or design envelope that tends to predetermine what the application will look like and how it will work. CASE tools that allow substantial flexibility in constructing applications tend to achieve high productivity only when substantial portions of the generated system are prefabricated into reusable objects such as Synon "functions," ADW/CWS "macros," or IEF "templates." Although preset design paradigms resulting from the definition and use of reusable objects are defined by developers, and therefore controllable, they're never the less restrictive. The productivity-to-flexibility trade-off, although true for all CASE tools, is more pronounced in Lower CASE, 4GLs and code generators.

### Productivity and methodology support

There's also a relationship between the breadth of the methodologies that a CASE tool can support and the value that the CASE tool will provide. CASE tools that provide high value to their users tend to be more methodology constraining then those that don't.

The origin of this dependency is that supporting multiple methodologies places limits on the number of value added rules and consistency checks that the CASE tool can enforce. For example, the narrow interpretation of information engineering derivative methodologies that IEF supports, permits the tool to be considerably more stringent in enforcing consistency checks than ADW, which supports a broader range of methodologies.

Although enforcing adherence to a specific methodology can enable high CASE tool value, taking advantage of that high value will be difficult unless the tool's users are prepared to live, not only with the methodology being

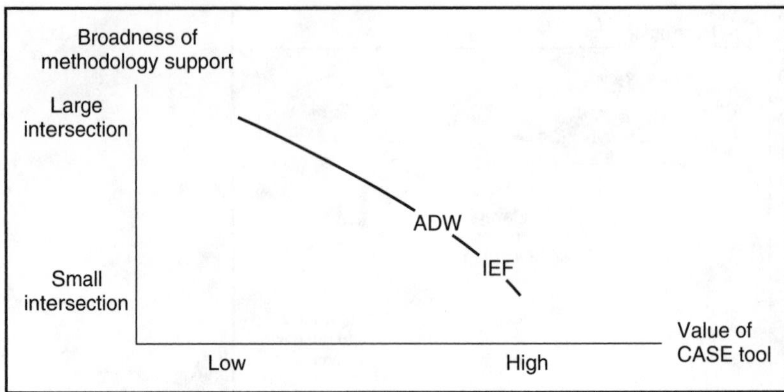


**Fig. 2.17** CASE tool value as a function of broadness of methodology support.

enforced, but with the CASE tool's interpretation of the methodology as well. (See Fig. 2.17.)

More narrow methodology interpretations decrease the latitude that companies have in adapting the tool-enforced methodology to their culture. CASE tools (such as IEF) that interpret their supported methodology narrowly, and rigorously enforce their narrow interpretation, can therefore be expected to have higher cultural impact than tools (such as ADW) that enforce the same methodology, but through a broader interpretation. Tools (such as System Architect) that are substantially methodology independent can be expected to have a correspondingly low cultural impact. (See Fig. 2.18.)

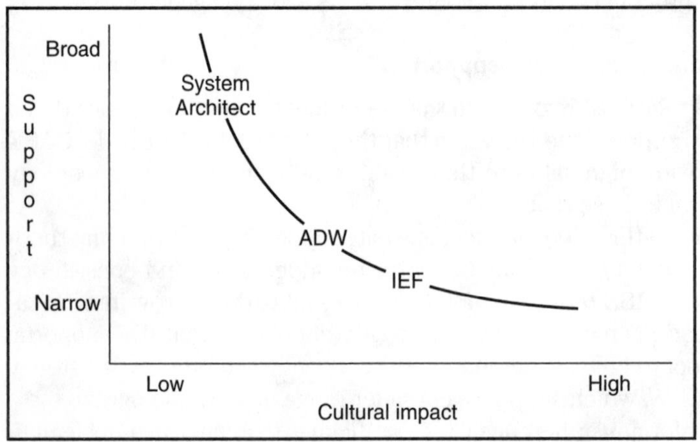


**Fig. 2.18** Cultural impact as a function of broadness of methodology support.

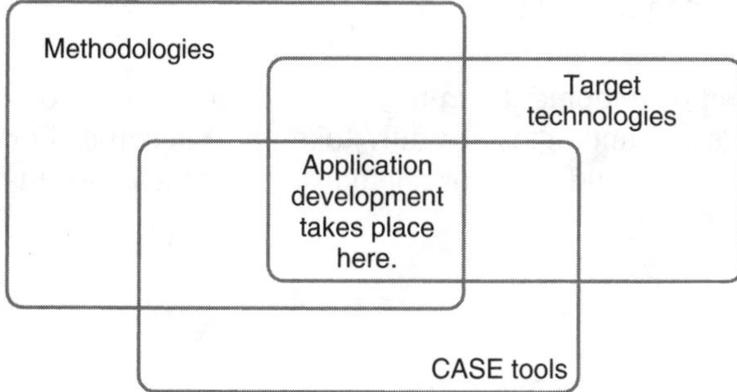


**Fig. 2.19** The intersection of methodologies, target technologies, and CASE tools is where CASE-based application development takes place.

### CASE tool, methodology, and target-technology trade-offs

In addition to being compatible with methodologies and techniques, CASE tools must support the target technology and information system architecture. Although technology dependencies are more pronounced for lower CASE tools such as 4GLs and code generators, technology dependencies also exist for Upper CASE and integrated CASE products. The prototyping, for example, provided by an Upper CASE analysis tool that targets a CICS type telecommunications environment will not be an appropriate choice for analysis if the application will eventually function on an OS/2 Presentation Manager, Windows, or Unix workstation.

Applications development methodology, target technology, and CASE tools therefore interact. Choosing one narrows choices for the other two, and choosing the second substantially narrows available choices for the third. Applications development requires all three, and it can take place only where methodology, target technology, and CASE tool support intersect. (See Fig. 2.19.) All CASE tools don't constrain methodology and technology in the same ways.

CASE-tool-to-technology interactions are not limited to versions of COBOL, user interface paradigms, or target technology environments; they cover development environments too. One company, which did all of its compiling and testing on its mainframe, found this out when they tried to employ a PC-based code generator. Although the generator worked well and generated lots of usable code, their companywide standard, requiring all compilation and testing to be mainframe based, meant that they had to constantly switch back and forth from PC to mainframe environments. The time required for switching back and forth between PC and mainframe development environments made the code generation process too cumbersome to be useful. All of its productivity gains were lost.

Successful CASE-based development can be achieved only when tools, methodologies, and target technologies are fully taken into account. For maximum latitude, all three should therefore be chosen, or at least evaluated, concurrently.

Chapter

# 3

# CASE Methodologies

"Stop the world . . . I want to get off, or I caught the golden ring while spinning round and round" read the headline on a newsletter sent to more than 1,000 information technology professionals at a large financial services company. The newsletter went on to describe the fundamental and far-reaching changes that were about to befall the company and to invite the frightened information technology staff to stay on and be part of what their organization was about to become. The newsletter was not preparing the staff for a hostile takeover. Nor was it preparing them for an impending merger, downsizing initiative, or monumental crash project. It was introducing their new information-engineering-based methodology.

Methodologies are consistent and comprehensive approaches to applications development. Methodologies define and order roles, responsibilities, milestones, tasks, activities, and techniques. Methodologies are mechanisms for ensuring that applications (developed by people with diverse backgrounds, preferences and skills) look and work in a consistent way, inside and out. Methodologies can also be vehicles for leveraging organizations' application development environments to maximum advantage.

Methodologies in use today are highly variable in how comprehensive and usable they are. Many address the entire applications development cycle, from enterprise-wide strategic planning through maintenance, although not all do. Methodologies also vary in the amount of guidance they provide to application developers, users, and management, as well as in the tools and techniques that they support.

Many successful applications have been, and continue to be, developed without the aid of a methodology. Indeed, some feel that the quickest and most efficient way to develop applications is to put a bunch of information technology "geniuses" in a room for a few months and let them do what they do best. For small, traditionally developed applications, there may be some truth to this, provided that sufficient quantities of "geniuses" are available, that the applications don't have to interface with other information systems, and that no one has to worry about, or pay for, maintenance. Where CASE is employed, the use of a methodology is mandatory.

CASE-based applications development is very different from its manual counterpart. Adopting CASE entails a substantial paradigm shift, not only for the information technology professionals who buy and use CASE, but also for the users and managers of CASE-developed applications. Without an appropriate and workable methodology to guide all who are affected by its use, employing CASE to develop applications is, with close to 100% certainty, doomed to failure.

Methodologies built around manual structured analysis and design techniques have been around since the mid 1970s[1], and many of the most prominent are still in use today. The Jackson structure charts developed during the early 1970s still represent an excellent way to view a program in terms of its sequence, logic, and iteration. Yourdon / DeMarco Structured Analysis and Gain / Sarson data flow diagrams are useful in analyzing what happens to the data that enter and leave a business area or information system, and Warnier-Orr diagrams remain an excellent way to decompose a business area or information system into its functional parts. (See Fig. 3.1.)

CASE tools and diagramming aids have been, and continue to be, developed to automate these techniques. But it wasn't until the mid 1980s that James Martin began to popularize the Information Engineering methodology developed by Martin and Finkelstein,[2] in order to leverage (the then emerging) PC technology to:

- Address the way information systems support a company, from strategic planning through application development.
- Integrate data and activity modeling techniques.
- Develop and use a centralized repository, or knowledge base, of business and technical information.

In short, the Information Engineering methodology tied existing automated techniques together and is the central idea behind today's Integrated CASE. James Martin formally defined Information Engineering as follows:

---

[1]Michael Jackson, *Principals Of Program Design*, Academic Press, London, 1975. See also Chris Gane and Trish Sarson *Structured Systems Analysis: Tools And Techniques*, Prentice Hall, 1977, Kenneth Orr, *Structured Systems Development*, Yourdon Press, 1977, and Tom DeMarco, *Structured Analysis & System Specification*, Yourdon Press, 1979.

[2]James Martin, Clive Finkelstein, *Information Engineering*, Savant, 1981.

- "An interlocking set of formal techniques in which enterprise models, data models, and process models are built up in a comprehensive knowledge base and are used to create and maintain data processing systems. These techniques depend on highly automated tools. The result is systems built with strong end user participation, that solve local problems, but that have horizontal integration so that they work together, and vertical integration, so that data processing systems are anchored into the top management goals and strategic plans of the enterprise."
- "An enterprise-wide set of automated disciplines for getting the right information to the right people at the right time."[3]

This is the Information Engineering methodology that formed the basis for development of the KnowledgeWare Information Engineering Workbench (IEW), predecessor of their Application Development Workbench (ADW), and the Texas Instruments Information Engineering Facility, (IEF).[4]

## The Methodology Market

Unlike ADW and IEF, which enjoy very high market profiles, CASE methodologies tend to be enigmatic. You can touch and feel each tool, and given the opportunity, marvel over its very impressive GUI. Methodologies, provided

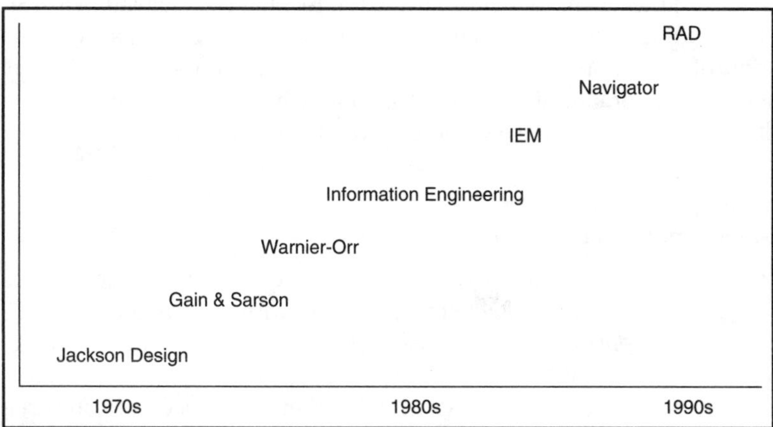


**Fig. 3.1** Evolution of several prominent methodologies and structured analysis techniques.

---

[3]James Martin, *Information Engineering* Volume 1: Introduction, Savant 1986, Section 1.2.

[4]James Martin, *Information Engineering*, Savant & Arthur Young, 1986. See also James Martin, *Information Engineering*, Books I and II, Prentice Hall, 1990 and Texas Instruments' marketing literature.

that you can see them at all, often exist as reams of seemingly incomprehensible documentation. Many methodologies, such as IEM, Summit / D, and Navigator, are sold by consulting firms, more as adjuncts to their consulting services than as off-the-shelf products. Others, in the form of books on tasks and techniques, seem to come along with CASE tools. Many methodologies, including some of the most successful for ADW and IEF, are homegrown and never even reach the market.

Because CASE tools are so much more visible than CASE methodologies, the tools can be perceived as being synonymous with CASE. Compensated on sales rather than on success, CASE sales organizations are tempted to leverage this misperception into higher sales revenues by de-emphasizing the importance of methodologies. Consequently, the initial acquisition of CASE technology sometimes begins and ends with a CASE tool purchase. Methodologies, if considered at all, are addressed only after the CASE tool "doesn't work."[5] It's paradoxical that CASE tools such as ADW and IEF, which were developed with the aid of James Martin to support a methodology, should so often be used without one.

## How CASE-Based Methodologies Fit in with Other CASE CSFs

In CASE-based development, the methodologies guide applications developers, users, and their management in using the techniques, enabled by CASE tools, to create and deliver efficient and high-quality applications. With the exception of the information technology personnel, who sit at CASE-tool workstations, the organization "sees" CASE largely through the eyes of the organization's application development methodology. (See Fig. 3.2.)

### How methodologies use CASE-tool-supported techniques

The ways in which tool-supported techniques are used by methodologies depends on the application development phase, with the same techniques sometimes put to entirely different uses by different phases. For example, information-engineering-based methodologies, such as IEM, use the association matrices, supported by the ADW and IEF matrix processors, in three different ways, each having a totally different effect on the organization.

In information systems planning, association matrices and affinity analysis are used to associate high-level business planning parameters, such as objectives, goals, problems, CSFs, locations, and information needs, with high-level functions and entity types, as well as with each other. This infor-

[5]Carma McClure & Johanna Ambrosio, "Methodology In Path From Art To Science," *Software Magazine*, June 1989.

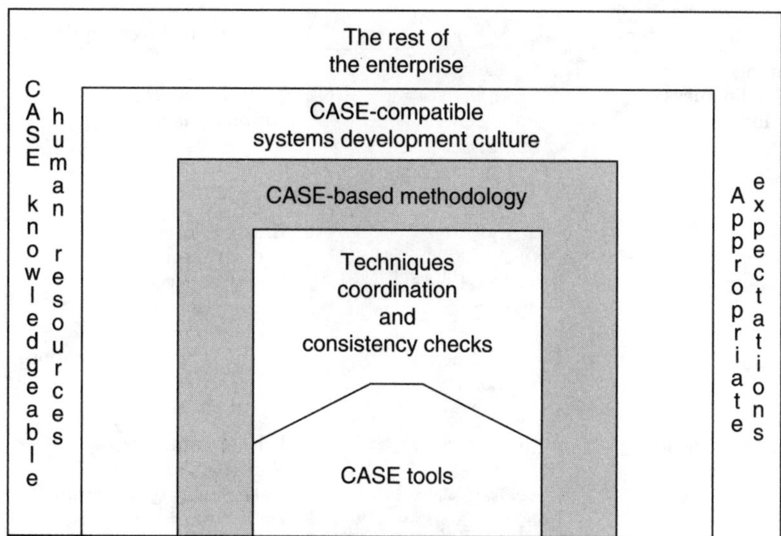


**Fig. 3.2.** How CASE methodologies fit in with the other CASE CSFs.

mation engineering requirement is typically reflected to top management in the form of very specific, information-technology-initiated interviews, models, and insights. To a management used to doing their own planning, and throwing the result "over the fence" for information technology to catch, this can represent a major change.

Prior to analysis, information engineering calls for the same matrix processor to be used to partition the required business functionality into multiple Business Area Analysis projects (BAAs, for short) based upon data to function affinities and dependencies.

Information engineering methodologies enable the size and order of the BAAs to be decided, not only on the basis of need, but also on the basis of development complexity, cost, and throwaway. Again, the methodology harnesses the tool-based matrix processor to affect the business, this time to alter the way information systems are developed. After analysis has been completed, information engineering once again calls for the same matrix processor to be trained, this time on normalized entity types and leaf-level processes. This is done to help decide which portions of the application will implemented first, second, and third, and sometimes, which portions will not be implemented at all. The point is that the powerful matrix processors provided by ADW and IEF, without a methodology to channel their use, are just powerful matrix processors—nothing more. The same concept applies to other CASE-tool-supported functions such as decomposition diagrammers, entity relationship diagrammers, central encyclopedias, and consistency checks. (See Fig. 3.3.)

| Phase & requirement | Methodology support | CASE tool techniques |
|---|---|---|
| Planning | | |
| IT to business alignment | Exec and operations interviews to obtain alignment parameters<br>Creation of association matrices | Matrix processing<br>Affinity analysis |
| Enterprise modeling | Data modeling | Entity relationship diagramming<br>Entity supertyping |
| | Functional decomposition | Decomposition diagramming |
| | Data-to-function alignment | C-R-U-D matrix generation |
| Analysis | | |
| Business modeling | Activity modeling<br>Data modeling<br>Consistency checking<br>User verification | E-R diagramming<br>Functional decomp<br>Dependency diagramming<br>Data flow diagramming<br>Prototyping<br>Action diagramming<br>Matrix processing |
| Design | | |
| System design | System flow design<br>Database design<br>Program logic | Structure charts<br>Database diagrams<br>Code generator specific action diagramming |
| Construction | Generation and testing of the system | Code generators<br>4GLs<br>Inquiry languages<br>Reporting environments |

**Fig. 3.3** How CASE tools and methodologies interact to support each phase of application development.

## How different methodologies can leverage the same CASE-tool-supported techniques for different purposes

In our previous examples, information engineering methodologies employed similar tool-supported techniques to accomplish entirely different objectives associated with application development. Different methodologies can also use the same CASE- tool-supported techniques to accomplish totally different purposes, some only peripherally related to application development.

The James Martin Associates' IEM methodology uses association matrices along with entity relationship data modeling and functional decomposition techniques, enabled by ADW and IEF, to develop applications that automate business requirements. In doing so, the business requirements that the developed applications will support are never questioned. CBPR, a methodology offered by Siberg Associates Inc., uses similar techniques supported by the same CASE tools, not for application development, but for business reengineering. Although no applications are developed, the way the enterprise conducts its business, along with its business requirements, can change completely.

The IEM and CBPR methodologies may use the same CASE tools and techniques, but the way they're used by each methodology has an entirely different effect on the organization; one methodology develops an application; the other reengineers the business.

## Major Methodology Issues

Since it's methodologies, not CASE tools, that interact with the organization implementing CASE, the use and procurement of methodologies are often shrouded in controversy. In terms of the information-engineering-based methodologies that are almost always considered, if not adopted, by users of ADW and IEF, the major issues fall into the four categories shown in Fig. 3.4. Let's explore each of these issues in terms of information-engineering-based methodologies and integrated CASE tools such as ADW and IEF.

### Integration requirements and support

CASE provides its highest payback when it's vertically integrated, so that the information systems developed through CASE support the company strategically and so that information learned in each phase of application development can be carried on to the next phase. Vertical integration occurs when:

- The planning phase provides high-level strategic models that are decomposed and made more detailed in analysis.
- The analysis phase provides detailed and rigorous models of applications that are used in design.
- The design phase provides a physical database along with machine-readable input for the code generator.

But how does this happen? And what does it really mean? When we speak in terms of models being passed from one phase to the next, we're referring

- Integration requirements and support
- Dealing with rigor and detail
- Analysis paralysis
- The methodology's effect on creativity

**Fig. 3.4** Major issues surrounding information-engineering-based methodologies.

| Phase | Passed to the next phase by ADW or IEF | Passed to the next phase by the methodology |
|---|---|---|
| Planning | Enterprise parameters<br>Data and activity models | A future view of the enterprise |
| Analysis | Business area data, activity and interaction models | The business accurately modeled<br>Business issues resolved<br>Technical issues resolved |
| Design | Database design<br>Input for the code generator | An operational view of the system |
| Construction | Executable code | A working system |

**Fig. 3.5** Information passed by CASE tools and methodologies in vertically integrated CASE.

to data, which are created and updated by the CASE tool used during the first phase, being read and used by the CASE tool that's used during the second phase. This happens quite automatically when tightly integrated CASE tools such as ADW and IEF are employed for each phase.

Execution of tasks that create and use integrated data, along with the meaning and accuracy of the models and data being passed, depend not on the CASE tools, but on the combination of the CASE tools and the methodology. Integrated CASE tools and an integrated methodology are required to achieve integrated CASE. The difference between the data passed by the CASE tools and the information passed by the methodology (via the CASE tools) is illustrated in Fig. 3.5.

The models created during a BAA, although detailed, rigorous and consistent, can be no better than the accuracy with which they represent the business area's requirements. The effectiveness of identifying business requirements, resolving issues, and translating the results into models is a function of the methodology.

Methodologies play an equally important role in horizontal integration within and across applications. For example, the ADW and IEF design tools are both equipped to make good use of reusable code. But reusing code is a lot less interesting than designing and writing code yourself. Consequently, relatively little code, if any, is likely to be reused unless the methodology specifically calls for and promotes it. Similar situations occur for functions and data that need to be shared across applications. (See Fig. 3.6.)

Achieving vertical and horizontal integration using integrated CASE tools without the guidance of an integrated methodology will be optional, depending on the orientation of each development team. While an integrated methodology may theoretically achieve integration without the use of integrated CASE tools such as ADW or IEF, meaningful integration is likely to be so labor intensive that it will not be worth the effort. Reaping the benefits of integrated CASE requires that both integrated CASE tools and a compatible integrated methodology be employed. (See Fig. 3.7.)

| Phase | Product of phase | Horizontal integration |
|---|---|---|
| Planning | Enterprise data model | Intersystem data sharing<br>Intersystem data consistency |
| | High-level functional decomposition | Common functions throughout enterprise |
| | C-R-U-D matrix | Data interactions and dependencies between systems |
| Analysis | Logical data model | Data sharing within the system |
| | Leaf-level processes | Common, reusable processes within the system |
| Design | Common modules, macros and action blocks | Common, reusable code |

**Fig. 3.6** How CASE-based methodologies support horizontal integration.

### Dealing with rigor and detail

Substantial rigor and detail are an inherent part of large-scale computer applications. Each is conserved over the application development cycle. They can be dealt with as corrective maintenance after applications are fully developed, as debugging during construction, or as corrections to business models during planning and analysis. But since they're conserved, they can't be substantially reduced or made to go away. Information-engineering-based methodologies work along with ADW and IEF to push the rigor and detail to the front of the application development cycle, during analysis, where they're at once more visible and less expensive to deal with. It's the added visibility that generates the controversy, and it's the reduced expense that forms the benefit. CASE methodologies are the mechanisms that call for and guide developers through the tasks necessary to push the detail and rigor to the front. CASE

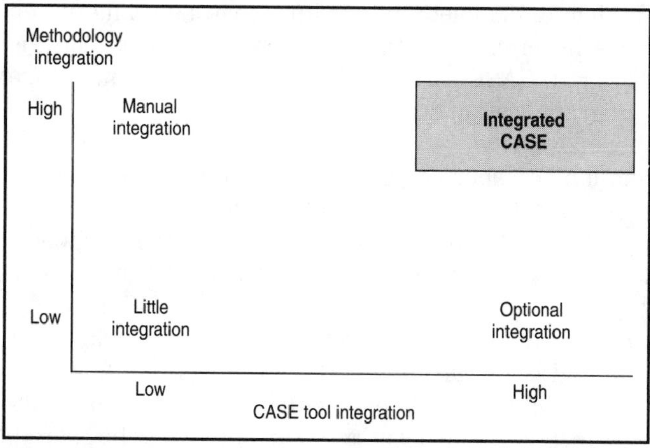


**Fig. 3.7** Integrated CASE tools + integrated methodology = integrated CASE.

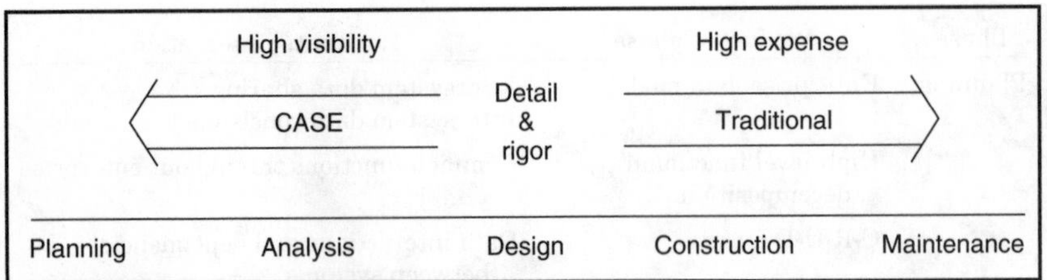


**Fig. 3.8** CASE methodologies and tools push detail and rigor toward the front of the application development cycle.

tools, via consistency checks, are the mechanisms by which detail and rigor are implemented and enforced. (See Fig. 3.8.)

During analysis, information engineering methodologies call for verification that the data model fully supports each process. Data flow diagrams are used by ADW to help ensure that all information coming into and leaving the application is supported by at least one process. Since each ADW data flow is tightly tied to (a view of) the data model, ADW data flows can be carefully checked to ensure that they support each process. IEF achieves a similar result through its Process Action Diagrams in which data accesses can be described only in terms of data-model-supported entity types and attributes. Either way, the combination of information engineering and ADW or IEF ensure that rigor and detail are dealt with during analysis instead of during design, construction or corrective maintenance—certainly, a desirable result.

### Analysis paralysis

There's another, less desirable and more controversial result of dealing with rigor and detail during planning and analysis. Planning, especially analysis, can take a very long time to complete. In a culture that judges merit and measures performance in terms of on-time deliverables, rather than the quality of what's delivered, CASE-based analysis can look a lot more like "analysis paralysis" than application development.

In many cases, the analysis paralysis results from inappropriate expectations, from information engineering's propensity to deal with rigor and detail toward the front of the application development cycle, and from a misunderstanding of the methodology. Although information-engineering-based analysis can't be conducted as quickly as a traditional analysis without sacrificing many of the advantages of integrated CASE, it can be accelerated by taking a flexible approach to the way the methodology is implemented. If time and effort are metered out to each methodology task based on the role it will ultimately play in developing and maintaining the application, a great deal of analysis time can potentially be spared.

Enormous effort, for example, often goes into textual definitions that are tangential to the application development process. Information-engineering-based methodologies, along with ADW and IEF, call for textual definitions of each modeled object. Entity types, attributes, relationships, functions, and processes must all be defined in terms of descriptive text. But aside from documenting the object's essence and purpose for developers who will deal with it later in the application development cycle, or even after the application has been delivered, textual definitions serve little purpose. The point is that once the textual definitions are understandable by any reasonable developer, they should be left alone. One or two sentences will usually suffice.

Information-engineering-based application development, therefore, doesn't have to be accompanied by analysis paralysis, although when analysis is carried to the extreme, analysis paralysis is the inevitable result. Too little analysis results in loss of the benefits associated with integrated CASE, since not enough information will be produced during analysis for the design and construction efforts to integrate with. If the amount of analysis is sufficiently low, integration ceases, and the integrated CASE tool becomes little more than an expensive, high-level language. (See Fig. 3.9.) We'll take a closer look at this trade-off in the chapter on analysis.

### The methodology's effect on creativity

As CASE tools and methodologies become more widely used, concern is often raised about the way CASE methodologies limit creativity on the

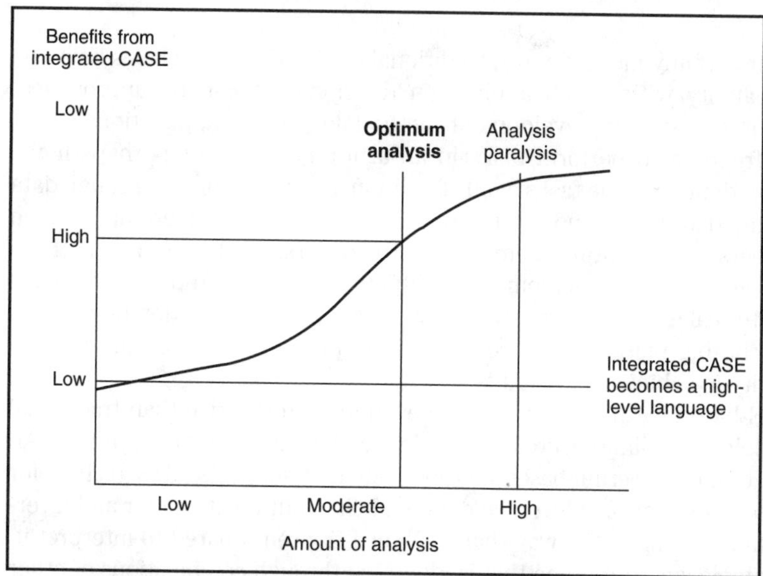


**Fig. 3.9** Integrated CASE benefit as a function of analysis.

part of information technology professionals. There are two sources for this perception.

The first has its origin in the way Lower CASE tools, such as code generators and 4GLs, achieve productivity gains over handcrafted coding, partially at the expense of flexibility. The desired functionality is achieved, but not necessarily the way the users or application developers would like. Therefore, in terms of the way the functionality is achieved, CASE can indeed limit creativity. This limitation is based in the (Lower) CASE tool, not in the methodology.

The second source of this perception originates from confusion between creativity in approach and creativity in achieving a desired result. Traditional, handcrafted application development, with no methodology, affords application developers the most creativity in approach. They can do whatever they like, whenever they like, in any order they like, so long as the application they're developing eventually works. The problem is that without the views and insights that CASE tools and methodologies enable, application developers, in exercising their creativity in approach, often unwittingly place limits on their ability to achieve a desired result. This is reflected to the companies they serve in ways that are all too well known:

- Applications that work well, but don't fully meet business requirements.
- High corrective maintenance costs.
- Limitations on ability to bring data in different applications together so that the company can leverage the result to further its objectives.

The use of any methodology, traditional or CASE-based, places limits on the creativity with which application development can be approached. Adoption of a system development methodology limits applications developers' freedom to perform tasks in an arbitrary order, or perhaps limits their freedom to tackle tasks at all. Traditional methodologies, through data modeling, data flows, and attention to detail, can help prevent application developers from painting themselves into corners, but traditional methodologies are often cumbersome and difficult to follow. And the effort required to make them work can impair the ability of application developers to see the big picture, to develop quality applications, to be productive. Creativity in achieving a result is stifled.

CASE-based methodologies can be even more restrictive than traditional methodologies in limiting creativity in application development approach. An information engineering-based methodology that supports ADW or IEF, for example, must not only leverage data modeling, but must call for and leverage data modeling in the way that ADW or IEF are prepared to interpret it. For example, an entity type that is identified through combinations of other entity types can be modeled using either foreign keys or identifying relation-

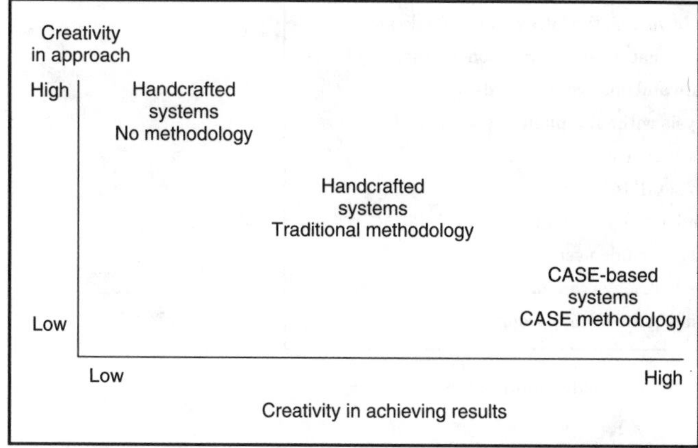


**Fig. 3.10** How CASE methodologies can affect creativity.

ships with equivalent results. But if the methodology supports ADW or IEF, the choice must be identifying relationships.

The same CASE methodologies can, within the bounds of Lower CASE tool design envelopes, potentially afford application developers the most creativity in terms of achieving a desired result. All information engineering methodologies call for high-level modeling of BAAs, along with the ways in which they can be fit together prior to beginning application development. With the ADW and IEF planning tools keeping track of the details, application developers, along with their business counterparts, are free to fit BAAs together to achieve what they want, often in ingenious ways. (See Fig. 3.10.)

## Ten Common Methodology Land Mines, and How to Avoid Them

The importance of methodologies in successful ADW and IEF-based CASE is reflected in the fact that there continue to be many methodology-based failures. The ten land mines presented in Fig. 3.11 have been, and continue to be, the most common ways in which methodologies fail.

### Believing that you have a methodology when you don't

Both ADW and IEF can appear not to require a methodology for their use. Both tools come with GUIs that make them easy to learn and to use; both vendors supply excellent training in using their tools, and both CASE tools are exceptionally well documented. In addition, ADW is touted by KnowledgeWare as being "methodology independent," and Texas Instruments offers a terrific

- Believing that you have a methodology when you do not
- Using a methodology that is not information-engineering-based
- Failing to coordinate and enforce standards
- Jumping into analysis without a planning framework
- Making the models 100% correct
- Going for too much detail too soon
- Separating data and activity modeling efforts
- Failing to adequately include users
- Not providing a methodology road map
- Training that is inadequate or inappropriate

**Fig. 3.11** Ten common methodology land mines.

book along with their CASE tool on how to develop applications using the IEF.[6] It's not difficult, given the considerable effort and expense involved in acquiring and implementing a methodology, to be beguiled into believing that, as an adjunct to purchasing either CASE tool, you'll have the equivalent of a methodology as well.

But you won't. You won't have the approaches, ordering, roles, responsibilities, milestones, tasks, standards, and work products.

And without these, many of the techniques that these CASE tools support can be difficult to use properly. You won't have guidance on how to:

- Use the matrix processor to define a reasonable number of data-independent BAAs.
- Identify and resolve business and technical issues that surface during BAAs.
- Use ADW/AWS Mini-specs to verify your data model.
- Present an ADW or IEF-based ERD to business users for verification,
- Leverage Library Modules and Common Action Blocks for productive code generation.

These are the providence of methodologies, without which the ADW and IEF CASE tools are practically useless.

### Using a methodology that is not information engineering based

Although ADW and IEF can be used in conjunction with a variety of methodologies, they work best when the methodology embodies, and is

[6]KnowledgeWare seminars and marketing literature. See also Dennis Minium, *A Guide To Information Engineering Using The IEF*, Texas Instruments Second edition, 1990.

based on, information engineering integration and techniques. The IEF consistency checks, which accompany each tool set, enforce information engineering concepts, a characteristic that enables IEF to provide substantial value to its users. ADW, through embedded Prologue rules that enforce information engineering concepts, achieves a similar result.

Methodologies that develop user requirements such as screens and reports prior to looking at data, for example, will therefore not work well with ADW or IEF. Neither will methodologies that develop applications based on modeling transactions and events. Such methodologies, while perfectly valid, are not consistent with the information engineering tenet that generic data and processes be modeled before operational views of the application are developed. Even structured methodologies, which seem to use ADW- and IEF-supported techniques, can be problematic.

An insurance company found this out when it tried to employ a widely used, but manually based methodology that used data flows for their ADW-based analysis. Although the ADW and methodology data flow diagrams were strikingly similar, their methodology called for data flow names to be entered with level numbers for each data flow, and ADW did not. The data flow numbers, which were needed to ensure that manual data flows were properly leveled, conflicted with the ADW "knowledge coordinator" that levels data flows automatically. The ease with which ADW data flows can be moved from level to level, in a highly interactive manner, was so compromised that the analysts on the project team soon found that they were unable to continue with ADW data flows. Only after altering the way their methodology approached and tracked data flows, did the ADW/AWS become a useful tool.

To be useful, methodologies must therefore not only use ADW- and IEF-supported techniques, but they must also be consistent with and use ADW- and IEF-supported model coordination and model management techniques.

### Failing to coordinate and enforce standards

Applications that are large enough to require multiple development teams will be successful only to the extent to which the ADW- or IEF-based models, developed by the different teams, fit together. For the application to work, entity types, attributes, and database tables, for example, which are common to more than one team's models, have to be modeled consistently. Inconsistencies brought about by different standards, or the same standards interpreted differently by different teams, can require extensive and costly retrofits. The cost of retrofitting inconsistent models, in terms of time and resources, can be comparable to CASE-based productivity gains. This is especially true when CASE is first being adopted and a substantial learning curve is involved.

The keys to successfully dealing with the coordination and standards land mine are to enforce a strict set of modeling standards and to hold interteam model coordination meetings on a frequent basis. One bank successfully ensured model coordination on the part of four teams, spread over two continents and developing complex IEF-based models, by requiring that all members on all teams get together and formally present their models for peer review on a weekly basis. The common understanding gained during their weekly reviews was the basis for numerous corrections to inconsistencies, many of which might have derailed the entire project.

### Jumping into analysis without a planning framework

A client of mine once observed that application developers, Americans in particular, have an almost uncontrollable urge to start building something right away. The idea of spending scarce time and resources in a planning effort, regardless of the result, somehow seems counter to our intuition. The consequence is that, in spite of the facts that ADW, IEF, and the methodologies that support them have planning components, many CASE-based development projects begin, not with planning, but with analysis.

For single-team efforts involving moderately sized applications, starting with the analysis phase may not be problematic. But for larger projects, beginning with analysis almost inevitably leads to difficulties with scoping and coordination. The reason is that without beginning with a planning effort, there's no way to ensure that the BAAs will be sized properly for completion of a meaningful amount of work within a reasonable time frame, yet be data-independent enough to be developed by separate (but coordinated) teams.

There are two solutions to this problem. The least risky, but most costly, is to conduct a full information system plan (ISP) prior to beginning analysis. In addition to developing a C-R-U-D matrix affinity analysis to scope out reasonable BAAs, a full ISP helps ensure that the business's objectives are met. For applications in which the developers are confident that they fully understand their company's business objectives and needs, a viable alternative is to begin with an abbreviated tactical ISP. In the tactical ISP, data and activity models are constructed, but they're not tied to enterprise parameters such as objectives, CSFs and information needs. An equivalent C-R-U-D matrix affinity analysis is developed, and workable BAAs defined.

### Making the models 100% correct

As discussed earlier, rigor and detail enable ADW, IEF, and the information engineering-based methodologies that they support to add value to application development; but, if carried too far, they can become counterproductive. The planning and analysis phases of information engineering methodologies can indeed take a very long time to complete, when conducted by a team that is dedicated to getting their models absolutely right.

Information-engineering-based methodologies model the business, and the applications that will serve it, in progressively more detailed phases, beginning with planning and ending with design and construction. Subsequent phases, either by going into more detail or by taking target technologies into account, often modify the products of the phases that preceded them. Trying to get early phases 100% right can therefore result in much wasted effort. Successful planning and analysis requires that a judicious compromise be struck between getting the models right and expending useless time and effort. The nature of the compromise varies from situation to situation, and there are no pat formulas that I can present for getting it right.

### Going for too much detail too soon

A methodology land-mine that is related to, but different from, trying to make the models 100% correct, is trying to deal with too much detail too soon. ADW and IEF have enormous appetites for detail of all kinds, and neither tool, nor many of the major methodologies that guide their use, is very particular about when in the application development cycle the detail is entered. This, coupled with our predisposition to try to provide whatever is asked for, is yet another cause of interminable analysis.

The solution is to address more and more detail in each methodology phase as the application proceeds through its development. A good rule of thumb is not to spend enormous amounts of time and effort modeling things that are likely to change in subsequent phases. As with trying to get things 100% correct, a judicious compromise is called for.

### Separating data and activity modeling efforts

Information-engineering-based methodologies call for modeling both data and activities during planning and analysis. Although data and activities can be modeled and entered into ADW and IEF separately, doing so tends to produce models that don't fully support one another. The result is a need for costly corrections during action diagramming, design, and construction.

The obvious solution is to develop the data and activity models together, with each team member participating fully in the development of each. But team-based modeling is difficult to implement since, in many companies, data modeling has traditionally been done not only by different people, but by a different organization as well. Data wars between Data Administration and application development teams over data modeling conventions and governance are the almost inevitable result, with the winners determining the degree to which information-engineering-based application development succeeds.

### Failing to adequately include users

The need for seemingly constant user access and involvement throughout the application development process is another consequence of the detail and rigor with which information engineering methodologies model a business and the application that will serve it. I have seen ADW and IEF analysis teams stopped in their tracks for weeks at a time while they await access to users in order to answer business questions with high model impact. The best solution, from an application development perspective, is development teams composed of both users and Information Systems personnel. Where this is not feasible, a means of assuring adequate user access must be worked out.

The problem is that high involvement of business users in information systems development represents not only a large paradigm shift in the way applications are developed, but also a strain on users and Information Systems personnel who may not be used to working closely with each other.

### Not providing a methodology road map

Information engineering methodologies are so different from traditional approaches to application development that without at least a rough understanding of how CASE-based development leads to a working application, many of those involved in the development project are likely to lose faith while only part way through. This need is every bit as important among Information Systems participants as it is among business users and management. A good way to provide the needed assurance is the combination of a series of one- to two-day introductory workshops, geared to the needs of each kind of applications development participant, coupled with one or more small, but fully developed, pilot projects.

### Training that is inadequate or inappropriate

Training for information-engineering-based methodologies can also be tricky business. Information engineering methodologies, and the tool-supported modeling techniques that enable them, are complex, very business oriented, and ordered differently than the traditional methodologies that they often replace. Assuming that the basics that apply to any training effort are in place, the four primary training CSFs for information engineering are:

- Training must cover the methodology as it will be implemented, which may be different from the way the vendor delivers it.
- Training examples must be relevant (banking examples for banks, retail examples for retailers, manufacturing examples for manufacturers).

- Allowance must be made for size (since small- and large-scale information engineering techniques are not necessarily the same).
- The training must be conducted, or at least refreshed, on a just-in-time basis.

## Factors to Consider When Choosing a CASE-Based Methodology

Choosing a methodology involves a complex set of trade-offs and compromises among CASE tools, technology, culture, orientation, support, and business. For the methodology to effectively serve the company, so that it derives maximum benefit from CASE, each must be taken into account. (See Fig. 3.12.)

### Methodology, CASE tools, and target technology

The first, and most obvious, factor when choosing a methodology is to choose the methodology along with the CASE tools and the target technologies. As described in the CASE tools chapter, the choices of any one of these factors limits options for the others. For maximum benefit using ADW or IEF, the methodology must support not only the information engineering development paradigm, but current and future tool-supported target technologies as well. As both ADW and IEF are on steep technology develop-

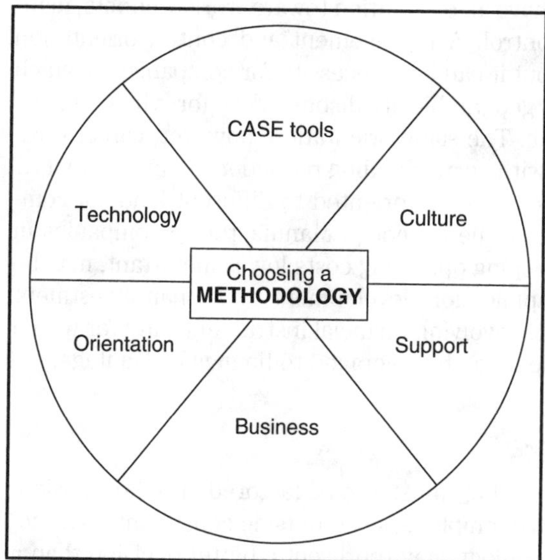


**Fig. 3.12** Factors to consider when choosing a methodology.

ment curves, with support for new target technologies announced each year, the methodology should be on a similar technology curve. It will do you little good if IEF develops tool sets to support the latest multitier fault-tolerant client/server architecture if your methodology remains mired in mainframes, DB2, and CICS.

### Culture

As we shall see in the chapter on a CASE-compatible culture, there are 10 principal ways in which CASE impacts developer, user, and management cultures. Since the cultural impact is felt largely through the methodology, methodologies represent one place in which (within bounds) the cultural effects of CASE can be controlled. All information engineering methodologies, for example, call for considerable user involvement, but not necessarily to the same extent. A methodology that calls for very high user involvement may not do well in a company in which operations personnel have been pared down to a bare minimum. But companies in which business users are actively reengineering their business may tolerate high user involvement if the methodology can develop applications for new business processes that are completely different from their current counterparts.

### Orientation

Methodologies are also oriented differently. Some methodologies, such as Ernst & Young's Navigator, have an orientation toward work products, management, reporting, and control. A management and control orientation may not only be desirable, but it can be a necessity for companies in which application development is geographically disbursed or for which consistency and control is an issue. The same orientation, however, can also require significant overhead, with corresponding reductions in productivity.

Different methodologies can also be oriented to different kinds of companies and different sectors of the economy. Manufacturing companies in mature industries, where keeping operating costs low is important, may be more tolerant of a slower application development cycle than investment banks that trade in constantly evolving financial instruments and for whom quick application development can be leveraged to financial advantage.

### Support

Support for the CASE methodology must also be factored into the decision. If hiring significant numbers of employees and outside consultants is anticipated, a widely used methodology may represent a better decision than a methodology with a narrower following. For companies with low turnover and a steady head count, that don't make extensive use of consultants, a

| Application development need | Degree addressed |
|---|---|
| Strategic planning | High |
| Small, nonstrategic applications | Low |
| Analysis | High |
| Purchase and reuse | Medium |
| Design | High |
| Construction | Medium |
| Testing | Low |
| Pilot production | Low |
| Maintenance | Low |
| Management & reporting | Low |

**Fig. 3.13** The degree to which CASE methodologies address ten common application development needs.

niche methodology may be an appropriate choice provided that it fits the other factors well, and that current staff can be trained to support it.

### Business

Finally, acquiring a CASE methodology is also a business decision. Price, licensing arrangements, and the stability of the methodology vendor should be factored into the choice.

## Customizing and Enhancing a CASE Methodology

CASE technology is still in the early part of its maturity curve, as are CASE methodologies. Consequently, methodologies tend to be far stronger in their support of CASE tools than they are in their support of the entire application development cycle. Although specific CASE methodologies can and do excel in specific nontool related areas, developers are left to use CASE methodologies in these areas as best they can. Figure 3.13 provides a rough guide to how well today's CASE-based methodologies address 10 common application development methodology needs.

A rating of high indicates that support for the function is commonly found in most CASE methodologies, and when found, is both comprehensive and well executed. A rating of medium indicates that the function is found in some methodologies. A low rating indicates that the function, in today's CASE methodologies, is a rarity. It's interesting to note that, of the ten common functions presented, five are rated low.

If the methodology is new to your organization, a good place to begin customizing and enhancing is in closing gaps caused by functions that are important to your organization and functions in which your methodology rates low. Customizing efforts, thus oriented, will provide needed value while leaving less understood tool-support features intact. Customizing the way a methodology supports sophisticated CASE tools, such as ADW or IEF, should not be attempted until substantial experience with the methodology and tools has been gained.

Chapter

# 4

# A CASE-Compatible Culture

"I can't understand why we keep revisiting the same material over and over and over again," bellowed the Senior Vice President of a billion-dollar service company and head of the steering committee for a major CASE project. "The application development team obviously doesn't understand our business!" The Line Manager of the development project, who, fortunately, was not at the meeting and was therefore spared the outburst, was just as unhappy, but for entirely different reasons. Although he could see his CASE-based models closing in on every detail of the complex business requirements, the Line Manager knew that he could have already had substantial portions of the application up and running had he been allowed to hand code the parts he understood. He had also seen a sample of the COBOL that his company's code generator had produced for another project, and he was not impressed.

The Senior Vice President and the Line Manager were both correct, in the context of their traditional corporate and application development cultures. But, when viewed from the context of a CASE culture, they couldn't have been more wrong.

Of the many effects that CASE has on a company and the way it interacts with information technology, the most profound, least understood, and most difficult to deal with, are the products of culture. Adoption of CASE involves nothing less than a fundamental paradigm shift for management, information technology professionals, and business users, who will each be called upon to approach applications development differently. For a company to derive value from CASE, the ways in which CASE impacts each of these cultures must be understood and addressed. But understanding and dealing with cultural impacts is not nearly as straightforward as purchasing CASE tools or adopting a CASE methodology. Many are subtle, although their effects on the value CASE has to a company can be substantial. Other cultural impacts may take time to be felt and may not fully surface until partway through analysis. By the time they do surface, Data Administration staff, the application development team, and the business users may already be in a three-way war with each other over issues that could have been avoided had CASE's cultural impacts been better understood.

## How Culture Fits in with Other CSFs

The impact that CASE has on information technology, management, and user cultures is primarily the product of CASE methodologies. Although CASE tools and the techniques they support do impact culture, their force is felt, not directly, but through the application development methodologies that they support. (See Fig. 4.1.)

CASE tools, for example, are used almost exclusively by application developers for whom the entry and analysis of tool-based information has relatively low cultural impact. Although their users and management may be aware of the CASE tools and techniques being employed, their interaction with CASE tools is typically limited to reviewing tool products in the form of diagrams and reports. However, the cultural effects of CASE-based

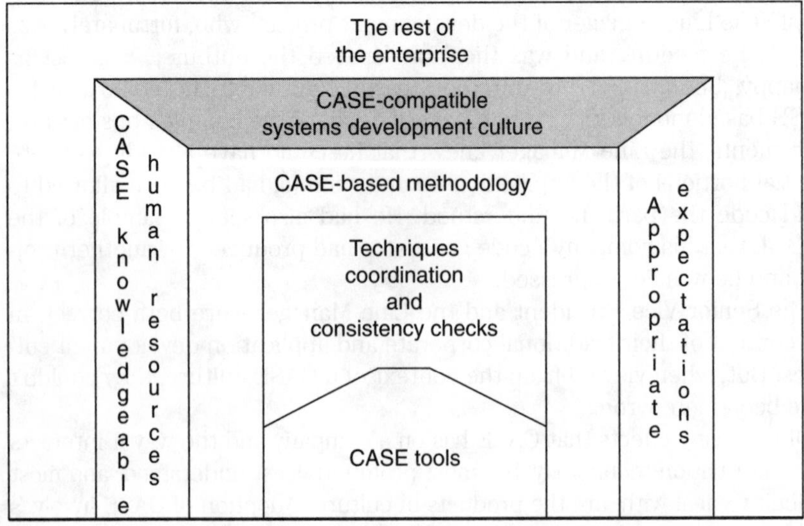


**Fig. 4.1** How a CASE-compatible culture fits in with the other CASE CSFs.

| CASE | | | Effect | Culture | | |
|---|---|---|---|---|---|---|
| Tools | Techniques | Methodology | Objectives<br>Tasks<br>Order<br>Emphasis<br>Work products<br>Evolution<br>Detail & rigor<br>Constraints<br>Roles<br>Control | Developers | Users | Management |

**Fig. 4.2** The ten ways CASE impacts developer, user, and management cultures.

methodologies that define the order, roles, responsibilities, activities, and tasks for everyone associated with application development, can be both substantial and direct. These effects are the origin of substantial cultural changes for all who come into contact with CASE. As we will see in the chapter on implementing CASE, they're also the source of the most significant management challenges facing companies trying to implement CASE.

### How CASE affects culture

CASE methodologies, along with the techniques and tools that support them, have 10 distinct and quantifiable effects on a company's business, management, and information technology cultures. (See Fig. 4.2.)

Although the nature and importance of each effect will vary with different methodologies, techniques, and CASE tools, as well as with the kinds of applications being developed, the 10 cultural effects presented in Fig. 4.2 must almost always be taken into account if CASE is to be a success. Consider, for example, the Information Engineering, ADW, and IEF requirement that data be modeled prior to designing the user interface (screens, dialogue, and reports). This seemingly innocent requirement affects application development culture via:

- Objectives (getting the data model right).
- Tasks (entity relationship data modeling and verification).
- Order (modeling the data first).
- Emphasis (placing equal emphasis on data and activities, and getting them both right).
- Evolution (dealing with a data model that evolves and changes throughout the application development process).
- Detail and rigor (defining, modeling, verifying, and checking for consistency, interminable numbers of entity types, attributes and properties).

- Constraints (taking target technology constraints into account while producing the data model).
- Roles (the application development team, not Data Administration, creates the data model as part of its analysis process).
- Abstraction and control (Everyone involved deals with abstract models of the business, its processes and its data).

Lets take a closer look at each of the 10 CASE-related cultural effects.

### How CASE affects objectives

The most fundamental way in which CASE impacts information technology, user, and management cultures is through altered objectives. Successful adoption of CASE requires that the most basic objectives regarding information technology, and the way the company interacts with it, must change. The information technology function is viewed in many companies as a cost center, with its prime application development objectives being to:

- Develop applications quickly.
- Develop applications at a low cost.
- Accomplish the development with minimum disruption to the rest of the organization.

In traditional application development, management has been able to further these objectives through deployment of productivity aids such as structured techniques, source-level debuggers, workstation-based development, 4GLs, and rudimentary code generators. But integrated CASE, using information-engineering-based methodologies along with an integrated CASE tool such as ADW or IEF, achieves high productivity not only through efficient code generation, but through better business-to-information technology alignment and reduced application development quality costs. It's largely by developing applications that are more relevant (a by-product of CASE-based planning), and by delivering the applications right the first time (a by-product of rigorous and detailed analysis coupled with high user involvement), that integrated CASE pays its users back. Deriving significant benefit from CASE, therefore, requires that management refocus its primary objectives to:

- Achieving business-to-information technology alignment.
- Increasing information system quality.
- Furthering user involvement.

Application developers must likewise refocus objectives, in this case from automating user specifications quickly and at a low cost, to:

- Understanding the business and its automation requirements.
- Accurately documenting the understanding while resolving issues and inconsistencies along the way.
- Delivering a high-quality, low (corrective) maintenance, product.

Regardless of the corrective maintenance (quality costs) that must be incurred before the applications provides value to the business, the traditional objective of delivering applications on time must be replaced with the objective of developing systems that are correct. This represents a fundamental cultural shift, one that is every bit as difficult as the shift that the manufacturing sector is going through as it refocuses on quality to become world class.[1] For users, the two primary information-technology-related objectives were: to develop application requirements (to be "tossed over the fence" for the application developers to catch), and to get back to their (real) jobs as quickly as possible. Those objectives must undergo a similar shift. (See Fig. 4.3.) CASE-based application development can succeed only if users get highly involved with the development process. It's through a high level of user involvement that the detailed and rigorous models that are fundamental to CASE-based application development will indeed accurately reflect the business requirements.

### How CASE affects tasks

In moving to a CASE environment, the predominant application development tasks shift from designing and coding the application to modeling the

| | Developers | Users | Management |
|---|---|---|---|
| Traditional objectives | • Automated users specs<br>• Low-cost development<br>• Fast development | • Develop the application requirements<br>• Finish quickly and get back to work | • Reduced IT costs<br>• Fast application development<br>• Minimum interruptions |
| Objectives with CASE | • Accuracy<br>• Business understanding<br>• High quality<br>• High productivity | • Make sure IT understands the business<br>• Get it right the first time | • Business-to-IT alignment<br>• Reduced maintenance<br>• High quality |

**Fig. 4.3** How CASE impacts objectives.

[1]Thomas G. Gunn, *Manufacturing For Competitive Advantage*, Bellinger Publishing Co., 1987.

business. CASE-based models are the link between the business requirements and the code generators that produce the application, and their importance in achieving a successful outcome can't be overemphasized. High-quality models that accurately reflect the business requirements ensure a high-quality application, while shortcuts in modeling always show up in code generation and testing—at up to 10 times the cost![2]

CASE-based developers therefore find themselves spending a substantial portion of their time working closely with users, trying to understand and model the business. This can represent a real culture shock for application developers, many of whom have built very successful careers working either alone or along with other application developers in an isolated, highly technical, environment. Business knowledge, interpersonal skills, abstract thinking, and ability to communicate ideas, become more important than technical prowess. For application developers, the cultural shift from an isolated technical implementation culture to a highly interactive abstract business modeling culture can be as traumatic as it is substantial.[3]

For business users, tasks shift from preparing requirements in a homogeneous and isolated business culture to working closely with information systems professionals to supplying details for and verifying models that are barely comprehensible. The combination of rigor, detail, and conceptual thinking associated with the CASE-based modeling process can add to this already challenging cultural shift. This is especially true for users who are used to dealing with the more concrete problems associated with business operations. One user, a very capable finance and tax analyst at a Fortune 100 company, found himself completely baffled for over two years by his project's IEF-based entity relationship diagram that "had no beginning and had no end."

Users who participate in CASE-based analysis and design will also be called upon to identify and document the (sometimes sticky) business issues that inevitably result from the modeling process. For certain companies, this too may run counter to user culture.

CASE-based development burdens management with new and challenging tasks as well. In addition to developing a quality-based culture as a primary means for achieving high productivity and reducing costs, management will have to free up users in line positions to participate in the development of accurate CASE-based business models. This too can represent a troublesome cultural shift for line organizations that have been developed as lean, cost-effective, highly focused units. Lots of grumbling and overtime is often the inevitable result. (See Fig. 4.4.)

---

[2]James Martin, *Rapid Application Development*, Macmillan, New York 1991, Pages 36-32.

[3]John F. Rockart, J. Debra Hofman "Improving System Delivery: A Managerial Perspective," Massachusetts Institute Of Technology CISR Working Paper No. 223, 1991.

| | Developers | Users | Management |
|---|---|---|---|
| Traditional tasks | • Analyzing requirements<br>• Writing specs<br>• Coding and testing | • Supplying requirements<br>• Acceptance testing | • Ensuring that time and cost objectives are met |
| Tasks with CASE | • Working with users<br>• Modeling<br>• Debugging and testing | • Supplying business expertise<br>• Identifying issues<br>• Verifying models | • Ensuring quality<br>• Freeing up line users<br>• Resolving issues |

**Fig. 4.4** How CASE impacts tasks.

## How CASE affects order

Not only are the tasks that accompany CASE-based development very different from their traditional counterparts, but the order in which the tasks are executed is different as well. Information engineering methodologies call for screens and reports, the tangible and understandable staples of traditional application development, to be designed only after substantial business modeling has taken place. We have a strong cultural inclination to measure progress based on how quickly we can see something work. This cultural inclination, the considerable time spent on modeling, and the abstract nature of the models themselves can make the order in which CASE-based applications are developed very difficult for developers, users, and managers to grapple with. (See Fig. 4.5.)

Business users, many of whom view the application as the screens and reports, have the worst time of all. They have little basis for understanding the enormous time and cost associated with redesigning a database when

| | Developers | Users | Management |
|---|---|---|---|
| Traditional order | • Screens and reports first<br>• Data and construction last | • Specify screens and reports first<br>• Testing last | • Sees tangible deliverables quickly |
| Order with CASE | • Business models and data first<br>• Screens, reports, and construction last | • Provide information for and verify models first<br>• Screens, reports, and testing last | • Sees business models first<br>• Waits a long time to see traditional deliverables |

**Fig. 4.5** How CASE impacts order.

unanticipated data requirements are discovered halfway through coding and testing. What they can and do understand is that their application looks like it's being developed backwards, with the important things postponed until last. They're likely to remain skeptical unless they're provided with credible material showing how and why CASE postpones the things they're most familiar with, bolstered by credible examples (pilot projects will do) and a culture that is focused on the future instead of on the immediate. And skeptics are not good sources of business modeling information.

Application developers, especially those participating in CASE-based development projects for the first time, can be equally dismayed by the postponement of what "really good" analysts and programmers have always been able to produce quickly. The cultural shift, of moving away from producing code quickly to developing high-quality business models, is a tough one for application developers who have built careers based on turning out quick code. They too are likely to remain skeptical until their management begins to develop the required cultural shifts by recognizing and measuring performance based on the CASE paradigm for application development.

For management, there's a threefold problem caused by reversing the traditional order in which application components are developed. Management must not only manage cultural transformations and new application development processes with which they're uncomfortable and unfamiliar, but they must also manage skeptical users and corporate management as well. Keeping users and corporate management at bay while planning and analysis modeling efforts are completed is achievable in many companies only by management putting their own careers on the line and making commitments that they may not be comfortable with. It's primarily for this reason that many CASE-based development projects are cut off partway through analysis.

### How CASE affects emphasis

Traditional application development cultures almost universally emphasize developing applications quickly and inexpensively, with well-structured code and minimum user involvement. The idea is to deliver a "functioning" application on time. Anything missed during development is set right after the system is delivered, during (corrective) maintenance. The emphasis on quick initial delivery is very much ingrained in user and management cultures, and it's often used as the yardstick to measure application development success—a successful application being one that is delivered on time, an unsuccessful application being one that is not. The resulting high maintenance costs associated with traditional application development, which often exceed 75% of the company's total information technology budget, are looked upon as an unavoidable consequence of information systems. With CASE, emphasis shifts from quick delivery to getting the application right the first time, even if it takes longer to develop. (See Fig. 4.6.)

| | Developers | Users | Management |
|---|---|---|---|
| Traditional emphasis | • Speed<br>• Readable code<br>• Corrective maintenance | • Speed<br>• Getting back to work | • Speed<br>• Reducing development costs |
| Emphasis with CASE | • Planning applications<br>• Understanding the business<br>• Correct data and activity models | • Identifying issues with IT to ensure that their models reflect the business | • Quality<br>• Reducing corrective maintenance costs |

**Fig. 4.6** How CASE impacts emphasis.

For application developers employing CASE, emphasis is first placed on planning the application to ensure that it will meet the business objectives, CSFs, and information needs before it's developed, and to properly scope out analysis projects (BAAs). During analysis, emphasis shifts to working with users so that the resultant business models, in which data and activities enjoy equal emphasis, are correct. In design and construction, emphasis again shifts, this time from producing well-structured code to ensuring that the ADW Modules or IEF Procedures, along with their action diagrams that comprise the code generator input, produces a correct and efficient application.

As the source code is automatically generated, the source code and its structure, which together comprise the centerpiece of many traditional application development cultures, are de-emphasized. If the models produced during planning, analysis and design are of sufficient quality, corrective maintenance is de-emphasized as well.

The emphasis shift for business users parallels the shift for application developers. Emphasis shifts to working closely with the application developers to ensure that their models accurately reflect the business so that the application will be delivered correctly the first time, and to identifying and resolving business issues that can affect the application after it's delivered.

For management, the emphasis must shift from reducing development costs by producing applications more quickly, to reducing corrective maintenance costs by developing applications correctly. The information system maintenance budget in most companies, when properly analyzed and presented, provides more than ample justification for this cultural shift.

### How CASE affects work products

The work products produced by CASE-based development are not only vastly different from their traditional counterparts, they're more abstract

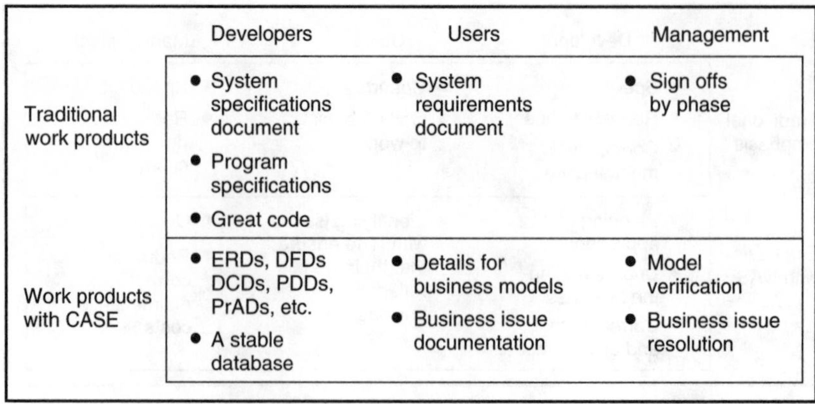

| | Developers | Users | Management |
|---|---|---|---|
| Traditional work products | • System specifications document<br>• Program specifications<br>• Great code | • System requirements document | • Sign offs by phase |
| Work products with CASE | • ERDs, DFDs DCDs, PDDs, PrADs, etc.<br>• A stable database | • Details for business models<br>• Business issue documentation | • Model verification<br>• Business issue resolution |

**Fig. 4.7** How CASE impacts work products.

and often meaningful only in the context of a specific CASE tool and methodology. Many can't even be viewed without using the CASE tool. (See Fig. 4.7.)

ADW and IEF-based entity relationship diagrams (ERDs), for example, describe the business information in a form that is very different from the way businesspeople, DBAs, or programmers would normally think of it. Data that businesspeople would recognize as pertaining to a customer, and that might be stored in a single DB2 table, may show up in the ERD as 10 different entity types, many of which are identified only by relationships to other entity types. Decomposition diagrams (DCDs and AHDs) depicting business functions and processes can be equally baffling unless the viewer understands what information engineering functions and processes are, and why they exist. Even viewing an entire ERD, without the use of an ADW or IEF workstation, can be close to impossible for anything but the smallest applications.

Application developers, who produce most CASE deliverables, can therefore have a difficult time presenting their work products to their understandably skeptical users and management. Managers and business users, whose applications will stand or fall based on models that, although far more detailed and precise than traditional requirements documents, are not nearly as understandable, have an equally difficult time with CASE work products. Many simply give up, or move ahead largely based on faith.

Even familiar work products, when produced by CASE, can be deceptively different. For example, COBOL or C source code is the product, not of coders, but of automated code generators that use models as their input. Although the COBOL or C work product still exists, and even looks similar to its handcrafted counterpart, the looks are deceiving. Its function, in a

CASE environment, is a lot closer to that of the assembler code produced by COBOL or C compilers than it is to the source code that it looks like. It's simply input to COBOL or C compilers, nothing more. The models and action diagrams, which represent the business rules and data accesses, are the CASE work products that functionally replace traditional source code.

The effect of the new work products on corporate culture is therefore twofold. They affect those who must produce the models, and those who must receive and interpret them. New skills (to build and interpret the models) and a new orientation (to understand and act on the models) are both required.

### How CASE affects evolution

Traditionally developed applications are built in a series of stages or phases, each associated with a set of work products that, once completed, tend not to change. A traditional requirements document, for example, represents the users' view of what the application will look like and the way it will work. Although the completed application may not fully conform to the requirements document, the requirements document itself remains fixed. If it doesn't, the developers have a difficult time completing the application as they continually try to make it conform to a moving target. The same thing holds true for other traditional work products such as the screens, reports, databases, and the technical specifications that programmers write code from. They're all fixed deliverables that, for well-run application development projects, don't change.

CASE work products, however, tend to be evolutionary. Many should and do change, sometimes substantially, throughout the application development process. In information engineering, the data, process, and data-process interaction models that comprise the work products of analysis, are built up in stages, as more and more is learned about the business area and its application. These models continually change, or evolve, throughout analysis. This is a normal part of CASE-based application development, and since CASE tools are very good at facilitating such changes, they are of little consequence.

But in many application development cultures, these changes are of major consequence. Business analysts, who are not used to or prepared for evolutionary deliverables, are often dismayed to see models that they carefully constructed, repeatedly replaced by new, and more correct, models. Business participants, who are used to line functions that are oriented to sequentially completed tasks, share their dismay. Managers, for whom changing work products has always been a danger sign that the project that produced them may be out of control, have perhaps the worst time of all.

Moving from fixed work products to work products that evolve therefore represents a major cultural shift. Application developers, users, and manage-

| | Developers | Users | Management |
|---|---|---|---|
| Traditional completed product | • Each work product is completed before moving on to the next | • Each area is completed before moving on to the next | • Progress can be measured in the form of completed work products |
| Evolving products with CASE | • Work products evolve as more knowledge is gained | • Constant need to revisit areas already modeled | • Progress can be measured by verifying models |

**Fig. 4.8** How CASE work products evolve.

ment will all need to be reoriented from task completion based on work products to task completion based on quality, or model correctness. (See Fig. 4.8.)

## How CASE affects detail and rigor

Moving the substantial detail and rigor associated with application development from coding, testing, and corrective maintenance, where programmers deal with it, to planning and analysis, where management, analysts, and users deal with it, is yet another source of CASE's considerable cultural impact. (See Fig. 4.9.)

ADW- and IEF-based planning forces managers to quantify and articulate how they want to run their company in ways that they may not be used to. Stating, as an objective, that management would like to increase penetration in an existing market from 35% to 50%, for example, is no longer good enough. CSFs, such as ability to match competitive pricing on a regional basis, and critical assumptions, such as a one-point fall in prime interest rate,

| | Developers | Users | Management |
|---|---|---|---|
| Traditional | • Leave the detail and rigor for programming and maintenance | • Little need to bother with detail and rigor in development | • Quick and easy delivery<br>• Expensive maintenance |
| With CASE | • Deal with detail and rigor up front during analysis | • Deal with detail and rigor up front during analysis | • Slow and frustrating delivery<br>• Inexpensive maintenance |

**Fig. 4.9** How CASE impacts detail and rigor.

which enable the increased market penetration, must not only be quantified and articulated, but also associated with subject areas, entity types, and functions. The combination of quantifying their visions in new and different ways, associating their newly articulated vision with ADW- or IEF-based models that they don't fully understand, and working closely with information technology to complete the process, can represent a substantial cultural shift for many companies. Business analysts, who have spent the largest part of their careers learning their company's business, can be dismayed to find themselves documenting business rules in the form of detailed action diagrams as part of a BAA. In cultures in which application developers rise from programmers to system analysts, to business analysts, this is not always a welcome experience, and it's not uncommon to hear complaints that action diagramming is a lot like the coding, that they (happily) graduated from many years ago.

Coding, of course, is precisely what action diagrams are. They're the high-level, machine-readable input that eventually drives the code generator. The concept is simple, and fundamental to integrated CASE. It's more productive for high-level analysts, who understand the business, to decide how applications deal with business rules, than to leave the same decisions to (lower level) programmers, who don't. This can be equally troublesome for business users, who for the first time come face to face with the detail and rigor associated with documenting their business rules in a form suitable for developing an application. CASE-based applications development, to them, can be a slower, more frustrating, and by inference, a costlier process than the manual development that they were used to. Although coding, testing, and maintenance costs are substantially reduced, the more immediate delays that a costlier analysis imposes on their application development projects is often difficult for business users and their management to tolerate. This is made worse when CASE has been sold to them on the basis of increased productivity.

### How CASE affects constraints

CASE-related constraints represent the exception to the rule that CASE tools impact culture through methodologies. When it comes to constraints, the tools have a more direct and pronounced cultural impact than do methodologies. CASE-related constraints come from:

- Reusable objects.
- CASE tool design envelopes.
- CASE tool target technology environments.

CASE methodologies such as Information Engineering and its derivatives achieve high productivity partially through reuse of objects. The cultural impacts are twofold. To application developers, who are used to employing their own ingenuity to handcraft custom solutions to business problems, reusing a general design to solve a specific problem can be constraining. Although reusing processes, modules, or procedure action blocks provides opportunities for being creative in reusing existing solutions in new ways and for new purposes, being creative in this way represents a significant cultural shift from developing a creative solution from scratch. A second, but related, impact that reuse has on developers is the need to take potential reuse into account when new objects are developed. This too represents a cultural shift for developers who are used to focusing only on immediate problems. Users of applications employing reused objects must undergo a corresponding and equally unwelcome cultural shift from purchasing expensive, handcrafted systems to purchasing applications that are ready-made.

While many 4GLs don't promote object reuse to the extent that ADW and IEF do, they nevertheless produce a similar set of constraints in which highly productive functionality can be achieved only in the way the 4GL was set up to deliver it. Whether a consequence of reuse or 4GL design envelopes, the resultant shift from demand-based functionality to availability-based functionality represents a major cultural change for many companies.

CASE tool target technology environments lead to constraints in two ways. The first and obvious constraints are the hardware, system software, and communications architectures supported by the CASE tool. Although both ADW and IEF are aggressively expanding the target technology architectures that they support, the available architectures themselves are expanding at an equally rapid rate. With two or more competing technologies often becoming available at the same time and for the same purpose, companies can easily find themselves torn between specific technologies supported by their CASE tool vendor and competing, or even incompatible, technologies that are required for other purposes. The unfortunate consequences of architecture incompatibilities can include anything from users having to reboot between CASE and non-CASE-developed applications, to being locked out of online access to important data. Companies adopting CASE for significant application development will, of course, have to live largely within CASE-tool-supported architectures.

A second, and less obvious, way in which target technologies constrain CASE-based development is by requiring that functionality be modeled in certain ways. Design tool action diagrams, such as IEF PrADs, provide a good example of how DB2 performance requirements can constrain design. In this case, alternate action diagram constructs can result in very different SQL statements being generated. Compound data access statements, such as extended reads that result in DB2 joins, may result in elegant-looking PrADs, but the SQL they generate may not work nearly as efficiently in a production environment.

| | For I/S | For users | For management |
|---|---|---|---|
| Traditional | • Can handcraft exactly what user wants<br>• Can choose any architecture | • Can dictate exactly what is wanted, the way it is wanted | • Exact fit is the prime objective |
| With CASE | • Can build the functionality that user wants<br>• Must address CASE-tool target architecture | • Must get what is wanted, but not necessarily the way it is wanted | • Engineering approach is the prime objective |

**Fig. 4.10** How CASE impacts constraints.

Since IEF data access statements originate not in design, but in BAA-based PADs, efficient transaction processing in a DB2 environment may well require that precautions be taken even during analysis. In this case, target technology-based constraints not only impact BAA PAD constructs, but with them, the ability to efficiently regenerate the application in alternate technologies.

In each of the previous examples, the impact is substantially the same. Choosing a CASE tool places constraints on not only the technology architectures that are available for development, but also on the CASE-based business models themselves. The cultural impact of these constraints are felt not only by the architects who must live within the confines of what the CASE tools support, but also by analysis and design teams who must take the constraints into account. (See Fig. 4.10.)

### How CASE affects roles

CASE changes the roles that different functions play in the application development process. For users, the shift from customer to participant can be traumatic. Application developers, who find themselves building abstract models instead of designing and writing applications, undergo an equally traumatic shift. Even support personnel, such as data administrators, must seek out new roles as application development teams usurp their functions.

The participatory role that users have in CASE-based application development projects is becoming an understood and accepted fact of life at many companies. Successful user participation in the development of their applications, however, requires a lot more than reassignment. Cultural implications, in terms of responsibilities, measurement and compensation, must be taken into account. One company, upon embarking on a large-scale ADW-based development project, reassigned key users from five different regions to participate in the applications development on a 50 percent basis. For close to a year, the users spent half of their time with the application development team, and the other half doing their regular jobs. The development team did well, producing accurate and well-documented models that reflected the company's business requirements. But as the organization was already very lean, their business responsibilities were not altered to take their new roles into account. When it came time for performance reviews, they uniformly got poor ratings. As their enthusiasm followed their ratings, the business analysts found that their second year's modeling efforts didn't go nearly as well as the first.

The moral is simple. For CASE to succeed, all who participate must have a common goal, and achievement of all goals must be measured based on the development project's success.

Changing roles, even within information technology functions, can also have serious consequences if the resulting cultural implications are not taken into account. On ADW or IEF analysis projects, for example, everyone on the BAA becomes skilled in data modeling. This is an outgrowth of the very tight coupling that ADW and IEF provide between the data model and the activity model. But this is a new concept, and for organizations in which Data Administration has always presided over data modeling efforts, friction over modeling techniques can easily result between project teams Data Administration.

For large-scale, CASE-based development projects, new functions must be defined and staffed to manage project encyclopedias and to coordinate data models and reusable objects between development projects. New roles must also be created to manage the new functions. (See Fig. 4.11.)

### How CASE affects abstraction and control

CASE increases the level of abstraction that everyone in application development has to deal with, and at the same time, decreases their control. The

| | Developers | Users | Management |
|---|---|---|---|
| Traditional | • Team builds system<br>• DA builds data model | • Active role in defining requirements | • Passive role in planning |
| With CASE | • Team builds system and all models<br>• Supporting function manages encyclopedia | • Team role in analysis, which includes requirements | • Active role in planning |

**Fig. 4.11** How CASE impacts roles.

| | Developers | Users | Management |
|---|---|---|---|
| Traditional | • Deal with screens, reports, COBOL, SQL, and databases | • Deal with the application from an operational perspective | • Sees the application develop toward an operational objective |
| With CASE | • Deal with abstract models | • Deal with seemingly irrelevant models | • Understands that high-quality models will result in a quality application |

**Fig. 4.12** How CASE impacts abstraction and control.

entity relationship data model is far more abstract than relational database tables, or a COBOL copybook. Foreign keys are implied instead of explicitly stated, and one can only guess at what the database might eventually look like. Activity decompositions, in ADW and IEF, are based on data and dependencies, not on operations, which is the way most of us think of applications. IEF action diagrams, for example, are not only more abstract than the COBOL and SQL statements that will be their result, but they're done in two parts with data accesses and basic logic being modeled before dialogue, screens, and reports. (See Fig. 4.12.)

Application developers therefore find themselves in a constant struggle between developing the abstract models demanded by their methodology and CASE tools, and developing the physical system that they know will be the result. The problem is compounded by the loss of control that results from allowing the CASE tool to translate the abstract models into compilable source code. To management, with backgrounds firmly steeped in traditional application development, the struggle between seeing their physical system emerge little by little, and having faith that high-quality CASE-based models will produce a high-quality (low-maintenance) application, can be an equally frustrating experience.

To users, for whom the application will be an operational tool, the abstract nature of the models that CASE forces them to deal with is frustrating, counter to their production-oriented cultures, and in many respects, irrelevant. The connection between the CASE-based models and their application is a difficult one for users to make if they come from line positions and cultures where almost nothing is abstract. Many of the application developers don't quite see how a usable system will result from their modeling efforts, and to users, the whole thing looks like a largely irrelevant exercise. Conflict and confusion among application developers and users is the typical result.

| | Assembler | COBOL | CASE |
|---|---|---|---|
| Objective: | Make the system work | Follow the specifications | Help the business |
| Emphasis: | Efficiency | Readability | Accuracy |
| Knowledge: | Machine and instruction set | System and language | Business and information |
| Interaction: | Programs and machines | Specs and COBOL statements | Business and abstract models |
| Information: | Bits, bytes, and words | Characters and numbers | Entities and relationships |
| Activities: | Coding & testing | Designing and coding | Analyzing and modeling |
| Work with: | Machine instructions | Program logic | Business requirements |

**Fig. 4.13** Application developer cultural shifts.

## Application Developer Cultural Shifts

The cultural shifts that application developers make in moving to CASE are analogous to the shifts that occur when moving from assembler language to COBOL. Moving to CASE is a logical extension of moving from assembler language to COBOL. Figure 4.13 summarizes the cultural changes that occur for information technology professionals as their application development paradigm shifts from assembler to COBOL, and on to CASE.

The assembler development paradigm put application developers in very close touch with hardware and system software, and afforded them substantial control over the way their applications worked. Efficient hardware use was the order of the day, and developers were considered successful if their applications worked within the narrow confines defined by the primitive hardware that was available to them. The resultant application development culture was one of bits and bytes, in which the heroes were the developers who could squeeze the most functionality out of the fewest cycles, memory, and disk space.

The COBOL development paradigm provided application developers with a degree of insulation from computer hardware and instruction sets, allowing them to focus on the application and the way it would work. The application development culture shifted from a very technical culture based on efficiency to a less technical culture based on programs, structure, and statements. The shift was a difficult one for the very technical, who were closest to the computer hardware, and not everyone made it.

With CASE, application development is once again being refocused, this time from programs, language and structure, to understanding and accu-

| | Traditional development | CASE-based development |
|---|---|---|
| Objective: | Hand off requirements | Develop requirements |
| Emphasis: | Requirements and testing | Planning and analysis |
| Interaction: | Arms-length relationship with developers | On a joint team with developers |
| Activities: | Documenting procedures | Model development |
| Work with: | Other businesspeople | IT Business specialists |

**Fig. 4.14** User cultural shifts.

rately modeling business rules and requirements. Programs that, along with their structure and statements, were the primary focus of the COBOL development paradigm, are automatically generated and therefore of only minor interest. The resultant cultural shift is once again away from technology and toward "a wholly new, totally business-oriented culture . . .," and once again those who can't refocus away from their technologies and toward the business and a higher degree of abstraction, will have trouble making the shift.[4]

## User Cultural Shifts

The application developers' shift away from technology and toward business requires that business users become more directly involved in the application development process. The arms-length customer-to-provider relationship, in which requirements were delivered to application developers who delivered a working application in return, is replaced by application development teams in which users work along with their information technology counterparts to develop the models that CASE tools turn into applications.[5] (See Fig. 4.14.)

The resulting CASE-induced cultural shift, in which users become personally involved in the modeling of their applications, is part of a general cultural shift in which business professionals are becoming more technically oriented, more computer literate, and more inclined to interact with information technology in a personal way.

## Management Cultural Changes

CASE affects management culture in two principal ways. Planning tools and methodologies provide a forum for user and information technology man-

[4]R. Jones, "Time To Change The Culture of Information System Departments." *Information And Software Technology*, March 1989 Volume 31.

[5]A. C. Gillies, "Humanizing The Software Factory," *Information And Software Technology*, Volume 33, November 1991.

| | Traditional development | CASE-based development |
|---|---|---|
| Objective: | Cost reduction | Competitive advantage |
| Emphasis: | Automate, reduce staff | Leverage information technology and company data |
| Interaction: | Other managers | Joint planning and analysis teams |
| Activities: | Set priorities, monitor progress | Resolve business issues, ensure quality |
| Work with: | ROI, cost reduction | Objectives, CSFs, and information needs |

**Fig. 4.15** Management cultural shifts.

agement to look at their company in new ways and to leverage their information and technology resources to further the business objectives. Analysis and design tools and methodologies achieve a similar result by surfacing business and technical issues, which management must resolve if the applications they produce are to be a success. (See Fig. 4.15.)

The second way in which CASE affects business and information technology management culture is by refocusing attention from the tactical to the strategic. Planning methodologies and tools promote strategic views of data across systems and organizational boundaries. Analysis methodologies and tools promote delivering correct, low-maintenance applications that serve the business. Construction methodologies and tools promote reuse instead of designing from scratch. The combination of a broader, more strategic and more business-oriented focus is the cultural impact of CASE on management.

Chapter

# 5

# Human Resources

Stories about failed CASE-based development projects permeate our collective CASE experience. Often associated with CASE are:

- Projects in which key analysis issues went unresolved because the analysis team couldn't access users who could answer their questions.
- Ventures in which over a third of the development effort went into model management.
- Endeavors that generated a system that didn't perform.

Although these problems are real, they're not the result of CASE. They're the predictable result of improperly deployed human resources.

Although CASE can be used to automate many of the tasks associated with developing information systems, the development process itself remains human-resource intensive. Successful implementation of CASE requires that application development projects be managed and staffed with appropriate individuals who have the skills and competencies required for CASE. The abstraction, detail, rigor, and business orientation of CASE-based models impacts not only application developers, but also users, management, and application development support personnel. Success with CASE is achievable only when all who are associated with the application development process are appropriately skilled and deployed.

## Human Resources and Other CASE CSFs

As with cultural impact, human resource requirements and constraints stem, not from CASE tools, but from the methodologies and techniques that

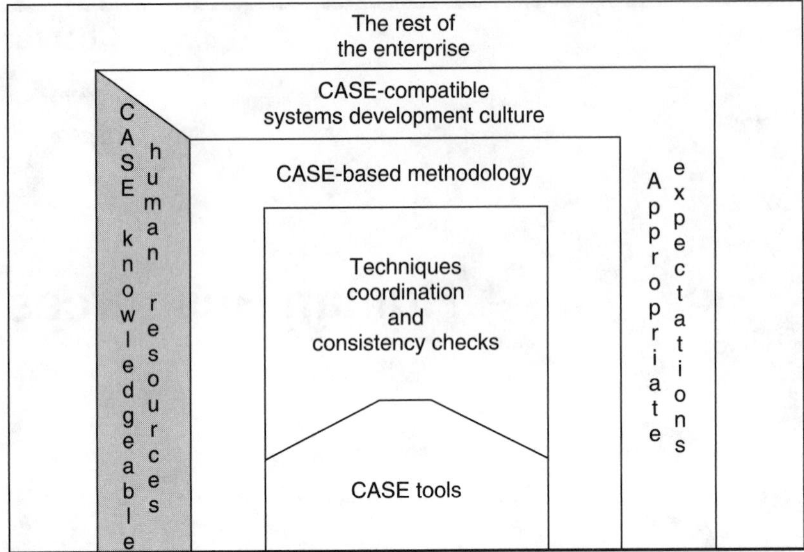


**Fig. 5.1** How human resources fits in with the other CASE CSFs.

the tools require and support. Indeed, CASE tools are used by only a small fraction of the people who are associated with, and affected by, CASE-based application development. (See Fig. 5.1.)

The emphasis that information-engineering-based methodologies place on business analysis, for example, requires that application developers and business users acquire new analysis and modeling skills. The models that must be developed for Lower CASE require analysts, designers, and coders to work with higher level and more abstract concepts—concepts that can seem far removed from the applications they seek to create. Support personnel such as database administrators (DBAs) must learn not only to interpret new and different tool-based data models, but also to use the new models to regenerate databases in days instead of weeks. Finally, because CASE-based models are the products of many participants representing a diverse array of business and information technology skills and interests, all must learn to understand and interact with new and different people, disciplines and bodies of knowledge.

## Skills, Competencies, and CASE Participants

Figure 5.2 summarizes the special skills and competencies that are required among information technology, business, and management personnel who participate in CASE-based application development. The skills are presented in order of importance.

- Abstract thinking
- Interpersonal and communication skills
- Business understanding and modeling skills
- Methodology and life cycle concepts

**Fig. 5.2** Skills required for CASE.

### Abstract thinking

The models employed by CASE can be very abstract, a fact that must be dealt with in all phases of ADW- and IEF-based development, from planning through construction and maintenance. Building and interpreting the models requires that all who interact with CASE be able not only to think and work abstractly, but also to take the abstract concepts and relate them to their company, its information systems, and its data. (See Fig. 5.3.)

In CASE-based planning, the business, along with its objectives, CSFs, and information needs, is modeled in terms of generic functions and data classes called "subject areas" that are independent of product, organization, geography, and current systems. Models can, and often do, cross over organizational and geographic boundaries, and if the models are to be of value, they must be understood not only by those who produce them, but also by the managers who have the power to act on the insights that the models provide. For example, the planning model for an East-coast manufacturing company viewed marketing, preproduction, manufacturing, and quality control specifications, which were stored in 12 different computer systems in five different countries, as a single subject area called Engineering Specifications. There were significant efficiencies to be gained from entering the Engi-neering Specifications only once and ensuring that the specifications didn't diverge as they passed through different operations. But the

| | | |
|---|---|---|
| Top management and planners | interact with | Abstract generic functions and data classes |
| Business users and analysts | interact with | Abstract activity data and interaction models |
| Business users and designers | interact with | Abstract operational models |
| CASE tools | interact with | Programs |

**Fig. 5.3** How participants in CASE-based application development interact with abstract models.

concept, along with the systems required to implement it, was difficult for management to grasp, and the project foundered. For CASE-based planning to yield meaningful results, the managers who use it have to be abstract thinkers so that they're able to interpret and act on the concepts that their planning projects present.

The models resulting from CASE-based analysis can be just as abstract. Here, the operational view of the system, which developers and users are comfortable and familiar with, is replaced by a set of abstract BAA models. The models view the application, not as an operational tool that does something useful for the company, but as abstract collections of data and processes that access the data in an unspecified order. To build, interpret, and manage these models, it's once again necessary to have the ability to think abstractly and to relate the abstract concepts to an operational view of the application being developed. Participants sometimes can't deal with the abstract models and make the required connection between their abstract view and the operational application that the abstract view will lead to. At best, these people have trouble participating, and at worst, they can bring down the entire project.

This is what happened when a line manager and CPA, who very successfully ran Headquarters Accounting for a Fortune 50 company, was tapped to run an IEF-based development project to produce an accounting system. Although the project proceeded well under a strong user and technical team, the abstract and evolving nature of the analysis models that the team produced made the CPA terribly uncomfortable. He was simply unable to see how the abstract information engineering processes and entity types in his models related to the ledgers, statements, and supporting schedules that he knew and understood. He couldn't relate to the models or the progress that their construction represented. Corporate management, who saw the project, not directly, but through the CPA's eyes, reacted to the apparent uncertain and halting progress in a sensible and predictable way. They canceled the project.

It's tempting to believe that by the time a CASE project reaches its design phase, the models that feed the code generator become a lot less abstract than the analysis and planning models that preceded them. Although this is generally true, the design models remain far more abstract than their conventional counterparts.

Designers using CASE tools such as ADW or IEF, for example, find that they can no longer think in terms of developing programs to directly access the data they seek, or even in terms of programming a database management system, such as DB2, to store and retrieve their company's data. They must instead think in terms of their CASE tool, which programs the database, which, in turn, accesses the sought-after data.

Accessing data using conventional means, a VSAM file, for example, is not abstract at all. Sought-after records, along with the way they're ac-

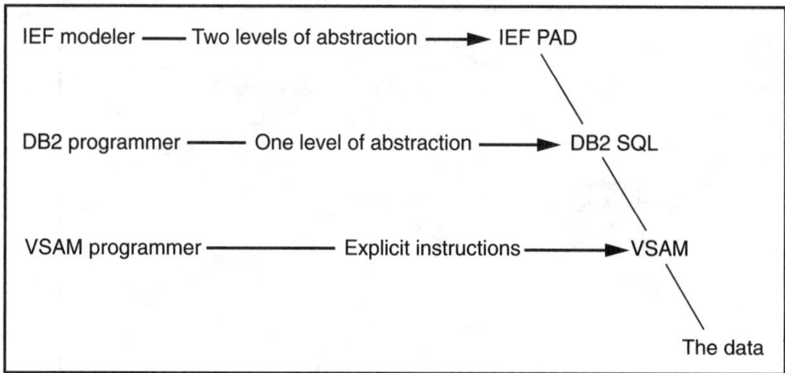


**Fig. 5.4** Levels of abstractions required for data access.

cessed, are explicitly programmed. Accessing similar data, contained in relational database tables, is more abstract. Although relational database query languages, such as SQL, can specify the data to be accessed (the desired result) the way the database management system goes about retrieving or updating the data is not explicit at all. DBAs, however, with some understanding of how SQL statements cause the relational database management system to access data, can write SQL statements that they know will execute efficiently to achieve the desired result. In an IEF Process Action Diagram (PAD), data access statements, which are two levels removed from the physical data accesses, are even more abstract. The PAD statements cause SQL statements to be generated, which, in turn, cause the database, such as DB2, to access the data and produce the result. The writer or the PAD, if it's to execute efficiently, must think not only in terms of the data being sought, but also in terms of the SQL that will be generated and the way DB2 will retrieve the data in response to it. (See Fig. 5.4.)

### Interpersonal and communications skills

Interpersonal and communications skills also become far more important for CASE project participants than for those who develop systems via conventional means. This is due to the abstract nature of CASE models, the unique combination of business and technical knowledge that the models reflect, and the newness of the CASE development process itself.

For CASE to work, the business and technical participants involved with the project must work very closely with one another so that all understand and buy into not only the detailed business concepts, but also the ways in which the CASE-based models represent the business's requirements, concepts, and technical constraints. Listening skills and the abilities to understand, present, and explain to a diverse application development team how

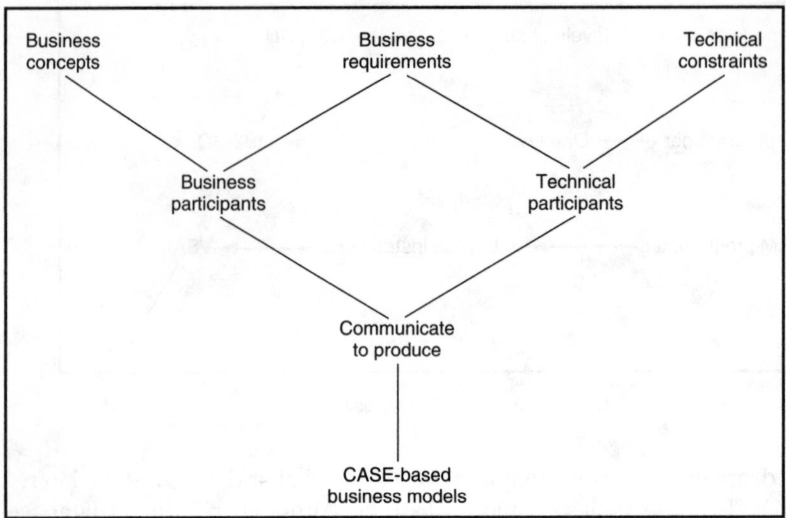


**Fig. 5.5** Business users and information technology personnel must communicate to develop CASE-based models.

CASE models work and how they reflect business concepts, are therefore critically important. (See Fig. 5.5.)

This was illustrated during a BAA for a financial service organization's reporting and accounting application. A combined team of 20 business and information technology executives was deadlocked for over two days while they tried in vain to understand how their "Posting" BAA would function. The problem was that Valuation, which is required for Posting, was being addressed, as part of another function called "Inventory Management." The operational (BSD) view, in which elementary processes associated with Posting and Valuation would become part of a single IEF procedure, remained elusive until an astute manager with an understanding of both information engineering and the business, realized that the problem was not a modeling problem at all, but one of semantics. The word "Posting" was synonymous with a well-understood physical operation, and neither the information technology or business participants could get past it. By splitting the "Posting" function into one called "Transaction Interpretation" and another called "Ledger Processing," and reserving the term "Posting" for a future BSD procedure, everyone understood, and the functions were immediately accepted. For CASE to work, business and information technology personnel can't work in isolation. They must learn to communicate.

### Business understanding and modeling skills

CASE replaces the conventional applications development paradigm in which user-generated requirements form the basis for applications that are designed and developed by the Information Technology function. The new paradigm is one in which the application is developed from detailed and rigorous models that are jointly developed. For the CASE-based models to work, both business and information technology participants must be conversant in and comfortable with both the business requirements and the models that reflect them. No one can accurately model a business that he or she doesn't understand, and no one can verify a business model that is not well understood and that doesn't make sense.

This means that the technical knowledge that served information technology participants in the past must be replaced by a combination of technical and business knowledge. Business objectives, customs, terminology, operations, and constraints must all be understood and assimilated before the business's requirements can be correctly interpreted and modeled.[1]

For business participants, this means becoming model literate. Sufficient modeling skills to understand modeling conventions and issues, and to accurately interpret the business models, must be acquired. One can't, for example, verify the business rules represented in IEF PADs or ADW mini-specs if action diagramming conventions are not understood, and without user verification, the PADs and mini-specs lose much of their value to the application development process. Business and technical participants must make the shift from operations to planning and thinking freely, from defined tasks to building abstract and evolving models, from executing procedures to questioning procedures and raising issues.

### Methodology and life cycle concepts

An understanding of the application development life cycle and the way it leads to a functioning system can't be taken for granted, and this is yet another consequence of the paradigm shift that results from adopting CASE. It's entirely possible, even common, for a development team and its management to go through an entire ISP or a BAA without really understanding the role that each will play in producing their application. Where integrated CASE tools such as ADW and IEF are employed, the life cycle is every bit as important as the models that are its products.

The functional decomposition and high-level data model produced during planning are a lot more meaningful if the roles they play in analysis are understood. The entity-to-function C-R-U-D matrix and affinity analysis, for example, are planning products that represent excellent vehicles for scoping BAAs. But scoping BAAs, without an understanding of how each BAA will be affected by the inclusion or exclusion of specific functions and entity

---

[1]Clive Finklestein, *An Introduction To Information Engineering,* Addison Wesley, 1989, Chapter 15. Also see Mark Duncan, "Preparing End Users For CASE," *Computerworld,* October 2, 1989.

types, is practically meaningless. Modeling BAA processes without understanding how they will be rearranged into IEF procedures would be similarly futile, as would be action diagramming for ADW modules without taking the needs of the target code generator into account. For integrated CASE to work, all participants need to have a fundamental understanding of the life cycle phases and how their products interrelate.

### CASE tool skills

Although CASE tools are the ultimate repositories for the models that are the backbone of the CASE paradigm for application development, much of the modeling that goes into them is likely to be generated outside of the tools, on white boards and flip charts. Hence, in spite of their high profiles, impressive GUIs, and value added consistency checks, the CASE tools are likely to be used only by a fraction of the total participants on a CASE project. While there's no harm in everyone associated with a CASE project becoming acquainted with the tools and their capabilities, CASE tool skills may not be needed by more than those participants who will be entering and updating the models and their encyclopedias. This is much less true for Lower CASE design and construction, in which technical and tool-related skills assume more importance. CASE tool skills and competencies remain an important requisite for teams engaging in Lower CASE-based application development.

## Skills, Competencies, and the Roles of CASE

Although it's desirable that all CASE project participants possess all of the above skills, the requirements for high competencies in specific skills are not equal for all project participants. Indeed, requirements in the ways in that specific skills are disbursed among project participants differ for Upper and Lower CASE. The business modeling efforts, which are the primary activities associated with Upper CASE planning and analysis, yield the best results when all participants understand the business and have minimum competencies in activity and data modeling. In Lower CASE design and construction, skills in specific technologies become important. Here, one or two individuals, who are very strong in action diagramming, teleprocessor, and database skills, for example, can keep an entire team going. (See Fig. 5.6.)

### Skill dispersion and Upper CASE

Upper CASE business modeling has two principal requirements: that the models accurately reflect the business, and that the models be consistent with each other. These requirements are most easily met when participants in the analysis and modeling efforts are sufficiently conversant in business

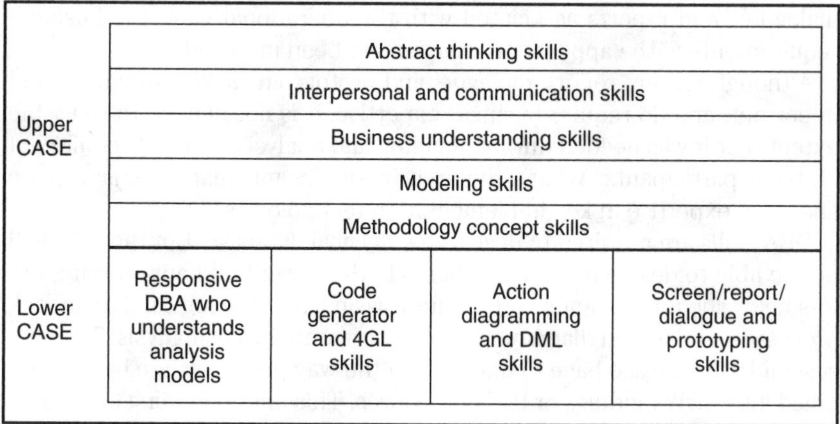


**Fig. 5.6** How dispersion of skills differs for members of Upper and Lower CASE project teams.

requirements and modeling techniques to be able to freely discuss modeling approaches, issues, and ideas with one other.

For example, to understand and correctly model their ideas, business participants who don't possess minimal communications or modeling skills become dependent on those who do. The extent to which their ideas are misunderstood or incorrectly modeled will be unknown and may not surface until design or construction, when many of the benefits of Upper CASE modeling will have been lost. With similar results, information technology participants who are skilled in modeling but don't possess more than a rudimentary understanding of the business, can easily find themselves correctly modeling incorrect ideas that they don't have sufficient knowledge to challenge.

Comparable problems can result when participants understand one model, but not another. Business rules, expressed as action diagrams, for example, can appear to be supported by the data model when they really are not. Without sufficient understanding of what the data model's entity types, attributes, and relationships mean, there's no way to verify the support. Once again, the important contribution that CASE-based analysis can make in terms of stable data and activity models, is lost. The modeling skills required for Upper CASE planning and analysis therefore tend to be horizontal skills in that all team members should possess reasonable expertise in each.

### Specific skills and Lower CASE

The mission of Lower CASE design and construction is one of rearranging the analysis models into an operational view of the application and implementing the operational view so that it performs efficiently in the chosen target technology. With the exception of designing the menus, screen dialogues, and reports associated with the operational view, the business requirements of the application have largely been modeled.

Although screen, report, dialogue, and prototyping skills are unique and important, and do require business expertise, it is not needed to the same extent that it was needed during planning and analysis. Nor is it required of all team participants. What's required in significant quantities is specific and deep expertise in key implementation technologies.

DBA skills are required to design the physical database. But the DBA will not be able to design a database that is both efficient and appropriate, unless he or she understands and has fully assimilated the logical data model, processes, and action diagrams that were created during analysis. The successful DBA will also have to understand the way processes are being combined into ADW modules or IEF procedures. This understanding takes time to develop, and for all but the most trivial projects, requires a close working relationship between the DBA and the analysis team.

A second requirement for DBAs for CASE projects stems from the capability of design and construction CASE tools to regenerate even sizable applications for a new database design in just a few hours. It's therefore both easy and common for a CASE-based development project to require responsiveness that the DBA function is not prepared to provide.

The traditional arms-length relationship, in which the development team provides the DBA with its requirements, and the DBA responds several weeks later with a database design, is therefore not appropriate for CASE. A CASE-knowledgeable DBA, who is either assigned to work on the development project along with the design team, or who is on call to make quick database revisions, is needed.

Code generator expertise is required for both design and construction phases. The expertise is needed not only to produce the action diagrams that comprise suitable input for the code generator, but also to help identify and create reusable code. The ADW/CWS code generator, for example, provides the greatest productivity when reusable DWS modules and CWS macros are defined near the beginning of the design process and the ensuing designs are developed to maximize their use. Depending on the teleprocessor employed, expertise on the teleprocessor and the way the code generator interacts with it can also be useful, as data model and action diagramming constructs are sometimes interpreted by the teleprocessor in surprising ways.

Needed along with code generator and teleprocessor expertise, is experience and expertise in action diagramming constructs and their DML implications. There are often a number of alternative ways in which the same logic, especially logic associated with accessing data, can be represented in module or procedure action diagrams. The difference is not in the functionality that the logic provides, but in the SQL statements, which the alternate action diagrams generate, and their database implications.

The required code generator expertise must therefore include not only the code generator and the action diagrams that program it, but also the ways in which alternate action diagramming logic are reflected through the generated SQL to the database.

The basic technical skills required for design and construction therefore fall into the four vertical categories shown in the lower portion of Fig. 5.6. Once these basic skills are in place, however, they can be leveraged by other information technology professionals who have reasonable competencies in basic database, coding, and ancillary technology skills. This requires that experts in each skill category are readily available to provide guidance and to help them over the rough spots.

## Staffing CASE-Based Development Projects

CASE-based application development projects tend to be front loaded, requiring significantly more effort during planning and analysis, and substantially less effort during design and construction, than do traditional projects. The relative effort required by each phase of a typical ADW or IEF project is illustrated in Fig. 5.7.

For our typical CASE-based application development project, for which the enterprise-level planning phase has been completed, this translates to the staffing requirements listed in Fig. 5.7. These numbers don't include the often substantial user participation in analysis and design, which can add as much as 100% to the total business analysis effort and 50% to the total physical design effort. They're also valid only for the medium-scale proj-ects that are the products of properly conducted information engineering C-R-U-D analysis. If large-scale analysis, design, and construction projects must be undertaken,

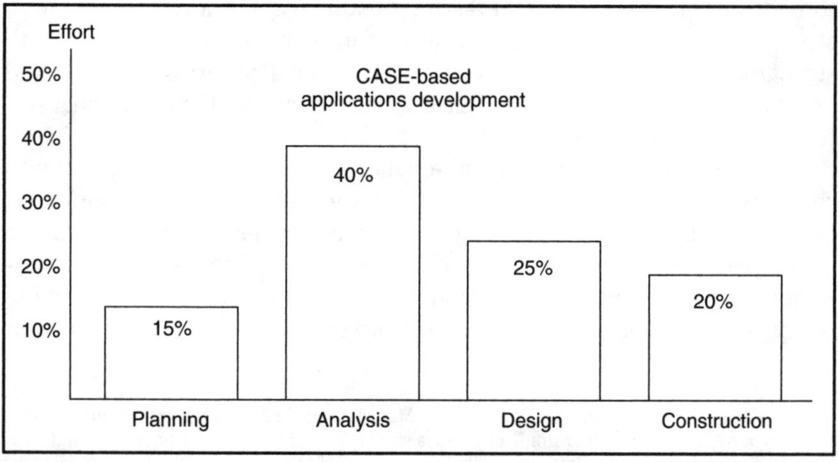


**Fig. 5.7** Effort allocated to each phase of a typical CASE-based applications development project.

generous allowances should be made for resolving more complex business issues during analysis and for more costly management overall. Staffing requirements, along with management problems and risk, can be expected to rise exponentially as projects become large. Figures are not presented for large-scale analysis projects, as it's my belief that such projects should always be broken into smaller, more manageable projects.

### The importance of strong management and a solid project team

As with the traditional projects that preceded them, CASE projects are sensitive to the quality with which they're managed and staffed. The difference is that, for CASE projects, the sensitivity is more pronounced. The increased sensitivity to staffing quality is the result of:

- The fundamental paradigm shift that accompanies CASE.
- The abstract nature of CASE-based models.
- The requirement for a very close working relationship among developers and business users.
- The ability of CASE tools to quickly propagate undetected errors throughout the application development cycle.

When CASE projects are managed and staffed by high-performance individuals who have the requisite skills, they almost always produce stunning results. CASE projects that are staffed by weak teams and poor managers do the opposite. To be successful, a CASE-based project must have either a strong team or an effective project manager, preferably both. Where both are not available, I have found the presence of an effective project manager to be far more important than a strong team (without a strong without a strong project manager). If a project team can't be put together with strengths in at least one of these areas, the results, in terms of quality and productivity, are likely to be significantly worse than with conventional system development.[2] (See Fig. 5.8.)

Where sufficient numbers of high-quality staff are not available, staffing a scaled-down CASE project with sufficient knowledgeable and experienced people will almost always yield significantly better results than staffing the larger project with armies of mediocrity. Teaming up experienced and inexperienced participants can be a good strategy for building CASE project experience while ensuring that current projects move forward with their

---

[2]John G. Sifonis, "The Landmark MIT Study: Management In The '90s," report published by Arthur Young, 1989, Page 26. Sifonis expresses similar ideas regarding strong teams and managers and weak teams and managers. While Sifonis found that the presence of a strong manager or team produces "above average results," I have found the presence of a strong manager to be more significant in determining project results.

| | Strong team | Weak team |
|---|---|---|
| Strong manager | Stunning results | Above average results |
| Weak manager | Below average results | Unacceptable results |

**Fig. 5.8** The impact of team composition on CASE-based development.

required skill sets. Pairing experienced and competent outside consultants with inexperienced internal staff members is sometimes a good way to seed the process.

### Components of a strong project team and effective management

The general staffing requirements for CASE-based application development projects can be expressed in terms of full-time project team participants

| Project participant | Planning | Analysis | Design & construction |
|---|---|---|---|
| Business Analyst | T | T | A |
| Business Expert | T | T | T |
| Business Line Managers | A | A | A |
| Business Modeling Expert | A | T | T |
| Business Operations Staff | — | A | A |
| CASE-tool Consultant | A | A | A |
| Code Generator Expert | — | — | P |
| Data Administrator | A | A | — |
| Database Administrator | — | A | T |
| Database DML Expert | — | A | T |
| Methodology Consultant | A | A | A |
| System Designer | — | A | T |
| Telecommunications Expert | — | A | T |

T = Full time project team member

A = Available to the team on an as-needed basis

**Fig. 5.9** Project team staffing requirements for each phase of ADW and IEF applications development projects.

and ancillary participants who should be available to the project, but not necessarily on a full-time basis. Figure 5.9 illustrates the kinds of project participants that lead to successful large-scale CASE-based development.

**Components of a strong project team.** Figure 5.9 shows the nonmanagerial staffing components for a strong CASE-based application development project team. As individual CASE projects differ substantially in magnitude and staffing needs, as do their environments, it's not necessary that each participant be present on each CASE project. Nor is it required that each staffing requirement be filled by multiple or different resources. These decisions must be made separately for each project. The participants presented in Fig. 5.9 are meant only to illustrate the classes of resources that are useful for large-scale CASE projects.

**Business Analyst.** The function of the Business Analyst is to work closely with the project's business experts to ensure that all the requirements are understood and properly modeled. A conceptually oriented systems person, with a good working knowledge of the business area, is best suited for this position. Good interpersonal and business communications skills are also required.

**Business Expert.** The Business Experts are the project's primary internal sources of business requirements and constraints. This position requires a businessperson with experience in, and a detailed working knowledge of, the business for which the applications are being planned or developed. The business expert should ideally be conceptually and analytically, rather than operationally, oriented, since he or she or she will be participating in the modeling of new, and possibly very different, applications. A good operational understanding of how the current system works can be helpful.

**Business Line Manager.** Access to line managers is required in planning projects to verify alignment with, and to add detail to, senior management's input. In analysis projects, line managers provide specific details for the models being developed, and in design and construction they can be extremely useful for verifying screens, menus, dialogue, and reports. Al-though line managers are seldom required or available on a full-time basis, their identification and participation will substantially benefit most CASE projects.

**Business Modeling Expert.** The Business Modeling Expert provides experience in the modeling techniques needed to produce high-quality data, activity, and interaction models that accurately reflect the business requirements. It's helpful if the Business Modeling Expert has taken previous CASE projects all the way through to design and construction using the methodology and CASE tool, so that the practical downstream consequences of modeling decisions can be understood and taken into account.

Note that a Business Modeling Expert is not the same as a Data Modeler.

Most CASE methodologies, and information engineering methodologies in particular, require modelers to be capable of modeling activities and activity-to-data interactions, in addition to modeling data.

**Business Operations Staff.** The rigor and detail associated with producing analysis and design models often requires access to business operations personnel, in addition to line managers, for verification and additional details. Their participation helps ensure that the application produced will be able to function in its intended environment without the customary corrective maintenance.

**CASE Tool Consultant.** Although the use of CASE tools is in many ways one of the more straightforward tasks associated with CASE, the elaborate system of consistency and integrity checks built into today's CASE tools can sometimes lead to confusion regarding why the tool is doing what it does. The services of a CASE Tool Consultant, with deep and current tool expertise, will therefore often be required to facilitate CASE projects. For projects staffed by experienced personnel, vendor telephone support may be sufficient.

**Code Generator Expert.** The Code Generator Expert is needed during design to ensure that the requirements, leverage points, and constraints of the code generator are fully taken into account. Functions performed by the Code Generator Expert include development of reusable code segments, development and provision of action diagramming guidelines and standards, and participation design reviews to ensure that the code generator is being used correctly. During construction and testing, a Code Generator Expert can be extremely valuable in helping team members test the right things in the right environment and to interpret errors in terms of the design models that comprise the code generator input.

**Data Administrator (DA).** Functions performed by the data administrator include participation in data modeling efforts for planning projects to help ensure alignment with other high-level data models throughout the organization. For analysis projects, the DA can help ensure that the data models developed by the analysis team don't conflict with other data models throughout the enterprise. The DA can also provide analysis teams with definition and data models of interfaces to other systems. As the analysis models for information-engineering-methodology-based projects require equal emphasis on both data and activity modeling, personnel such as data administrators, who are very data oriented, should not play a major role in modeling the application.

**Database Administrator (DBA).** DBAs play critical roles in analysis, design, and construction of CASE-based applications. During analysis, they ensure that the information being provided is sufficient to support the design of an efficient database. During design and construction, the DBA must not only design efficient and appropriate databases in response to the design team's requirements, but also work closely with the DML expert to ensure that the database is being efficiently accessed. Because CASE-based applications can be efficiently designed and constructed in small increments, and because CASE-based design and construction can respond more quickly to database changes than traditional projects, DBA services may be called upon often, with requirements for very quick response.

**Database DML Expert.** Database manipulation language (DML) expertise is required during analysis to provide guidelines for module and procedure action diagram data access constructs. During design and construction, the DML expert is needed to ensure that the action diagrams, which comprise the code generator input, generate SQL statements that can be efficiently executed by the database management system. The DBA and DML are often the same person.

**Methodology Consultant.** Information-engineering-based methodologies are sufficiently complex and unintuitive that methodology questions inevitably arise on CASE projects, especially during planning and analysis. Also, since not all methodologies are a good fit for the corporate culture or the application being developed, issues involving trade-offs among different approaches to tasks specified in the methodology will have to be analyzed, and project decisions made. Having the services of a consultant who is well versed in the methodology and its practical application, is therefore almost always a good idea.

**System Designer.** On CASE projects, the primary role of the system designer is to develop a physical system design that can be executed within the design and construction-tool capabilities. A second, but equally important, responsibility for the system designer is to take the lead in making decisions regarding which parts of the system to construct within and outside of the CASE tool, and to fully specify construction that will be hand coded.

**Telecommunications Expert.** Specifying screen data structures and using the CASE tool's screen painter to define the system's screens, although quick and easy, may not be adequate. Depending on the user interface requirements and the telecommunications environment, (e.g., CICS, Windows, DDE) the design and construction team may require the services of a person who fully understands not only the telecommunications environment being employed, but also the way the design and construction CASE tool interfaces with it. Telecommu-nications expertise should be available to each CASE project during design and construction.

**Components of strong project management.** The human resource components required for successful large-scale CASE-based application development are presented in Fig. 5.10. As with project team resources, not every

| Project participant | Planning | Analysis | Design & construction |
|---|---|---|---|
| Boundary Manager | T | T | A |
| Development Coordinator and Model Manager | A | T | T |
| Project Manager | T | T | T |
| Project Sponsor | A | A | A |
| Testing Manager | — | A | T |

T = Full-time project team member
A = Available to the team on an as-needed basis

**Fig. 5.10** Project management staffing requirements for each phase of ADW and IEF applications development projects.

management component will be required on each CASE-based project, and there's no requirement that each component be staffed by a different person. The project participants presented in Fig. 5.10 should, however, be carefully evaluated, especially for large-scale CASE-based development covering large organizational and geographic territory.

**Boundary Manager.** Planning and analysis modeling efforts, as well as the design of the application's user interface, often require that specific business and operational requirements be sought and taken into account. The function of the Boundary Manager is to develop and manage the boundary between the project and the rest of the enterprise so that its business and operational personnel will be available to the project. The Boundary Manager needs to have (or be able to develop) working-level contacts with managers and operations personnel in each business organization that uses or is potentially affected by the applications being planned or developed. A boundary manager is especially important for large organizations and for projects that cover substantial geographic areas.[3]

**Development Coordinator and Model Manager.** For all but the smallest of projects, a Development Coordinator and Model Manager will be required to ensure that portions of the models are available to team members who need them and to ensure that the models produced by different teams, projects, or even different members of the same team, are consistent with each other and not subject to conflicts or double updates. For large-scale CASE proj-ects, the development coordinator will be needed to manage version control for, and interfaces between, different development efforts that may progress at differ-

[3]The idea of a "Boundary Representative" to represent ". . . the many categories of people in an organization who will be at least peripherally affected by an information system. . . " was presented by John Sifonis in "The Landmark MIT Study: Management In The 90s," report published by Arthur Young, 1989, Page 25.

ing speeds. The Model Manager should therefore have stewardship of all models and sharable objects, including views, common action blocks, screen templates, subsets, uploads, downloads, merges and consolidations, backups, and recovery. Coordination of conversion and bridging requirements can also be included within the development coordinator's governance.

**Project Manager.** Although the responsibilities of CASE Project Managers parallel those required of traditional projects, some significant differences exist. The front loading of CASE projects, coupled with the propensity of information technology and business management to prejudge progress based on traditional criteria, mean that setting and managing expectations must assume a larger and more important role if the project is to be successful. A related, and equally significant, difference is that planning, scoping, and business modeling play a more important role in application development, and must therefore be given more attention and emphasis than their manual project counterparts.

**Project Sponsor.** The Project Sponsor is the owner of the project, and is responsible for the interface between the project and both business and information technology management. CASE-related functions carried out by the project sponsor typically include scheduling interviews and resolving business and scoping issues, as well as formulating and enabling the project team.

**Testing Manager.** The functions of the Testing Manager parallel those of traditional projects. The difference is that for CASE-based development, code development (e.g., IEF PADs for the code generator) can begin during analysis, far earlier than on traditional projects.[4] Therefore, while the governance of the Testing Manager will include development of test cases and the construction and execution of a test plan, they're also likely to include analysis model testing and verification as well. When strategic support of business objectives is an issue, the testing manager may also need to test and verify CASE-based planning models.

## Team and Management Continuity

Although applications are modeled from very different perspectives in CASE-based analysis and design, the two sets of models remain very much interdependent. The logical data model created during analysis is the basis for the physical database structure created during design; analysis process action diagram and mini-spec work products become the building blocks for design-based procedures and modules. Continuity of key analysis and design participants represents a good way of ensuring that the models created during design preserve and reflect the work done during analysis.

[4]Don Kelleher, "Testing In The Information Engineering Methodology," James Martin & Company, internal document, 1991.

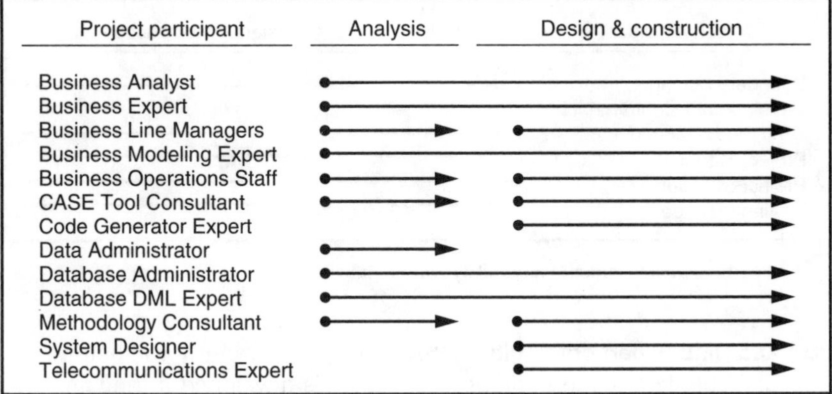


**Fig. 5.11** Project team continuity requirements for CASE.

### Project team continuity

To preserve analysis-to-design continuity among project team members, key design team participants should be carried over to design and construction from the analysis project. Figure 5.11 illustrates analysis-to-design-and-construction continuity requirements. This doesn't imply, however, that these skills are needed in the same quantity as they were during analysis. Note also that while methodology and case tool consultants are required during both phases, they can be effectively filled by different personnel, as can business line managers and operations staff requirements.

**Business Analyst continuity.** Continuity of business analysis expertise is needed to ensure that the business rules embedded in the analysis models, along with the reasoning and thought processes that they represent, are fully understood by the design team. Business Analysts are also useful in verifying that the application's screens, dialogue, and reports truly reflect the business rules and concepts.

**Business Expert continuity.** Continuity of business expertise will help to ensure that the design and analysis models reflect a single vision as well as a consistent set of business rules. Serious discontinuities between analysis and design business perspectives, if allowed to develop, can potentially render the analysis models close to useless.

**Business Modeling Expert continuity.** The Business Modeling Expert can also be valuable in helping to ensure that analysis models are properly interpreted. Maximum design utility can be derived from the process action diagrams and mini-specs, for example, only to the extent that they're fully understood.

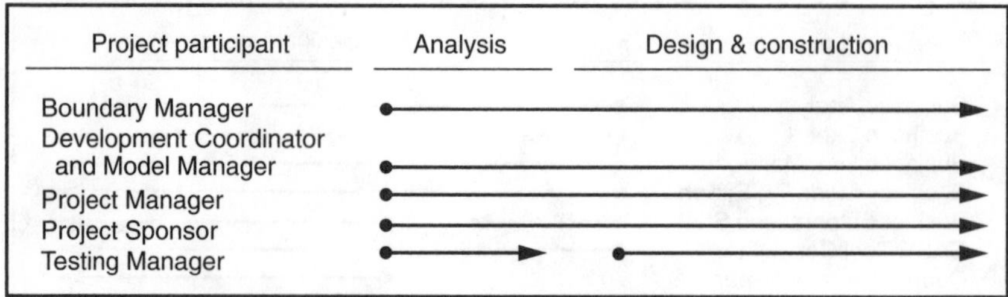


**Fig. 5.12** Project management continuity requirements for CASE.

**DBA and DML Expert continuity.** DBA and DML continuity will help to ensure that the data models and accesses models developed during analysis are understood and reflected during design.

### Project management continuity

As with project team participants, it's important to have management continuity between the analysis phase and the design and construction phase of CASE-based application development. With the exception of the Testing Manager role, which can be effectively filled by different personnel over the two phases, continuity of the entire management team is important. (See Fig. 5.12.)

**Boundary Manager continuity.** Design and analysis teams should share the same boundary manager so that hard-won interfaces between the project and working-level organizations, developed during analysis, remain intact. Although line operations personnel may differ, maintaining continuity with contacts developed during analysis can facilitate required contacts during design and construction.

**Development Coordinator and Model Manager continuity.** As physical design proceeds, Model Manager continuity will help to maintain the models in the CASE tool and ensure that the logical models developed during planning and analysis are updated to reflect decisions made during design. Development Coordinator continuity during design and construction will facilitate interfaces with other projects that may still be in analysis and more effectively tie conversion and bridging designs into the analysis models.

**Project Sponsor and Manager continuity.** Continuity of project ownership and management is required to present a consistent interface with the application's users, to oversee and facilitate resolution of business and technical issues that surface during the design, and to help prevent finger pointing between analysis and design teams. Sponsor and management continuity also helps to ensure that a single, consistent vision of the application is maintained.

Chapter

# 6

# Appropriate Expectations for CASE

"You lied to me yesterday! You lied to me the day before yesterday! And you lied to me the day before that! Why should I believe you now?" roared the Controller of a Fortune 10 company as the horrified analysis team looked on. Their IEF-based BAA had just entered its sixth month, and management was losing patience fast. The company was not inclined to stick with a project that had an overrun that was pushing 300%.

But the BAA was on schedule and doing well, from a CASE perspective. From a traditional perspective, which was the way management saw it, the analysis was taking three times longer than it should have, and therefore wasn't doing well at all. Both management and the team were right. The difference was one of perspective, and their different perspectives were the unavoidable products of their very different expectations.

Setting and managing appropriate expectations for CASE can be the most difficult of the CSFs to achieve. The difficulty stems not only from the CASE development paradigm being so different, but from the relatively long time required to reap CASE's benefits, coupled with the fact that CASE is often sold to management as a means for raising productivity. When viewed from a short-term perspective, raising productivity is precisely what CASE doesn't do.[1]

[1]Kristiina Sorensen, "Despite A Slow Start, CASE Goes The Distance," *Digital Review*, October 2, 1989.

For CASE to be successful, the expectations of information technology, user, and management personnel must be properly set and carefully managed. If not, CASE will in all likelihood not last long enough for its benefits to be realized. Applications development will revert to the traditional paradigm, and the CASE tools and methodologies will become "shelfware."

## Expectations Management and the Other CASE CSFs

The need to set and manage expectations is a natural consequence of the methodologies, techniques and tools, that make up CASE. CASE methodologies tend to be front loaded, often requiring many times the planning and analysis effort than do traditional methodologies. The techniques that support the expanded planning and analysis phases of CASE methodologies produce deliverables that are unfamiliar, abstract, and difficult to interpret. High-value CASE tools, such as ADW and IEF, support and enforce the prolonged early phases and unfamiliar techniques through rules, analyses, and consistency checks. (See Fig. 6.1.)

## Expectations and the CASE Application Development Cycle

CASE's benefits, in terms of productivity and quality, tend to be long-range. Many are not realized until development projects reach their design and construction phases, at which point development projects require less effort and proceed much more quickly than traditional projects. Still others

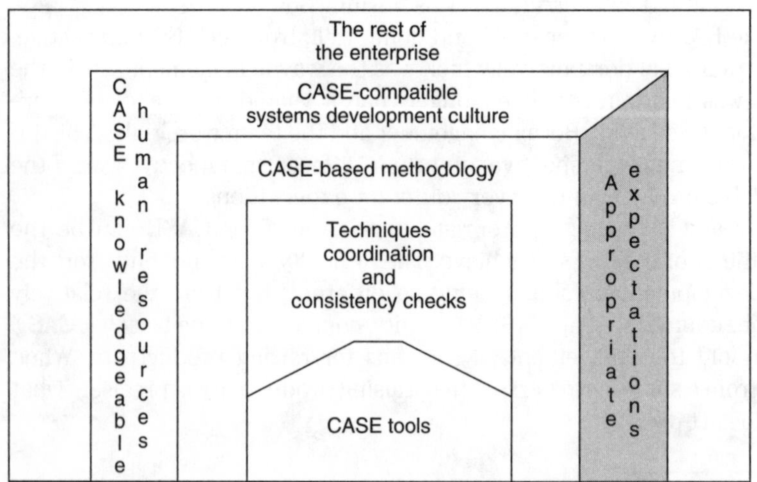


**Fig. 6.1** How CASE-appropriate expectations fit in with the other CASE CSFs.

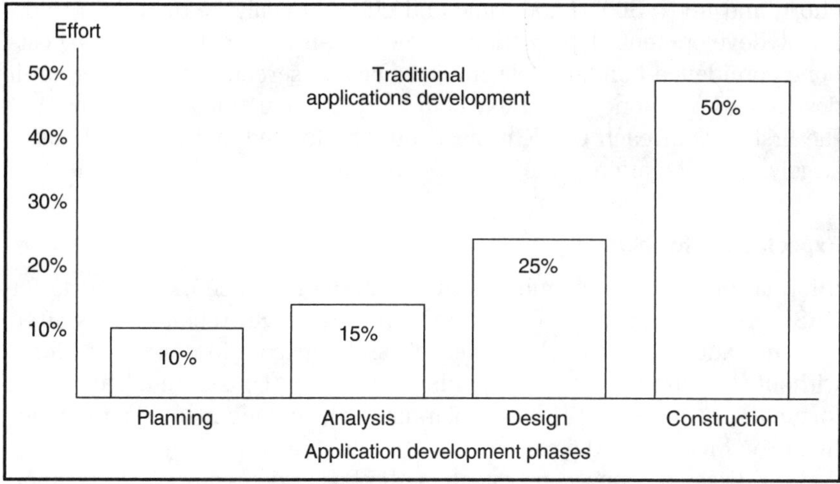


**Fig. 6.2** Effort allocated to each phase of a typical traditional applications development cycle.

are not realized until after the application has been delivered, when corrective and adaptive maintenance are substantially reduced. What's realized immediately is the investment, learning curve, and risks associated with a new technology coupled with an application development cycle that is heavily front loaded.

As Figs. 6.2 and 6.3 indicate, the front loading of the CASE-based application development cycle can typically require 50% more planning time and

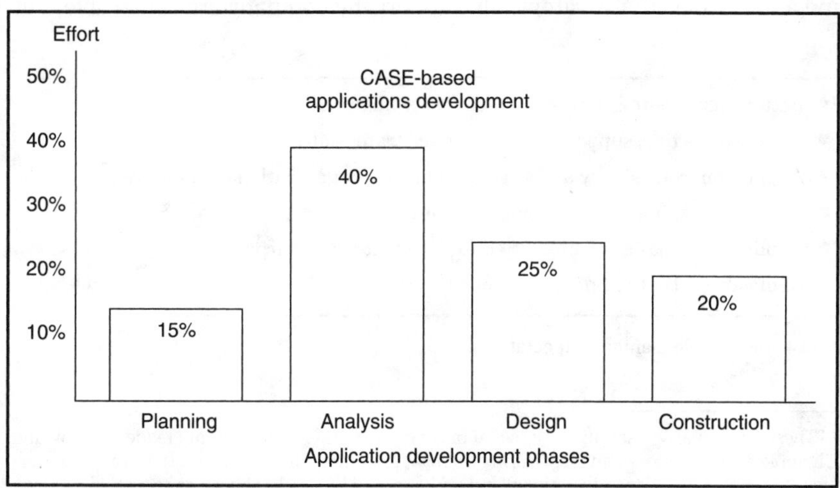


**Fig. 6.3** Effort allocated to each phase of a typical CASE-based applications development cycle.

effort, and up to 300% more time and effort in analysis, than does traditional development. Information-engineering-based methodologies postpone confidence-building deliverables, such as screens and reports, until design, and postpone executable code until construction. This means that the first 50% of each CASE project must be funded and executed based largely on expectations![2]

## Expectations for planning

Information systems planning is the one area in which expectations for CASE are almost universally too low. Indeed, CASE technology is often sold and adopted for analysis, design, and construction of applications, without its potential use for planning even being considered. This is unfortunate, because CASE-based planning can provide many useful benefits. (See Figs. 6.4 and 6.5.)

CASE-based planning can promote better business-to-information technology alignment via identifying, quantifying, and analyzing strategic business parameters such as objectives, goals, CSFs and information needs. Planning methodologies and tools employ sophisticated matrix processors and affinity analysis techniques to analyze the ways in which business parameters can be supported by the generic data and functions that make up existing and potential applications.

Taking advantage of these CASE-enabled techniques, however, requires not only a well-articulated business plan, but also a business plan that is verified and documented in terms of the quantifiable parameters with which CASE tools and methodologies work.

Expectations of better business-to-information technology alignment and applications that strategically support the company are achievable, but

- **Better business-to-information technology alignment**
- **Applications that support the enterprise strategically**
- **Application consistency across geographic and organizational boundaries**
- **Better leveraging of the company's information asset**
- **Applications that are better fitted for their intended purpose**
- **Applications that are properly scoped**

**Fig. 6.4** Achievable planning expectations.

[2]These figures are based upon personal observations and measurements made at ADW and IEF application development sites during the past six years. Similar observations on the differences in emphasis between traditional and CASE-based life cycle phases were made by Eileen Souza, "The Impact Of CASE On Software Development," *Journal of Information System Management*, Winter 1991, Pages 17-23.

- A faster, less expensive planning process
- A detailed and well-documented business plan is not required
- Little or no need for business management involvement
- Easy acceptance across organization, geographic, and governance boundaries

**Fig. 6.5** Unachievable planning expectations.

not without a detailed and well-documented business plan. To be useful for CASE-based planning, the business plan must be documented in terms of quantifiable objectives, CSF's information needs, and risks that are suitable for populating ADW or IEF matrices. In many organizations, the development of such a business plan and sharing both the plan and the planning process with information technology management may not be expected, or even welcome.

By applying matrix processing techniques to the company's generic data and functions, data and activities can be made more consistent across geographic, organizational, and system boundaries. Once achieved, the additional consistency can be used to develop applications that leverage the company's data and information technology resources.

But achieving the consensus and consistency required to do this can be problematic, especially in large organizations that are decentralized and geographically dispersed. Disputes over conflicting initiatives, business autonomy, and data governance, coupled with hardware and system software incompatibilities, get in the way. Strategic business support is a lofty and achievable goal, but it will not be realized in most companies without strong business management sponsorship, deep commitment, and active participation of all constituencies that may be affected. Appropriate expectations should include lots of time and effort on the part of business and information technology management to build and enforce the required consensus.

It is a valid and achievable expectation that the planning-enabled C-R-U-D matrices produced by ADW and IEF be useful for defining and scoping application development projects. But it is not a valid and achievable expectation that the tools and methodologies can define and scope application development projects without manual intervention. The scoping of reasonable and consistent BAAs that support the business is the product of not only substantial manual manipulation, but also equally substantial input from business and information technology management. Manual intervention is almost always required to supplement the clustering algorithms provided by today's CASE tools. The size and order of the clustered BAAs that result must be further adjusted to provide acceptable value to the business without undue application development "throwaway" costs. The common complaints are that C-R-U-D analysis yields "one enormous BAA," "too

- Applications that are a better fit for the business
- Applications that are right the first time
- Fewer logical errors and "program bugs"
- Lower enhancement costs
- Better documentation

**Fig. 6.6** Achievable analysis expectations.

many tiny BAAs," or a plan that doesn't support the business, but these grievances cease to exist when C-R-U-D analysis expectations are properly managed and these required inputs are taken into account.

## Expectations for analysis

Analysis is the phase in which the expectations and realities of CASE are often furthest apart. Not only does CASE-based analysis take substantially longer than traditional analysis, but it also requires more business and information technology resources. These requirements stand in sharp contrast to the common perception that CASE raises productivity and reduces cost. The result is that many companies, having justified CASE based on increases in productivity and reductions in application development costs, are forced to terminate CASE projects while partway through analysis. For such companies, the benefits of a prolonged and costly analysis are lost because they don't show up until design and construction. (See Figs. 6.6 and 6.7.)

Although a CASE-based analysis that takes up to 300% longer, uses more resources, and yields models that are hard to understand, may be a foreign and distasteful concept to management, the concept of making substantial investments with a long-term payoff is not. Nor are the concepts of becoming more involved in or dealing with technologies that they don't fully understand. These concepts are fundamental to any company that has adopted CAD/CAM or CIM, developed new financial instruments, reengineered a business or developed a high-technology product.

- Faster and less costly analysis
- Business participation at or below levels required for traditional analysis
- Reducing time and effort spent on analysis will result in quicker application development
- Models that are understandable to anyone but CASE-trained professionals
- A quick learning curve

**Fig. 6.7** Unachievable analysis expectations.

The issue is not one of prolonged and costly analysis, high levels of business user participation, unfamiliar procedures, a prolonged learning curve, or technologies that are hard to understand. The difference is that CASE is often purchased and deployed without the expectations of time, investment, involvement, and risk being properly addressed.

For CASE to be successful, information technology and user participants, along with their management, must understand and be prepared to deal with the following CASE-related issues.

- CASE-based analysis is more costly and labor intensive, often by up to 300% or more. It forces business and information technology participants, along with their management, to openly deal with data, business rules, and issues at a much more detailed level than they may be used to.
- The data, activity, and interaction models that CASE produces are a much more solid basis for designing and implementing applications than are conventional specifications, but these models are new and difficult for people not used to them to understand. Familiar analysis products such as screens, menus, and reports are not part of the CASE-based analysis repertoire.
- The detailed and rigorous modeling required to complete analysis can involve a substantial learning curve. Specialized training, supplemented by external consultants, may be required before sufficient numbers of CASE-knowledgeable internal resources can be developed.
- The quality of the models produced during analysis directly impacts the gains in quality and productivity that can be realized during design, construction, and maintenance. Shortcuts taken during analysis, however tempting, are multiplied many times in terms of lower quality and productivity during design and construction.

### Expectations for design and construction

Design and construction are the phases in the CASE life cycle where expectations can be, and often are, met. This is where the substantial productivity gains that CASE can provide over conventional application development show up. Expectations in terms of reusable code, reduced corrective maintenance, and the ability to regenerate applications for different target technologies are all achievable in these phases. Even the deliverables, such as screens, menus and reports, are comfortable and familiar. There are, however, some caveats, and a number of design and construction expectations that can't be achieved. The high productivity afforded by ADW and IEF code generators, for example, is not achievable in the absence of a high-quality and fully completed analysis. Nor are they achievable if the code generator is not tightly integrated to the design tool, and the design tool tightly integrated to the tool used for analysis. The substantial investment made during analysis can indeed

- High productivity
- Reuse of code and objects
- Ability to regenerate for different target technologies
- Deliverables that are understandable and easy to relate to
- Lower corrective maintenance costs

**Fig. 6.8** Achievable design and construction expectations.

pay off during design and construction, but only to the extent that quality and integration permit. (See Figs. 6.8 and 6.9.)

Design and construction expectations that are not achievable include doing away with the need to code detailed business rules and logic, deriving immediate benefits from reusable code, generation of code that meets predefined standards, and high performance without tuning the DDL and database. With the exceptions of screen painting, which provides substantial productivity gains over manually coding screens, and reusing data access statements that were written during analysis, much of the detailed procedural logic must still be coded in the form of action diagrams for modules or procedures. Although both ADW and IEF provide mechanisms for reusing action diagrams, deriving benefit from their reuse is far from automatic. The expectation that reusing code will provide immediate value to development projects must be mitigated by the time it takes to develop a viable library of reusable code and by the creation and administration of a design and development environment that promotes and facilitates reuse.

Compilable source code, which is a principal product of the design and construction process, can also be the subject of inappropriate expectations. The problem stems from coding standards that, although absolutely necessary for handcrafted code, are not appropriate for code that is produced by a code generator. Generated code, in the CASE paradigm for application development, is nothing more than input to compilers, which provide input to binders, which provide input to loaders. The quality of generated code should be measured, not by its structure, over which CASE tool users have little control, but by the way it performs when compiled, linked, loaded, and executed.

- High productivity without high quality and tightly integrated design and analysis
- No need to code detailed business rules and logic
- Immediate benefits from code reuse
- Code that conforms to manual coding standards

**Fig. 6.9** Unachievable design and construction expectations.

## CASE Expectations and the Organization

CASE technology is purchased, introduced, and adopted by the information technology function, often without much notice by the rest of the organization. Yet CASE can profoundly affect not only the information technology function, but the way operations and management deal with information technology, and in some cases, the way they do their jobs. Setting and managing appropriate expectations of management, information technology, and user organizations, is therefore critical to the success of CASE.

### Management expectations

For CASE to provide substantial value to a company, management expectations must include a realistic view of CASE, not only as a means for boosting application development quality and productivity, but also as a strategic business tool. (See Figs. 6.10 and 6.11.)

Competitive advantage, enabled by the close business-to-information-technology alignment that CASE-based planning facilitates, can't be realized if management is unaware of what CASE-based planning is, or how it can contribute to better alignment. Nor will it become a reality if management is not prepared to make CASE, and with it information technology management, an integral part of the company's planning process.

Management expectations for CASE-based planning need not be limited to better information technology plans and strategic alignment. The order of magnitude of improvements promised by business process reengineering, for example, becomes a lot less elusive when the reengineering effort is supported by CASE-based business models. Generic data, functions, and processes, which are modeled as part of CASE-based planning and analysis, can provide valuable insights into information resources that exist outside of current organizations, procedures, and geographic dispersion. The same models can be just as useful in understanding the data and generic process-based constraints under which reengineered business processes, if they're to be successful, must operate. If management expectations for CASE don't address the key support roles that CASE technologies can play in business

- Better business-to-IT alignment
- Business process reengineering support
- High productivity
- High quality
- Faster delivery
- Lower corrective maintenance

**Fig. 6.10** Achievable management expectations.

- Business planning without IT involvement
- Business reengineering without IT involvement
- Lower IT costs (they will be absorbed by the backlog)
- Low turnover

**Fig. 6.11** Unachievable management expectations.

process reengineering, many of the potential advantages of not only CASE, but of business process reengineering, can be lost.

Management expectations, in terms of information technology cost reductions, are both valid and appropriate. But if they're to be fulfilled, expectations for cost reductions must take into account the substantial learning curve that accompanies CASE. They must likewise account for how and where the cost reductions can be achieved.

Expectations for cost reductions during design, construction, and maintenance should be tempered by expectations of higher planning and analysis costs. It's the failure to properly set this expectation that causes management to sour on CASE, often solely on the basis of a more costly analysis. A cursory look at most information technology budgets will reveal the disparity between the enormous amounts of money spent on maintenance, compared with funds spent on analysis. After increases in planning and analysis costs have been fully discounted, the net reductions in application development costs afforded by CASE can still be substantial. There are no valid reasons for not taking increased planning and analysis costs into account. (See Figs. 6.12 and 6.13.)

Net reductions in information technology costs, associated with development of individual applications, may be more than offset by the increased numbers of, and the complexity of, the applications delivered. It's therefore necessary, when setting information technology cost reduction expectations, to take the application backlog into account. The combination of application backlog reductions, and the ability to deliver applications more quickly, can have a substantial and positive effect on operating costs. Faster delivery of new applications, can not only enable the company to be more competitive through new products and entry into new markets, but it can also reduce the time required to realize application dependent cost reductions. These substantial and positive effects notwithstanding, the net application development costs are likely to go up for companies with large application backlogs.

### Information technology expectations

Although CASE is an information technology, the gap between expectations for CASE and what CASE really does is often widest among information technology professionals. This paradox is the result of the newness of

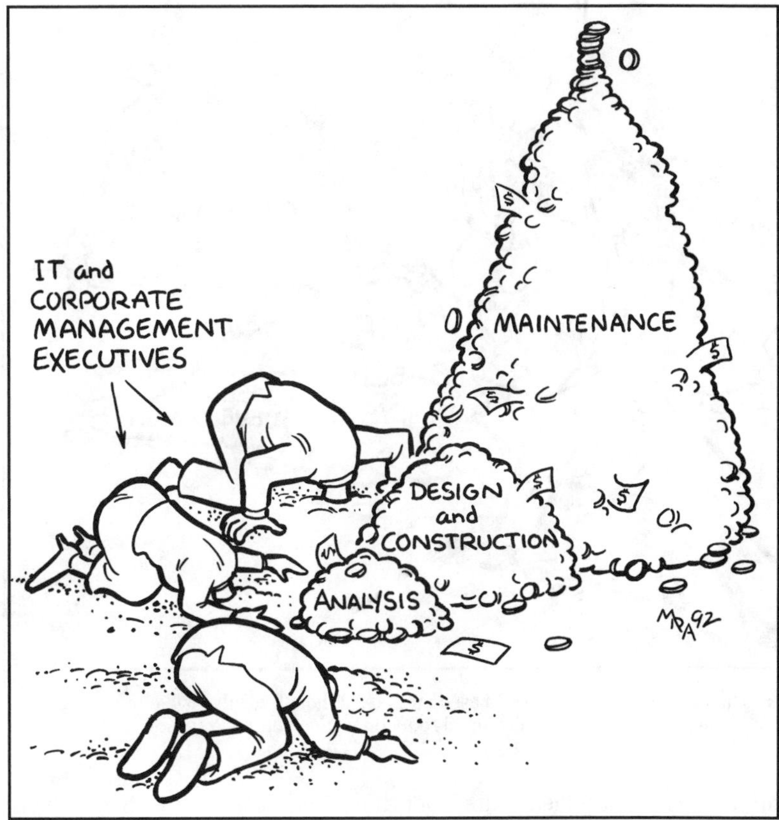


**Fig. 6.12** The increased cost of CASE-based analysis, although highly visible, can be more than offset by substantial reductions in maintenance costs— a fact that's lost on many corporate management executives.

CASE, coupled with the profound way in which it can affect the way information systems are developed. Companies can therefore anticipate significant problems in making a success of CASE unless they properly set and manage the expectations of the programmers, analysts, project managers, data administrators, and database administrators, who will be most directly affected by the adoption of CASE. (See Figs. 6.14 and 6.15.)

Becoming proficient in CASE involves a substantial learning curve. A significant amount of hands-on project experience is typically required before the light bulb comes on, and information technology project participants begin to feel comfortable with their new technology.

For moderately sized projects, this generally takes about six months. In ADW- or IEF-based analysis, for example, project participants often begin feeling comfortable during mini-specs and process action diagramming, as team members experience potentially costly, even catastrophic, logic and

**Fig. 6.13** The increased cost of CASE-based analysis, although highly visible to management, can be more than offset by substantial reductions in maintenance costs.

data model inconsistencies being identified and resolved with relatively modest effort. Some team members, as a result of catching and resolving significant problems early on, become so enthusiastic about CASE that they leave their companies to join their CASE vendor! Keeping the benefits of CASE in perspective, and expectations at realistic levels among project participants, requires alert and careful management.

In addition to a significantly longer learning curve than one might expect, adoption of CASE requires a high level of commitment and support. With CASE, it's not appropriate to expect that new technologies can be evaluated and adopted without direct involvement of high-level, experienced informa-

- **High productivity**
- **High-quality applications**
- **Low corrective maintenance**
- **More efficient enhancements**

**Fig. 6.14** Achievable information technology expectations.

- Short learning curve
- Balanced view among CASE project participants
- Implementation without active high-level participation and support
- Information technology roles will not be significantly altered by CASE
- High compatibility between CASE tools
- Applicability of current methodologies and latitude in choosing new methodologies
- Unrestricted utilization of technologies, system integrators, methodologies, and CASE tools
- Highly productive design without high quality and tightly integrated analysis
- Freedom and latitude in design and construction

**Fig. 6.15** Unachievable information technology expectations.

tion technology participants, although this can be achievable for productivity-enhancing technologies such as development workstations, diagramming aids, and debuggers. A good rule of thumb is that if the level of commitment and involvement is not sufficient to manage and achieve the CASE CSFs presented in this book, even for a pilot project, it's insufficient for CASE.

Information technology expectations should also take into account the high-level involvement needed to redefine and manage the changes in roles within the information technology organization. This will be required to make CASE a success. Programmers and analysts will find themselves not only working at higher and more abstract levels, but in close cooperation with business users who actively participate in the analysis process.

Data modelers, with the understandable expectation that CASE tools are yet another step in a continuing evolution of quicker and more graphic data-modeling aids, can easily find themselves out of touch with their company's CASE projects. Data administrators who produce planning and analysis models using ADW or IEF, for example, will have to produce business models as members of project teams, where activities and data are given equal weight. Not only database administrators, but the entire DBA function may have to be reengineered so that it can work with CASE tool products and provide the additional responsiveness (hours and days, instead of weeks) required to support CASE-based design and construction projects.

Compatibility between CASE tools, and between CASE tools and methodologies, is another area in which dangerous gaps often exist between information technology expectations and reality. The competitive nature of CASE tool and methodology markets, the natural desire to work with a combination of the very best, and the abundance of customer-developed interfaces, serve to fuel expectations that one can successfully mix and match tools and methodologies from different vendors and wind up with a viable result.

The reality is that CASE tools offered by different vendors, although often compatible in some sense, are rarely sufficiently compatible to make the combination worth the effort. CASE tool interfaces, many of which have been developed by customers to address specific requirements and constraints, tend to vary greatly in quality and completeness. While screens (the easy part, in a 3270 or GUI environment) tend to come over intact, the logic and data components of the interface can be much more problematic. Differences in the way data are represented, and in logical constructs, especially between procedural and nonprocedural tools, make the fulfillment of this expectation chancy, at best. Fulfillment of compatibility expectations between CASE tools and methodologies can be just as elusive.

An insurance company found this out when they tried to use their ADW Analysis Workstation with a methodology that was built around the modeling of events. Although the methodology vendor was able to demonstrate that the tool could support the required event modeling, the tool's data-to-activity integration and consistency checks could not be applied. The result was that while their CASE tool, which adds significant value when supporting methodologies that are based on activity and data, could support the event-based methodology, it did so by functioning as little more than a elegant diagramming aid. The principal advantages of CASE were lost, and the project floundered.

A similar set of problems and constraints applies to expectations that systems integrators, who are conversant with one CASE tool along with the techniques and methodologies that it supports, will be able to competently develop applications using other tools and methodologies. Such expectations, if they're to be realized, must be tempered by the systems integrators' experiences and successes with the specific CASE tools, methodologies, and techniques to be used. CASE tools and methodologies tend to be very specific in their requirements, with the result that knowledge and experience are not always totally transferable.

Expectations for high productivity often don't include expectations for the tight integration between design and a high-quality analysis, on which the productivity increases depend. Indeed, the alacrity with which CASE-based applications can be designed, constructed, redesigned, and constructed again, can easily mask the importance of this requirement, with the result that many application development projects are completed without realizing the full benefits of CASE. Development project managers, for whom integration-related expectations have not been properly set, are tempted to proceed quickly to design and construction, without bothering to complete a time-consuming, high-quality analysis.

When an IEF development project at a medical service company proceeded directly to design and construction, where their application was designed, constructed and redesigned three times without the benefit of a completed analysis, the resulting productivity gains were only 10%.

Although they were dazzled by the ease and speed with which they were able to design and redesign their application, and therefore duly impressed with CASE, the result was well below what can be achieved using IEF.

The loss of freedom and latitude during design and construction can be dismaying to information systems personnel who are not prepared for it. Expectations for freedom and latitude in how desired functionality can be achieved, which are based on handcrafted application development, are not always achievable using CASE. Design tools, particularly where significant reuse is sought, can be far more restrictive than are languages such as COBOL or C. If this expectation is not correctly set, the compromises demanded by CASE in achieving required functionality will not be successfully struck, and much time will be lost trying to force CASE tools to develop screens and dialogue formats that the tools are not designed to support.

### User expectations

Adoption of CASE affects the way users participate in the application development process as well as the applications that the process generates. The combination of the high level of user participation demanded by CASE analysis, the unintuitive nature of CASE application development life cycle phases, the work products that CASE-based projects produce, and restrictions that design and construction tools impose on the way functionality can be achieved, can be devastating to users for whom expectations are based on experiences with handcrafted development. Although CASE provides the user community with substantial and welcome benefits, such as faster application delivery, applications that function correctly when first delivered, and more responsive enhancements, care must be taken to ensure that users understand and expect the changes that CASE will bring about. (See Figs. 6.16 and 6.17.)

The arms-length relationship, in which users define their application requirements and information technology produces applications that satisfy the requirements, is comfortable for most users. However old-fashioned and inefficient from a CASE perspective, this relationship has produced the array of applications with which the users successfully conduct their day-to-day operations. CASE imposed requirements that users should not only participate in application development right along with systems and business analysts, but also that they delve deeply into the underlying rules and

- Faster application delivery
- Applications which function correctly when first delivered
- More responsive enhancements

**Fig. 6.16** Achievable user expectations.

- **Continuance of an arms-length relationship with application development projects**
- **An intuitive approach to applications development**
- **Easily understandable work products**
- **Handcrafted functionality**

**Fig. 6-17.** Unachievable user expectations.

issues behind their requirements in order to produce models. Users have difficulty understanding these models, and these CASE-imposed requirements are therefore unexpected and unwelcome.

The generic, nonoperational view that ADW- and IEF-based analysis requires is difficult for operationally oriented users to understand because they have spent their careers performing operationally-oriented activities. Probing and challenging underlying principals and rules behind user requirements, however beneficial to analysis models, may be regarded by such users as something close to insubordination. Unless time is taken to set and manage the expectations of operationally oriented users so that they understand the reasons for the altered relationship, a difficult and marginally workable user relationship can easily result. These users should be made to understand what will be expected of them, why their requirements will be challenged, and how their efforts will benefit both their company and their operations.

User expectations for screens, dialogue, and reports must also be managed in terms of restrictions that CASE tools may impose on what they look like and how they work. Line managers, who would not be inclined to spend additional time and money to build custom-made, handcrafted buildings, equipment, tools or supplies, may not be aware of the fact that this is precisely the way their computer applications have been built. Although the compromises that CASE imposes on the way functionality is achieved are generally no more severe than analogous compromises in these other areas, users should not be expected to go along with such compromises unless their expectations are properly set in terms of handcrafted versus machine-generated functionality.

## Expectations, Facilities, and Support Requirements

Expectations are seldom realistic or appropriate in terms of the facilities and support required to derive significant benefit from CASE. The need for specialized facilities and support, if it's considered at all, is often addressed only as an afterthought.

Although ADW and IEF will function on slower workstations, neither tool should be used that way, as productivity losses resulting from even moderate performance workstations can be considerable. A few minutes spent watching analysts and designers using ADW or IEF on i486 workstations, for example, will reveal that an appalling amount of idle time is spent waiting for the tool to catch up to its user's demand. Expectations, in terms of workstation support should be set, not by the CASE tool vendor's minimum requirements, or by the desire for workstation consistency throughout the organization, but by the high potential cost of nonproductive time.

Expectations for mainframe and LAN server capacity and support requirements are almost universally too low among first-time CASE users. Both ADW and IEF mainframe components, for example, can require surprising amounts of mainframe CPU and disk space, especially for large implementations that involve many uploads and downloads. Care must therefore be taken to ensure that mainframe capacity estimates are adequate. Initial expectations and estimates of significant mainframe and LAN server usage are almost never appropriate.

Although development facilities have been an ongoing problem in most companies, the problem is worse with CASE.[3] The reason is that the models produced by CASE are very tightly linked and don't generally lend themselves to isolated work. The linkage of the models, combined with the close interaction between analysts, modelers, and users needed to complete them, requires substantially more meeting space than did traditional applications development.

Inclusion of facilities that promote communication and group activities are almost never inappropriate for CASE. Automatic white boards, JAD rooms, projection monitors, plotters, and high-speed printers and duplicators, for example, all help. Where geographic dispersion permits, highest productivity can be attained when combined user and information technology teams are located in close proximity to the system's users.

## CASE Initiatives and Expectations

Management of CASE-related expectations, as we have seen, is critically important to the successful use of CASE. Although certainly not universally achievable, most CASE-related expectations can be successfully managed once they're acknowledged and their causes and effects are understood.

Figure 6.18 summarizes the major CASE-related initiatives and expectations common to most companies as they go through the process of adopting CASE for their information systems planning and development. It's my hope that insights gained through tying each expectation to the CASE initiative most often associated with it, will help CASE implementors to achieve this important CSF.

---

[3]T. DeMarco & T. Lister, *Peopleware, Productive Projects And Teams*, Dorset House, New York, 1987.

| CASE initiative | What you should expect |
| --- | --- |
| Bring in CASE based on quick productivity gains | Disappointed users and management during analysis |
| Bring in CASE based on information technology cost reductions | Information technology cost reductions offset by money spent on reducing information system backlog |
| Utilize CASE tools and methodologies produced by different vendors | Compatibility and integration gaps |
| Utilize resources with experience on different CASE tools and methodologies | Problems in transferring their knowledge to your situation |
| Promote high levels of user participation on CASE projects | Difficulties in establishing user-to-developer relationships |
| Promote low levels of user participation on CASE projects | Flawed planning and analysis projects |
| Utilize CASE for information systems planning | Information systems that are more relevant and provide better business support<br><br>A poorly articulated business plan without the specific information called for in your CASE tool and methodology<br><br>Problems formulating new relationships and consensus with business management |
| Utilize CASE for analysis | Higher analysis costs<br><br>Lower design and construction costs |
| Shortcuts during analysis | Flawed design and construction |
| Utilize CASE for design and construction | Higher design and construction productivity<br><br>Less design latitude in achieving a desired result |

**Fig. 6.18** Major CASE-related initiatives and expectations.

Part

2

# Utilizing CASE

Chapter

# 7

# Using CASE for Information Systems Planning

Working with large numbers of companies that are using CASE quickly reveals that CASE is currently used mostly for analysis, design, and construction of information systems, and the role that CASE can play in information system planning is almost universally misunderstood, undervalued, and underused. Indeed most strategic information system planning is still conducted manually, without the aid of CASE, and the overwhelming majority of CASE-based application development projects still begin without the benefit of a tactical plan. When CASE is used for planning, it's most often applied incorrectly by organizations and project teams that have not achieved the critical success factors required to make CASE-based planning pay off.[1] Yet, CASE-based planning can pay off, and when correctly employed, has the potential to add considerable value to the information systems planning process, and to substantially lower the risks associated with CASE-based application development.

## Types of CASE-Based Planning

There are two kinds of CASE-based planning: strategic, and tactical. While both are supported by similar tools, techniques, and methodologies, they per-

[1]John C. Henderson, Jay G. Cooprider, "Dimensions Of I/S Planning And Design Technology," Massachusetts Institute Of Technology CISR Working Paper No. 191, September 1990.

form very different functions. Strategic CASE-based planning develops information technology strategies and helps align the information technology function with the business. It's typically performed at the corporate or division level, where it promotes leveraging of information technologies and the company's information assets, while promoting better integration of the organization's applications. Tactical planning goes by many names, including "Business System Architecture Definition," "Mini ISP," and "BAA Scoping." It is most often performed below strategic planning, at the departmental or project level where one or more new CASE-based applications are being defined. It provides a framework, in terms of function, low-level models, dependencies, and scope, that is mandatory for defining the CASE-based application development projects if they're to be executed with minimum risk. (See Fig. 7.1.)

Strategic and tactical CASE-based information system plans can be executed separately, for individual divisions, departments or projects, or in multiple tiers throughout the entire enterprise. Although CASE-based planning provides value either way, when it's performed at multiple tiers in a corporate hierarchy, CASE adds additional value by storing the results of each planning process in a centrally maintained encyclopedia. The encyclopedia can then be accessed by individual planning tools to ensure that the multiple plans are consistent with, and fully support, each other. (See Fig. 7.2.)

One CASE-based strategic planning project at the corporate level can be a starting point for several strategic planning projects in divisions, using the central encyclopedia and association matrices to ensure that the division and corporate plans are in alignment. In Fig. 7.2 a business planning project is shown alongside each strategic information system planning project to emphasize the need for executing both projects in parallel as a requisite for achieving business-to-information technology alignment. Division-level strategic planning projects provide direction for departmental-level planning, where the need for applications is defined.

| Strategic | Tactical |
|---|---|
| Business-to-IT alignment | BAA functionality |
| An informational view of the company, division or department | Low-level data and activity models |
| An objective assessment of current IT support | BAA dependencies |
| IT integration and business support requirements | BAA order and scope |

**Fig. 7.1** Objectives of strategic and tactical information system plans.

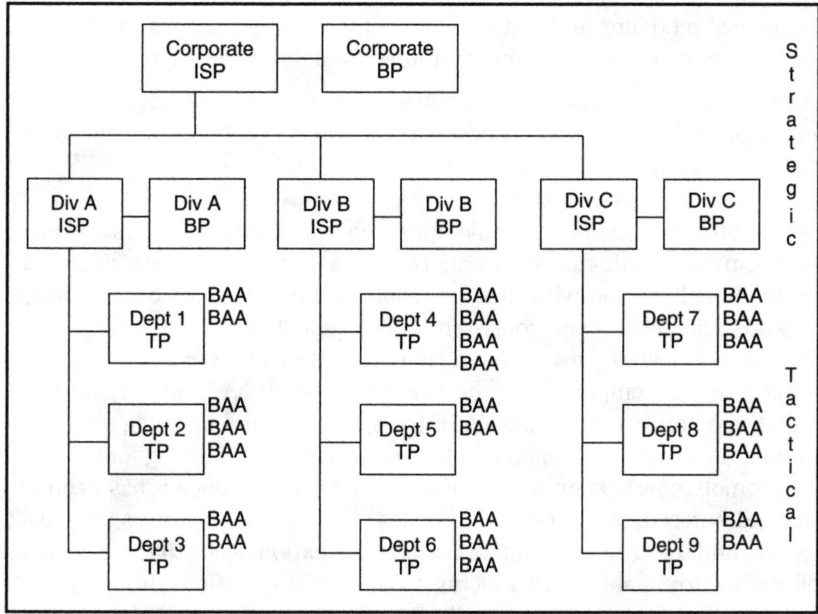


**Fig. 7.2** Tiers of strategic and tactical information system plans.

Departmental-level tactical planning provides the framework for executing application development projects by defining and scoping their analysis phases, or BAAs.

## CASE-Based Strategic Planning

According to John Sifonis and Beverly Goldberg, the goals of strategic information system planning are to develop strategies that ensure that the information technology function and infrastructure are aligned with, and support, the business, and that information technologies and the company's information assets can be leveraged to support its business's mission.[2] CASE-based strategic planning methodologies, along with the CASE tools that support them, can add substantial value to, the strategic planning process by providing:

- A consistent methodology and framework for developing and documenting planning parameters.
- Highly graphical, planning-object-oriented tools for entering and reporting on planning information.

---

[2]Beverly Goldberg and John G. Sifonis, *Looking Beyond Tomorrow: A Pragmatic Approach To Dynamic Planning,* Oxford University Press, forthcoming.

- Enhanced modeling and analysis capabilities and techniques, such as matrix processing, data modeling and functional decomposition.
- A centralized repository or encyclopedia for storing, organizing, and making accessible the myriad of information that is created and used by the strategic planning process.

Although there are many viable approaches to information system planning, the use of CASE enables the adoption of a common and consistent planning methodology, and with the methodology, a common set of techniques. The value-added rules and consistency checks built into CASE tools such as ADW and IEF help to ensure that a common, information-engineering-based approach will be employed by the planners at each level and organization within the enterprise. Planning CASE tools, via GUIs and planning object orientation, do more than facilitate entry and retrieval of planning information; they promote consistency as well. For example, a CSF, once it has been defined and entered, can appear in matrices showing the objectives or goals it supports and the critical assumptions and information needs that impact it, as well as the current and future functions, data, and applications that support it. The CASE tool ensures that, regardless of where it appears or which planning function it serves, each CSF is one object, defined in a singular and consistent way. When a CSF is altered, the tool ensures that the changed CSF is automatically propagated into every plan in which it's used.

The modeling and analytic capabilities enabled by CASE methodologies and tools are both formidable and fully integrated. Methodologies add consistency to modeling and analysis efforts by defining:

- Objects from which the models will be built.
- Methods used to build the models.
- Techniques by which the models can be analyzed.
- Ways in which each model and analysis contributes to the plan.

While information-engineering-based enterprise models such as data models and functional decompositions can be built and documented using diagramming tools, white boards, and paper, CASE tools make it much easier and a more productive process to enter, define, move, store, report on, and redefine the objects that compose the models.

Finally, the encyclopedias and repositories, which are centrally maintained by CASE tools such as ADW and IEF, make planning parameters, models, plans, and conclusions accessible by other CASE users (of the same CASE tools) throughout the enterprise. For companies large enough to require multiple strategic planning efforts, this means that each plan will be constructed based on a singularly defined, consistent, and fully updated set of planning parameters and assumptions. For all companies, a central encyclopedia provides a consistent starting point, and guidance for, tactical planning efforts, integration projects, and applications.[3]

### Business and information technology alignment

CASE methodologies and tools employ a combination of models and association matrices to help ensure that information system plans are in alignment with business plans, and that the information system plans created by different divisions and departments are in alignment with each other. For example, by defining and entering the business goals and CSFs for the business organization, and similar information for the information technology function that supports it, tool-based matrices can be constructed to show the degree to which each:

- Business CSF supports each business goal or objective.
- Information technology goal or objective supports each business CSF.
- Information technology CSF supports each information technology goal or objective.

Thus populated, association matrices can show the cascading of:

- Business goals and objectives into business CSFs.
- Business CSFs into information technology goals and objectives.
- Information technology goals and objectives into information technology CSFs.

These matrices are also useful in developing insights into how each business CSF supports its goals and mission, how well the information technology goals are aligned with the business CSFs, and how well information technology CSFs are aligned with their own goals and objectives. (See Fig. 7.3.)

Once entered, information technology goals, objectives, and CSFs from different divisions and departments can also be used to test the degree to which they're in alignment with each other. Where close alignment is indicated, the potential for sharing data and commonly developed applications can be explored. Common data and functions can be identified and developed more directly by constructing CASE-based enterprise data and activity models that provide an informational view of the organization being modeled.[4] (See Fig. 7.4.)

---

[3]James Martin, *Information Engineering* Book II. Prentice Hall, 1990.

[4]James Martin, *Strategic Data Planning Methodologies* Prentice Hall, 1982. Contains excellent examples of C-R-U-D matrix analysis. See also Dennis Minium, *A Guide To Information Engineering Using The IEF,* Texas Instruments, First Edition. Appendix B provides insight into the history of matrix-based clustering, along with its implementation in the IEF.

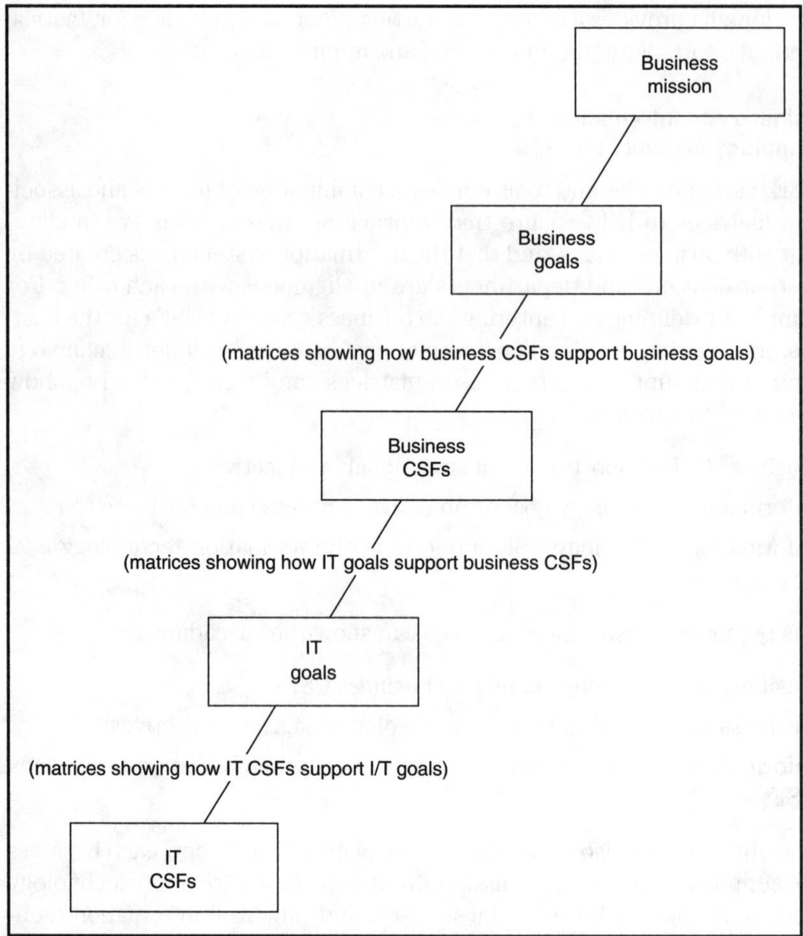


**Fig. 7.3** Use of association matrices to show the relationship between I/T CSFs, I/T goals, business CSFs, and business goals.

## An informational view of the company, division, or department

Most companies, along with their divisions and departments, have a good understanding of what they look like from an operational perspective, and with it, a clear picture of their missions, organizations, locations, procedures, products and markets. CASE, through the enterprise modeling that it enables, can provide a very different picture—one based on generic functions and data.

By supporting functional decomposition through graphics, rules, consistency checks, and object-oriented storage in a central encyclopedia, ADW and IEF can be used to develop a hierarchical view of a company, division, or de-

| | Increase productivity 35% | Improve customer satisfaction | Expand the product line | Exceed competitive standards | Increase sales | Control inventory | Improve product quality | Increase profitability |
|---|---|---|---|---|---|---|---|---|
| Manage human resources | ✓ | | | | ✓ | | | ✓ |
| Market and sell the product | | ✓ | | ✓ | ✓ | ✓ | | ✓ |
| Fabricate the product | | | | | | ✓ | ✓ | ✓ |
| Support the company | | ✓ | | | | ✓ | | |
| Hire employees | | | ✓ | | ✓ | | ✓ | |
| Train employees | ✓ | ✓ | ✓ | ✓ | ✓ | | ✓ | ✓ |
| Plan the product | | ✓ | ✓ | ✓ | ✓ | | ✓ | |
| Market the product | | ✓ | ✓ | ✓ | ✓ | | | ✓ |
| Sell the product | | ✓ | ✓ | ✓ | ✓ | | | ✓ |
| Support the product | | ✓ | ✓ | ✓ | ✓ | | ✓ | |
| Acquire raw materials | | | | | | ✓ | ✓ | |
| Manufacture product components | | | | ✓ | | ✓ | ✓ | ✓ |
| Assemble components | | | | ✓ | | ✓ | ✓ | |
| Assure product quality | | ✓ | ✓ | ✓ | ✓ | ✓ | ✓ | ✓ |
| Supply and process information | ✓ | ✓ | | ✓ | ✓ | | | ✓ |
| Plan strategic direction | | ✓ | ✓ | ✓ | ✓ | | ✓ | |

**Fig. 7.4** ADW association matrix showing functions supporting goals.

partment, populated by generic activities that are independent of its organization, procedures, and locations. In an information engineering functional decomposition, the children of each function performed by a company, division, or department, need only support the parent function. No consideration is given to where, how, or in whose organization each child function might reside. The function Product Engineering, for example, might appear as a single function within a manufacturing company's generic Engineering function, instead of under the company's Sales & Marketing, New Product Development, Preproduction, and Production Engineering departments where product engineering may be performed.

In addition to providing a starting point for tactical planning and CASE-based analysis, functional decomposition, through association matrices, shows where, and in which organization each generic function is performed, and in many companies, reperformed. Generic functions provide additional support for the strategic planning process by identifying opportunities for:

- Developing generic applications once, and reusing them to serve the needs of multiple organizations and locations.
- Business processes reengineering, based not on current locations or procedures, but on what the organization really needs.
- Integrated applications that, though they may be currently housed in different organizations, produce a common outcome.

Enterprise data modeling, enabled by similar CASE tool and methodology support, models a company, division or department's generic data. Data, represented as groupings of like information called "entity types" and "subject areas," are modeled based solely on their support of current and future generic functions, without regard to governance, location, database or file structures, hardware platforms, format, or accuracy. The idea is to get at the data that are required to support the current and planned functions for the organization. Once the generic data have been defined, and the central encyclopedia populated, association matrices can be employed to analyze not only which goals, CSFs and information needs they support, but their locations, current systems, databases, hardware platforms and quality.

The data models and association matrix analyses support the planning process by identifying:

- Information that's generic to the organization and its mission, and that therefore tends to be stable.
- Information that's needed, but not yet available.
- Information that's available, but is not fully leveraged by one or more of the company's organizations.
- Opportunities for supporting reengineered business processes.
- Opportunities for better integration of information systems.

### An objective assessment of current information technology

Once entered and verified, the planning parameters, data models and activity models in the central encyclopedia become an objective framework for assessing current applications and data. Association matrices can be used to analyze current information systems with respect to their:

- Location and organization.
- Usability, technology, responsiveness, reliability, maintainability and age.
- Support of goals, objectives, CSFs, and information needs.
- Support of generic functions.
- Database accesses.

As even the most ambitious of plans must be executed within time and budgetary constraints, this kind of objective appraisal of current applications can be extremely valuable in determining which current information systems might be replaced, and in what order.

### Integration and business support

Small and moderately sized companies that have not fully used information technology to automate their operations can benefit substantially from new applications. For large, diverse, and fully automated organizations, much of the opportunity for leveraging information technology lies not in new applications, functionality, or better interfaces, but in better integration. For example, increasing functional integration can help fully automated companies decrease inventory expense and reduce time to market new products by enabling them to take advantage of integrated operations such as just-in-time inventory management and concurrent engineering. (See Fig. 7.5.) Increased data integration can also enable companies to service customers

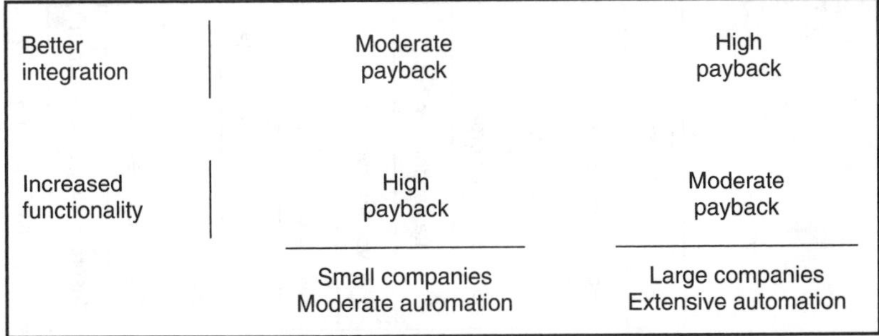


**Fig. 7.5** Potential payback of added functionality and integration for moderate and large companies.

| | Product | Product inventory | Location | Customer | PO | Shipping vendor | Customer agreement | Order | Salesperson | Packing list | Product component | Vendor | Employee | Customer shipping address |
|---|---|---|---|---|---|---|---|---|---|---|---|---|---|---|
| Process customer orders | RU | CR | RU | RU | RUD | | R | RUD | R | RU | | | | |
| Receive customer orders | R | | | CR | CD | | CRUD | C | RU | | | | | CRUD |
| Fill customer orders | RUD | CRUD | R | RU | RU | | | RUD | | C | RU | | | R |
| Ship customer orders | | | | | UD | R | R | | | RUD | | | | RU |
| Validate vendor invoices | | | | | RU | | | | | | | RUD | | |
| Pay vendor invoices | | | | R | R | RU | | R | | | | RU | | |
| Bill customer | | | | U | RU | | R | U | | R | | | R | R |
| Identify potential customers | | | | RU | | | RU | | | | | | | |
| Contact potential customers | | | RU | R | | | | | RU | | | | | |
| Solicit potential customers | | | R | R | | | | | R | | | | | |
| Insure customer satisfaction | R | | | R | RU | | RU | RU | | | | | R | |

**Fig .7.6** ADW entity-type-to-process C-R-U-D matrix.

CASEBEN: BUSINESS_FUNCTION/ENTITY_TYPE - Matrix

Diagram Edit Detail View Options Window

Cell Value:
= No reference
C = Create
D = Delete
U = Update
R = Read only

| Function \ Entity Type | FINISHED GOOD STOCK | COMPONENT STOCK | COMPONENT | PRODUCT | COMPONENT USAGE | SUPPLIER | PURCHASE ORDER | PURCHASE ORDER LINE | CUSTOMER | INVOICE | SHIPMENT | SCUSTOMER ORDER | CUSTOMER ORDER LINE | SALES PERSON |
|---|---|---|---|---|---|---|---|---|---|---|---|---|---|---|
| MATERIALS PURCHASING | U | U | U | R | R | U | C | C | R | R | | | | |
| RAW MATERIAL WAREHOUSE | R | U | R | R | R | R | U | U | | | R | | | |
| PRODUCT TESTING | U | R | R | R | R | R | U | U | | | | | | |
| ACCOUNTS PAYABLES | | | R | R | | U | U | U | | | R | | | |
| ORDER PROCESSING | | | | | | U | U | U | R | R | | | | |
| ACCOUNTS RECEIVABLE | | | | | | U | | | R | C | U | R | R | R |
| DISTRIBUTION | U | U | R | R | | R | | | | R | U | R | R | |
| FINISH GOOD WAREHOUSE | U | | R | U | R | R | | | R | R | R | R | R | |
| PRODUCT DEVELOPMENT | C | C | R | U | R | R | | | | | | | | |
| PRODUCT ASSEMBLY | U | U | U | U | U | R | | | | | | | | |

**Fig. 7.7** IEF entity-type-to-function C-R-U-D matrix.

who purchase goods and services from multiple divisions and departments via a single and consistent interface.

The data and activity models developed during the planning process can be used to identify opportunities for both kinds of integration. By defining interactions between generic functions and data, activity-to-data association matrices, known as "C-R-U-D matrices" can be formed. (They're called C-R-U-D matrices because of the Create, Read, Update and Delete interactions that populate them). C-R-U-D matrices can be used to cluster generic functions and data, which interact heavily with one another, into highly integrated collections of applications; these collections then create opportunities for integrated applications.[5] (See Figs. 7.6 and 7.7.)

## CSFs for CASE-Based Strategic Planning

Although the potential benefits of CASE-based strategic information system planning are both desirable and impressive, making it work, so that it adds value to the planning processes of a real company, can be tricky.

---

[5]Chris F. Kamerer, Glenn Sosa,"Systems Development Challenges In The Strategic Use Of Information Technology: Some Cautionary Lessons From Experience," Massachusetts Institute Of Technology CISR Working Paper No. 186, February 1989. Contains a wealth of anecdotal information on the kinds of things that go wrong with the strategic information planning process.

1. Senior management commitment and support
2. An accurate business plan
3. Senior management involvement
4. Use of a methodology
5. The right skill set
6. Interviewing at multiple levels within the organization
7. Developing one and only one plan at the enterprise level
8. Making the plan implementable
9. Implementing the plan—following through
10. Keeping the plan current

**Fig. 7.8** The ten CSFs for strategic information systems planning.

Indeed, strategic information system planning can be difficult to achieve even in a traditional environment due to the many and varied things that can go wrong[5] and the subtle, but significant ways in which business and information technology strategies and infrastructure can interact.[6] John Sifonis captures the most common strategic planning land mines in the form of the ten CSFs shown in Fig. 7.8. These are generally applicable to all strategic planning efforts.[7]

Although these CSFs hold true for both CASE-based and traditional strategic planning, using CASE brings an additional set of CSFs to bear on the strategic information system planning process. Figure 7.9 lists the six CASE-related CSFs that must be achieved, over and above those associated

1. A business plan quantifiable in terms of CASE-based strategic planning parameters
2. Senior management involvement, sponsorship, and absolute commitment
3. Methodology consistency
4. CASE tool compatibility
5. Detail management
6. A mechanism for keeping the planning models current

**Fig. 7.9** The six CSFs for CASE-based strategic information system planning.

---

[6]John C. Henderson, N. Venkatraman, "Strategic Alignment: A Framework For Strategic Information Technology Management," Massachusetts Institute Of Technology CISR Working Paper No. 190, August 1989. Contains a strategic alignment model that provides useful insights into business-to-information technology strategy and infrastructure interactions.

[7]Conversations with John Sifonis.

with strategic planning efforts, if a company is to derive significant benefit from using CASE in its strategic planning process.

### Business plans and CASE-based strategic planning parameters

For association matrices to work, the company's strategic business mission and direction must first be expressed in terms of quantifiable planning parameters that can be used to populate CASE tool matrices. Association matrices that show how generic functions and data support CSFs, or how CSFs supports business goals and objectives, can't be produced if this information is unavailable or not known. Each goal, objective, critical assumption, CSF, problem, and information need must therefore be defined and quantified, both individually and in terms of its relationship to the others. For example:

- Goals, critical assumptions, problems, and information needs must be numerically ranked in terms of their strategic importance.
- Critical assumptions must be described in terms of stability—the degree to which management believes they might, or might not, change with time.
- CSFs must be related to the specific goals and objectives that they support, and the degree to which each CSF supports each goal or objective must be documented as well.

But many companies don't have missions, directions, and business plans that are articulated and documented well enough to be meaningfully quantified in terms of the goals, objectives, critical assumptions, CSFs, problems, and information needs that CASE methodologies and CASE tool association matrices require. Executive interviews and JAD sessions can be used to make up the deficiencies, but only to the extent that the company's planners and executives are comfortable with the process, and with the increased level of involvement of their information technology function. A well-documented business plan is the best way to start.

### Senior management involvement, sponsorship, and absolute commitment

Even with a well-documented mission and business plan, expressed in terms of quantified strategic planning parameters, direct involvement of senior management in the planning process will be needed. Although senior management commitment, involvement, and sponsorship are identified as CSFs for all strategic information systems planning, they take on even greater significance for CASE. There are two reasons for this added importance.

The first is that the rigor and detail with which CASE tools and methodologies document and analyze the planning parameters almost always lead to requests for clarification of information contained in the plan, and often for additional information. Such information should not be shaded by interpretation, and should therefore be supplied directly by management.

The second reason for management's direct involvement comes from the need to verify the models and matrices that the CASE-based planning process develops. Management verification is an essential mechanism for ensuring that the CASE-based models, upon which the strategic plan will be based, are accurate and fully represent the company's strategic mission and direction.

Direct involvement in the planning process, although important, is not sufficient. Management needs to sponsor the planning project as well. Management sponsorship not only ensures that executives will be available for participation in interviews and JAD sessions, but also helps ensure that the models, which may cross over organizational, governance, geographic and political boundaries, accurately reflect an enterprise view. Management sponsorship raises the planning process above these boundaries and ensures that the models, and the plans that evolve from the models, are not tainted by rivalry and politics.

### Methodology consistency

For CASE-based strategic planning to work at the enterprise level, consistent planning methodologies must be used throughout the organization. For CASE-based planning to add value to information system development, planning methodologies must be compatible with development methodologies as well.

Divisional and departmental models, for example, if they're to add value to the enterprise as a whole, must be consolidated into, or at minimum, reconciled with, strategic planning models at the enterprise level, so that common threads can be spotted and integration opportunities identified. This can't take place if the models result from different methodologies that view planning parameters, activities, and data in fundamentally different ways. Different information-engineering-based methodologies, for example, all decompose activities generically, with the result that their high-level functions can be easily combined into companywide functions at a still higher level. But if some departments use a methodology that decomposes activities generically, while others use a different methodology that decomposes activities based on organization, the functions will not combine in a meaningful way, even though they may have been documented using the same CASE tools. Duplications and omissions are likely to result, and with the duplications and omissions, false insights and opportunities.

If the methodologies used for planning and development are not consistent, the starting point that the planning models provide for CASE-based application development projects may be lost, or even worse, misleading, since it's the methodologies that provide the context within which the tool-based models are interpreted. There's probably no better way to undermine application development than to provide application development projects with detailed, rigorous and precise models that look like they mean one thing, but really mean something entirely different!

### CASE tool compatibility

Although less dangerous than inconsistent methodologies, use of consistent, even identical methodologies, when supported by planning CASE tools that are not fully compatible, can also be problematic. The main difficulties in working with incompatible CASE tools stem from bridging and migration software that doesn't fully, accurately, or consistently populate the target tool's encyclopedia.

A large global securities company recently found this out when they tried to migrate their ADW-based planning models over to IEF, the CASE tool that they chose to complete their planning and application development. Although they used proven migration software with a good track record for success, and each of the entity types and attributes in their data model came over intact, the relationships and properties didn't. Their functions didn't migrate over at all. As the planning model was a large one, containing several thousand objects, the migration, which was scheduled for one week, took over two months to complete, with many of the objects being migrated manually.

This is not a single or an uncommon event. For large organizations with many planning models, each populated with hundreds, even thousands, of objects, the discontinuity and lost productivity associated with cleaning up poorly migrated models can make the maintenance of consistent, coordinated, models into a daunting and expensive task. The inevitable result is inconsistent planning models in different parts of the company, and a compromised strategic planning process.

### Detail management

Most CASE tools, including ADW and IEF, have the ability to accept and store planning models in an astounding amount of detail. Each planning parameter, function, entity type, attribute, and relationship, for example, can be painstakingly described using paragraphs of carefully worded text. Although planning methodologies generally provide direction regarding where to start a functional decomposition, how deep the decomposition should go, at what level data should be modeled, and the kinds of details to document for each planning object, managing the level and detail at which information system plans are developed remains problematic. Tendencies, especially among new CASE users, are to either manage to meet unrealistically short deadlines, leaving important information out of the planning process, or to get carried away with their CASE tool's capabilities, and plan so deeply, and in so much detail, that large parts of the plan's models become irrelevant and superfluous.

A strategic planning team, operating at the divisional level of a large financial services company,"completed" its IEF-based strategic planning project in two full-day JAD sessions. Although they succeeded in making their deadline, the plan that resulted from their abbreviated planning process used objectives and CSFs developed in a different, noninformation engineering and non-IEF project.

They decomposed functions to only 4 levels, and modeled only some of the data. In terms of defining workable strategic directions along with applications to be developed, the plan was close to useless. They derived no benefit from CASE.

An oil company, using the same CASE tool and methodology, erred in the opposite direction, spending over seven months planning a program that resulted in the initiation of eleven application development projects. The project, which was staffed with five full-time information technology people and four full-time users, produced an accurate and usable strategic plan. The care with which they defined each function, entity type, and attribute, however, was far greater than required, a fact that they discovered when much of the information they so carefully developed was discarded by the application development projects.

Successful CASE-based strategic planning requires careful management of the details that go into each model. Planning parameters need to be entered, and their effects on other planning parameters documented, only where it makes sense to do so. The criteria should be relevancy to the requirements of the plan being developed, not the time being allocated, the capability of the CASE tool, or the breadth of the planning methodology. One to two sentences are generally sufficient to define a planning object, the criteria for a good definition being that all stakeholders have a common understanding of what the object is and does.

Although there are many factors that can influence the size of a strategic planning project, if detail is properly managed, an ADW- or IEF-based strategic planning effort, using an information-engineering-based methodology, should require no more than two to four months to complete. Information gathering, not modeling, should drive the time required to complete the strategic plan.

### A mechanism for keeping the plan current

The business climate in which many companies operate is no longer stable. Changes in competition, technology, global politics, products, and regulatory requirements can cause the strategic planning parameters upon which the strategic plan is based, to change at an alarmingly increasing rate. If the plan is to remain a valid mechanism for setting information technology strategic direction, the planning parameters on which the plan's association matrices are based must be periodically revisited, and where necessary, updated. The plan's models and association matrices can then be used to propagate the changes into an updated plan.

Although it's a CSF for all strategic information system planning, a mechanism for keeping the plan current is nevertheless included among the CASE-related CSFs. The reason for this inclusion is that during CASE-based application development, the high-level data and activity models developed during the planning process are analyzed to a much finer level of detail, and often change as a result. For the plan to remain accurate and relevant, the changes, which are built into the applications, must be reflected back into the planning models. If the strategic planning models are not periodically reconciled with their analysis counterparts, the plan will become less and less relevant as each application is developed.

## CASE-Based Tactical Planning

The purpose of CASE-based tactical planning is to provide a framework within which the planning parameters, activities, and data, defined in the strategic planning process, can be turned into one or more executable BAAs. Where CASE-based strategic planning models don't exist, tactical planning can be used to improvise the required models from an application development perspective. Although high-level data and activity models, thus improvised, may not serve the same planning functions as their strategic counterparts, they can provide a viable starting point for CASE-based application development.

CASE-based tactical planning projects use planning-tool modeling and association matrices to:

- Verify, and if necessary, develop, high-level activity and data models that can be used in C-R-U-D matrix analysis and that form the starting point for BAAs.
- Develop and use C-R-U-D matrix analysis to properly define, scope, and order one or more BAAs.

The functional decompositions and high-level data models produced by the strategic planning process, while appropriate for setting strategic direction, may not be detailed enough, or developed at a sufficiently low level, to serve as a good starting point for business area analysis. For example, analysis methodologies that are based on information engineering call for the decomposition of low-level functions down to "elementary" or "sequential" processes, as well as for the development of fully normalized data models that support the decomposition. But the functional decomposition produced by strategic planning may not go all the way down to low-level functions, and the high-level entity types defined in the strategic data model may not be a suitable starting point for developing a normalized data model.

The activity and data modeling components of the tactical planning process have a singular purpose: to ensure that the data and activity models, which represent the starting points of the BAA modeling process, are in place, regardless of the level or completeness with which the strategic planning models may have (or may not have) been developed.

With low-level functions and entity types defined, C-R-U-D matrices can be developed in which low-level functions and the entity types that support them are clustered into an optimal number of BAAs. When properly executed, BAAs defined using a C-R-U-D matrix:

- Support the business and its priorities.
- Are reasonably scoped.
- Are reasonably independent from one another.
- Are ordered such that early BAAs produce the data required by BAAs that follow them.

This is done by manually manipulating the C-R-U-D matrix's functions and entity types to make them cluster into one or more BAAs, so that for each BAA:

- Its functions represent a viable application that serves the business's needs and priorities.
- The entity types that its functions create, delete, and update are contained within its scope.
- Its scope represents a reasonably sized project, for which the BAA can be completed in less than six months and a functioning application can be delivered within a year.
- It creates and updates entity types that will be read by BAAs that follow it, and reads entity types that are created and updated by BAAs that precede it.
- Its entity types fully support each of its low-level functions.
- Its entity types have a high degree of interdependence within the BAA, but a low degree of dependencies with entity types in other BAAs.
- Its functions have a high degree of interdependence within the BAA, but a low degree of dependencies with functions in other BAAs.

These are high ideals, and as you might expect, the process of manipulating functions and entity types to define BAAs can involve significant compromises and trade-offs. If executed properly, however, the BAAs that

1. Articulated and documented objectives and scope
2. Business and information technology participants
3. Sufficient time to develop the plan

**Fig. 7.10** The three CSFs for CASE-based tactical planning.

result from this process will form the best possible basis for beginning CASE-based analysis and development.

Given the contributions that it can make to setting up of viable, low-risk BAAs, perhaps the most surprising thing about CASE-based tactical planning is that it's rarely done. Whether it's because its role in defining viable BAAs is not well known, it's assumed to have been done as part of strategic planning, or because tactical planning is viewed as something that gets in the way of starting application development, the results are the same:

- BAAs that are large and risky, or too small to be of real value.
- Model management contention between BAAs that share many of the same entity types.
- BAA projects that have trouble getting off the ground because they lack the starting points that their analysis methodologies assume exist.

### The three CSFs for CASE-based tactical planning

Making CASE-based tactical planning work in a real company environment is not an easy or sure process. While there are many factors that contribute to tactical planning risks and successes, the three CSFs shown in Fig. 7.10, when achieved, will provide a solid basis for executing a tactical planning project.

**Articulated and documented objectives and scope.** Without an understanding of, and agreement on, the objectives and scope of the applications being planned, none of the modeling and analyses required for CASE-based tactical planning are likely to work. Functions, for example, can't be decomposed down to their lowest levels, and included in a C-R-U-D matrix, if team members are not sure which strategic planning functions to decompose. Trade-offs and compromises between functionality, size, and order of the BAAs defined using C-R-U-D analysis must also be made against a backdrop of the planning project's objectives and scope. Although this requirement seems fundamental and obvious, it's not always met, especially in companies in which serious differences exist regarding what the applications being planned will be expected to accomplish.

When the project has been preceded by a CASE-based strategic plan, the objectives and CSFs associated with the planning-level functions and entity types can be easily associated with their C-R-U-D matrix counterparts to form a solid basis for defining objectives and scope. They should, however, be verified, especially if more than six months has elapsed between formulation of the strategic plan and the tactical planning project, or if any of the organizations associated with the strategic planning functions or entity types have reengineered their business processes. Where no strategic planning has been done, planning parameters will have to be actively sought, through executive interviews and JAD sessions; also, the results will need to be documented and verified, as they would be for a strategic planning project.

**Business and information technology participants.** The trade-offs involved in defining, scoping and ordering BAAs are, to a large extent, trade-offs between business and information technology interests. Business requirements, for example, may dictate that applications be delivered in an order that demands that BAAs that read certain data precede the BAAs that create the data. The information technology function may be concerned about limiting BAA scope, as a strategy for making implementation projects more manageable and reducing risk.

For the tactical planning project to be successful, BAA planning decisions can't be made by business or information technology interests alone. They should be the result of careful compromise based on an understanding of the business and information technology implications of each decision. There's nothing in a C-R-U-D matrix analysis that astute business and information technology participants can't easily understand, and each should be represented in the process.

**Sufficient time to develop the plan.** With the singular exception of not doing a tactical information system plan at all, the most common problem associated with BAA planning is not allowing sufficient time to execute it. Tactical planning projects typically require only three to six weeks to complete, provided that the team understands the CASE tool and the analysis, both business and information technology interests are represented, and that a strategic planning project recently preceded it. Since a single tactical plan can affect years of application development projects, the three to six weeks that it takes to complete the tactical plan will be time very well spent.

Chapter

# 8

# Using CASE for Analysis

The project's users were furious! After three months of so-called "business area analysis," they still hadn't seen the first screen of what was supposed to be their new application, and their tolerance for reviewing the meaningless data model for yet another time was growing thin. The data model wasn't doing much better in the eyes of the project's analysts. They knew that implementing a data model in DB2, which at their consultant's insistence was in third normal form, would lead to a system that wouldn't perform; it might lead to the loss of their jobs as well. Management had consented to using ADW to improve application development productivity, but it now appeared to them that the use of the CASE tool and information engineering was doing precisely the opposite. Instead of a productivity improvement, what they were witnessing looked a lot more like a productivity loss.

The last twenty years have taught us a lot about the benefits of analyzing a business and its requirements prior to designing and constructing the information systems that serve it. As a result, the need to perform analysis is almost universally understood and accepted by both business and information technology professionals—and CASE-based analysis, like traditional analysis, is called upon to fulfill that need. When CASE is adopted for information system development, inclusion of analysis tools and methodologies is the rule rather than the exception, a rule that approaches 100% compliance for integrated CASE tools such as ADW and IEF.

But, unlike its manual counterpart, ADW- and IEF-based analysis often leads to disappointment. Indeed, when evaluated in terms of productivity improvement, often the primary motivation for CASE, analysis is nothing short of a disaster. CASE- based analysis does lead to productivity improvements, and quality improvements as well, but they're long-term rather than short-term improvements, and they don't show up until design, construction, and maintenance.

## What CASE-Based Analysis Is

Using ADW or IEF, an information engineering analysis addresses the identification, analysis, and documentation of what the information system is to accomplish, prior to deciding on the best way of accomplishing it. This is done by constructing a series of extremely detailed and rigorous "logical" business models. The term "logical" is used to emphasize the fact that ADW and IEF analysis models represent business logic and rules, and don't address report layouts, screens, menus, dialogue, or prototyping, which are the "physical," implementation-dependent products of design and construction.[1] These logical models, along with related business and technical issues, are the product of CASE-based analysis.

The tremendous detail and rigor associated with the logical models, and the lack of tangible screens, menus, and reports tend to make analysis products difficult for operationally oriented information technology, user, and management personnel to relate to. The time required to construct the models, and the often sticky business issues that they uncover, make construction of models difficult for management to tolerate.

In the ADW and IEF integrated CASE application development cycles, analysis follows tactical planning. Since it precedes design and construction, analysis is considered Upper CASE. While strategic planning addresses how information technology can be used to support the enterprise, and tactical planning defines and scopes the applications to be developed, analysis nails down precisely what each application, defined during tactical planning, is to accomplish. When properly scoped, analysis can be limited to a specific business area delineated by a small number of business functions and entity types on the tactical planning C-R-U-D matrix, and is therefore often referred to as "Business Area Analysis," or "BAA" for short. Because neither the business functions nor the entity types on the C-R-U-D matrix take location into account, the geographic area covered by a BAA can be large, sometimes spanning many countries and continents.

Just as a single tactical plan can identify a number of BAAs, a single BAA can spawn more than one design and construction project. There's no in-

---

[1]There are two exceptions to this rule. The first involves the use of the ADW/RAD tool that spans analysis and design and uses analysis models to develop sophisticated prototypes showing the way the application might function. The second exception is that the IEF can also be used to develop prototypes during analysis, although the tool is usually not used in this manner.

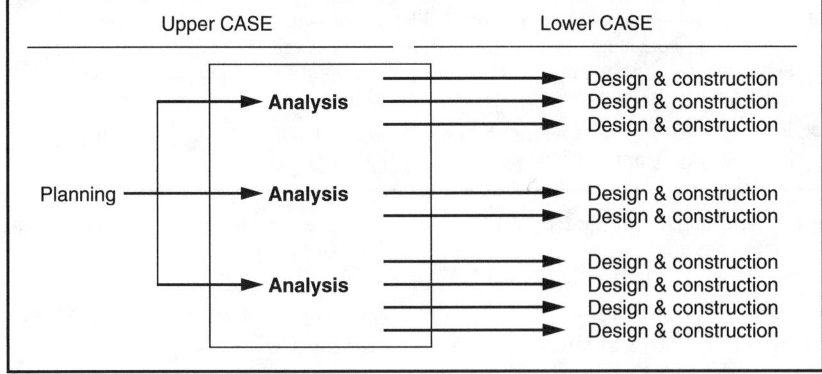


**Fig. 8.1** Where analysis fits into the integrated CASE-based application development cycle.

formation engineering, ADW, or IEF requirement that the entire analysis be implemented at once. (See Fig. 8.1.)

## What ADW- and IEF-based analysis does, and how it works

The models constructed during an ADW- or IEF-based integrated CASE analysis have two principal objectives. (See Fig. 8.2.)

These objectives are achieved through a series of process, data, and process-to-data interaction models that are constructed during analysis and used during design and construction. Detailed business requirements are modeled using techniques that are similar to those employed to construct information engineering planning models. The differences are that in analysis, the modeling and model verification processes are far more rigorous, and a much finer level of detail is sought. The objectives are to:

- Flush out and document all of the business opportunities, rules, and requirements, especially those that might not come to light during design and construction, when the application is modeled from an operational perspective.
- Develop a stable data model that completely supports the business area's rules and operational requirements,
- Provide input for design and construction of applications that meet the business area's requirements.

ADW and IEF analysis models meet these objectives through a combination of process and data granularity, careful definition and consistency checks, resolution of business and technical issues, and integration with design and construction tools. (See Fig. 8.3.)

- Develop, verify, and document detailed business requirements early in the application's development life cycle, when gaps between the business area's actual needs and the application development team's understanding of the business area's needs are least expensive to close.
- Provide machine readable input for designing and generating code for the business area's application.

**Fig. 8.2** ADW and IEF integrated CASE analysis objectives.

**Process and data granularity.** Process granularity is achieved by decomposing each of the business functions contained within the business area down to leaf-level processes (known as "sequential" processes in ADW and "elementary" processes in IEF), each representing a very small unit of work. Data granularity is achieved by modeling the data that support the leaf-level processes, in "third normal form."[2] This is a representation that causes the small number of large entity types, used during tactical planning to define the business area, to be broken into many smaller entity types, each containing only a few data elements called "attributes." Granularity in process and data models:

- Allows each small unit of work to be separately scrutinized, analyzed, and given a precise definition.
- Permits the data required to support each leaf-level process to be precisely defined in terms of specific entity types and attributes.

If business events are modeled, then frequent and response-critical transactions, inquiries, and reports can also be modeled in terms of the very granular leaf-level processes and entity actions that support them. Although this analysis is not supported by current releases of ADW or IEF, it can be easily

- Process and data granularity
- Careful definition and consistency checks
- Resolution of business and technical issues
- Integration with design and construction tools

**Fig. 8.3** How ADW and IEF achieve analysis objectives.

---

[2]For a clear discussion of third normal form and the data normalization process, see James Martin, *Information Engineering* Book II, Prentice Hall, 1990, Pages 221-244. James Martin, *Strategic Data Planning Methodologies* Prentice Hall, 1982, contains detailed instructions on data model normalization along with a reprint of some of E. F. Codd's normalization work.

accomplished using a technique known as Process Logic Diagramming or Data Navigation Diagramming, in which the actions of each leaf-level process are shown on the entity relationship data model,[3] with the actions tabulated using a spreadsheet. The result is a solid basis for designing a physical database that is specifically optimized for crucial business needs without making unnecessary trade-offs in other areas.

**Careful definition and consistency checks.** An ADW- or IEF-based analysis therefore represents a time-consuming and labor-intensive process in which large numbers of small, granular processes are defined and verified, along with many entity actions involving large numbers of small, granular entity types. Separate definitions and verifications for each entity type and relationship, as well as for each process and attribute, add to the labor intensity of this already arduous task.

Methodology and CASE tool value added consistency checks can be brought to bear on the models to ensure that:

- All parts of the definition of each process, entity type, relationship, and attribute are present, internally consistent, and consistent with one another.
- The data model is robust enough to fully support the data access requirements of each leaf-level process.

The additional rigor imposed by the methodology ADW and IEF value added consistency checks can add substantially to the already large effort required to complete the analysis.

**Resolution of business and technical issues.** The third factor that contributes to the large amounts of time and effort expended during an ADW- and IEF-based analysis involves the combination of business and technical issues that this kind of close and rigorous scrutiny inevitably raises. I have never participated in an ADW- or IEF-based analysis that didn't send the business and information technology participants scurrying to:

- Figure out precisely how the logic of leaf-level processes will handle specific situations.
- Precisely define the data that a process requires or creates.
- Work out the myriad of issues involved in resolving an anomaly or taking advantage of an opportunity that was discovered during the analysis.

---

[3]Dennis Minium, *A Guide To Information Engineering Using The IEF,* Texas Instruments, 1990, Pages 206-214.

- An implementation-independent view of the business area's functional requirements
- A technology-independent view of the business area's data requirements
- Data access logic for code generation

**Fig. 8.4** Design and construction requirements addressed by ADW- and IEF-based analysis.

An insurance company, for example, found that when their claims processing business function was decomposed independent of organization, operations, and geographic area, the IEF-based decomposition contained a single claims payment process. Although the consistent customer interface and cost reductions derived from analyzing and implementing their claims payment operations in a single process were desirable, proceeding with the single claims payment process analysis meant that organizational and business issues had to be addressed. Several issues had to be worked out: those centered around common governance of the single process over a number of different organizations, and common requirements and the implication that the common process might not be fully optimized for each organization's claim processing needs.

**Integration with design and construction tools.** When integrated CASE tools and methodologies are employed, the data models, process decompositions, and action diagrams, produced during analysis provide machine readable input for database design and code generation. Design and construction tools can then be used to implement the analysis models in the desired technology. (See Fig. 8.4.)

For example, the fully normalized data model constructed during analysis can be read by ADW and IEF design tools that can be used to turn the data model into a viable design for the application's physical database. IEF process action diagrams, and to a lesser extent, ADW mini-specs, for leaf-level processes can also be read by their respective design and construction tools to become part of the input for automated code generation. The ADW RAD tool uses the analysis data model as a basis for developing and prototyping the application's dialogue and screens.

### How ADW-based and IEF-based analysis differs from other analysis paradigms

The information-engineering-based analysis supported by ADW and IEF can differ considerably from traditional manual and automated paradigms for analysis. Although there are many minor variations, even between ADW and IEF, the major differences tend to involve:

- Additional effort and visibility.
- Concentration on data, rules, and logic.
- Equal emphasis on modeling data and activities.
- Integration with other CASE tools for information engineering life cycle phases.

**Additional effort and visibility.** The granularity, detailed definition, consistency checks, and issue resolution associated with ADW- and IEF-based analysis add substantially to the required time and effort. Relative to the total effort expended, it's not uncommon to have expenditures of over 300% more time and effort than have been required for traditional analyses. (See Fig. 8.5.)

Where a traditional manual analysis might consume as little as 15% of an application's total development costs, the corresponding cost, in the information engineering paradigm for application development, can reach 40% or more.[4]

The additional relative time and cost of an ADW- or IEF-based analysis, as explained in the chapter on methodologies, is not the result of additional detail and rigor associated with integrated CASE, for rigor and detail are an inherent part of application development and are conserved over the application development life cycle. CASE simply forces detail and rigor to the

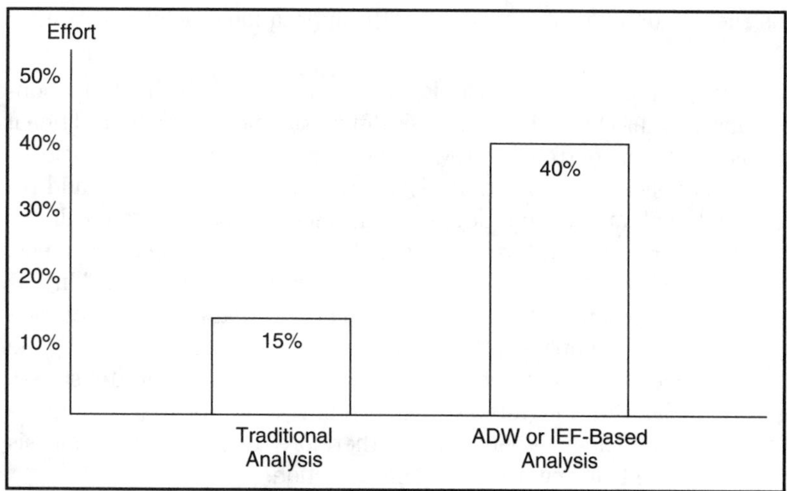


**Fig. 8.5** CASE-based analysis can require 300% more effort than traditional analysis.

[4]Based upon personal observations and measurements made at ADW and IEF application development sites during the past six years.

| Application development phase | Visibility of an error | Cost to correct an error |
|---|---|---|
| Analysis | High | Low |
| Design | Low | Moderate |
| Construction | Low | High |
| Production | Extremely High | Extremely High |

**Fig. 8.6** Relative viability and cost of correcting an error in each phase of an application's life cycle.

surface and deals with them during analysis, where they're least expensive to address. Analysis, however, along with production, is also one of the two places in an information system's life cycle where detail and rigor are most visible. It's the added visibility and expanded relative size of a CASE-based analysis, not necessarily its actual size, that causes it to loom as large as it often does. (See Fig. 8.6.)

Involvement of business users and management in the analysis process means that the visibility of misunderstandings, issues, and errors addressed during analysis can be significantly greater than would be the case if they were addressed during design and construction, where no one outside of the information systems development team may know about them. The cost of correcting the errors and misunderstandings during analysis, however, can be significantly less than the cost of making the same corrections during design or construction, or as "maintenance after the application is delivered."[5]

**Concentration on data, rules, and logic.** A second way in which information-engineering-based ADW and IEF analysis differs significantly from traditional analysis is that it concentrates on the business area's data, rules, and logic instead of the application's operations—its screens, windows, menus, and reports. Traditional application development methodologies often call for analysis of requirements in terms of technology-dependent menus, screens, and reports, as part of "external design" or "requirements definition." In this application development paradigm, the design phases that follow concentrate on figuring out how to implement the business rules, which are implied by the screens and reports, but not necessarily modeled, or even explicitly stated. Using ADW or IEF for integrated CASE, screens, windows, menus, and reports that are technology dependent, are therefore dealt with after analysis has been completed, during design and construction.

The objectives of an ADW and IEF analysis are understanding and model-

---

[5]James Martin, *Rapid Application Development,* Macmillan Publishing Company, 1991, Pages 26-30. Also see Clive Finkelstein, *An Introduction To Information Engineering,* Addison Wesley, 1989, Pages 5-7.

ing the business's detailed rules and requirements, irrespective of how they might be met. As with the additional detail and rigor associated with integrated CASE-based analysis, this difference is highly visible, and for those not used to CASE, the difference is often unwelcome as well. (See Fig. 8.7.)

Addressing what the business rules are, along with what the application will do, but not how the application might work, enables analysis teams to concentrate on the business, along with its fundamental rules and issues, unclouded by approaches or technologies. It makes the analysis models stable and independent of physical implementations, which can change over time as business processes are reengineered and new information technologies emerge.[6] Technology and business process independence can be important considerations for companies that have to implement the same application simultaneously, in different locations (possibly with differing technologies), or take advantage of emerging technologies, such as client/server, without having to reanalyze the business.

**Emphasis and integration.** Information-engineering-based analysis using ADW and IEF can also differ significantly from traditional software engineering (SE) and structured analysis. Although many of the techniques, such as

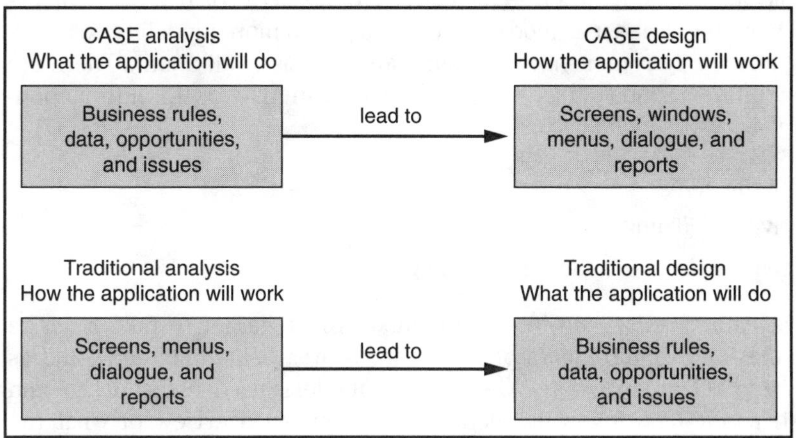


**Fig. 8.7** Objectives of integrated CASE and traditional analysis and design.

[6]The distinction between business "processes" and information "processes" is important. Business processes represent specific approaches to achieving desired outcomes for portions of a business. Business processes can include organization, geography, procedures, and work flow. Information engineering processes represent generic activities carried out by the business, independent of organization, geography, procedure, and work flow. Michael Hammer, "Reengineering Work: Don't Automate, Obliterate," *Harvard Business Review*, July-August 1990, Pages 104-112 provides a good introduction to reengineering business processes.

functional decomposition, data flow diagramming, and entity relationship modeling, upon which the analysis is based, may seem familiar, the way they're used and integrated into the analysis is likely to be different. The most significant differences fall into two categories: emphasis and integration.

Instead of emphasizing the analysis of either data or process, as many SE and structured approaches do, information engineering places equal emphasis on data, process, and their interaction. ADW and IEF data, process, and interaction models are not complete until each of the others have been fully analyzed and verified with the application's users. ADW and IEF models can also be much more tightly integrated than their SE or structured analysis counterparts. Although both ADW and IEF can be used to support traditional, data, and activity analysis, it's when they're used as integrated CASE tools that the substantial investments that they represent can be realized. In this context, an information engineering analysis represents one part of a tightly integrated planning, design, and construction effort as opposed to separate structured or SE analysis and diagramming techniques designed to enhance analysis.[7]

## Business Modeling

If I had to succinctly describe the essence of an ADW- or IEF-based analysis, I would describe it as modeling, modeling, and more modeling, for modeling succinctly represents what such an analysis is all about. There are three different kinds of modeling that occur in an ADW or IEF information-engineering-based analysis:

- Data modeling.
- Activity modeling.
- Activity-to-data interaction modeling.

The data, activity, and interaction models fit together to fully describe the rules and requirements of the business area being analyzed—and as ADW and IEF are integrated CASE—each model is used during design and construction. The following sections represent an overview of what the analysis models are, how they work, what they do, and how they're supported by ADW and IEF. A more in-depth description of how information engineering analysis models work, along with precisely how they're sup-

---

[7]Robert G. Fichman & Chris F. Kemerer, "Object Oriented And Conventional Analysis And Design Methodologies: Comparison And Critique," Massachusetts Institute Of Technology CISR Working Paper No. 230, November 1991, and James Martin, *Strategic Data Planning Methodologies* Prentice Hall, 1982, Pages 15-20, contain excellent examples of C-R-U-D matrix analysis. For a more complete information engineering overview, see James Martin, *Information Engineering,* Books I and II, Prentice Hall, 1990.

ported by ADW and IEF, can be found in Dennis Minium and Rick Napier's excellent books on the subject.[8]

### The information engineering data model

Most data are modeled using variations of the entity relationship diagram developed by Peter Chen in 1976, long before the advent of CASE.[9] Although the notation is different, this is the basis of the data modeling techniques supported by ADW and IEF.

CASE tools and methodologies add significant value to the data modeling process by supplying a convenient means for entering, storing, and retrieving each data model object (e.g., entity type, relationship, attribute, domain) and by automatically propagating changes made to data model objects throughout the data model and into other CASE-based models that interact with it. They add additional value by ensuring data model consistency through checking data model objects against each other and by associating each data model object with the processes that it supports.

The objectives in building an ADW or IEF information engineering data model for the business area are to:

- Capture information about the business area's data in machine readable format.
- Fully and accurately describe the data needed to support the business area's activities—independent of procedures and constraints imposed by current information systems and technologies,
- Capture the business area's rules and logic that can be described in terms of data.
- Provide the basis for designing a stable database that will support the business area's information requirements.
- Gain a better understanding of how the business area's data can affect application performance.
- Identify and resolve data-related business and technical issues.

Without the logical data model created during the BAA, CASE would be a lot less productive, and integrated CASE wouldn't exist. The physical database would have to be developed during design and construction, just as it is in traditional application development, and for large and complex ap-

---

[8]Dennis Minium, *A Guide To Information Engineering Using The IEF,* Texas Instruments, 1990. Also see Rick Mapier, *Information Engineering & Application Development Using KnowledgeWare's CASE Tool Set,* Prentice Hall, 1991.

[9]Peter Chen, "The Entity Relationship Model: Toward A Unified View Of Data," ACM Transactions On Database Systems, 1976.

| Entity relationship diagram | Shows | Doesn't show |
|---|---|---|
| Business rules and logic represented as data | x | |
| The information used and impacted by the business area | x | |
| Details about the information | x | |
| When the information is used or impacted | | x |
| How the information supports the business area's activities | | x |
| How the different kinds of information are related | x | |
| How the information might be stored | | x |

**Fig. 8.8** What an entity relationship diagram shows.

plications, redeveloped over and over as new data requirements and constraints are discovered and issues resolved. With each regeneration of the database, many of the application programs, which access the changed database, would have to be modified and retested as well. Productivity would rapidly decline, even with powerful Lower CASE tools that can generate and regenerate programs quickly. For applications requiring multiple team development, the data access and interface specifications for each team's program would diverge during programming and unit testing, causing much confusion and reprogramming during integration testing, substantially prolonging the testing process.

Because the analysis data model is a logical model, it doesn't represent an operational view of the business area or its applications. Although it shows precisely which data support each of the business areas processes, it tells little about how, when, or in what order the support takes place, or even where or how the data might be stored. For those not versed in data modeling, it can be very difficult to relate to the combination of the lack of physical information and the data model's representation in third normal form, a necessity for making large models accurate and controllable, and for achieving sufficient granularity. Data modeling, however necessary and productive, remains the bane of many business users who participate on teams conducting business area analysis. (See Figs. 8.8, 8.9, and 8.10.)

### The information engineering process model

The information-engineering-based process model supported by ADW and IEF involves decomposing the functions, which are included in the business area, into smaller and smaller pieces, until leaf-level processes, each representing a single unit of work, are reached. Although the concept of functional decomposition, in the form of Warnier-Orr charts and HIPO diagrams, has been around for a long time,[10] the CASE-based process decompositions cre-

[10]Kenneth Orr, *Structured Systems Development*, Yourdon Press, 1977. Also, IBM lectures and presentations on Hierarchy Input Process Output (HIPO) techniques for describing programs during the early 1970s.

ated during analysis are unique in that they decompose and validate processes based on, and verified by, data. The analysis decomposition therefore represents the business area's activities in terms of many small, granular, leaf-level processes, each serving a unique logical function based on their interaction with the logical data model.

As with data models, there's much confusion over what the logical process model does and shows. Care must be taken to ensure that the process decomposition doesn't represent the business area from an operational or organizational view, since this is the way most people normally think about it. Indeed, it's not uncommon for business and information technology analysis team participants to lapse into an organizational or operational view and have to go back and correct the decomposition several times during the process modeling effort. (See Figs. 8.11, 8.12, and 8.13.)

Not only does the process model capture and illustrate information showing how the business area's activities break down based on data, but a substantial amount of descriptive information about each process is

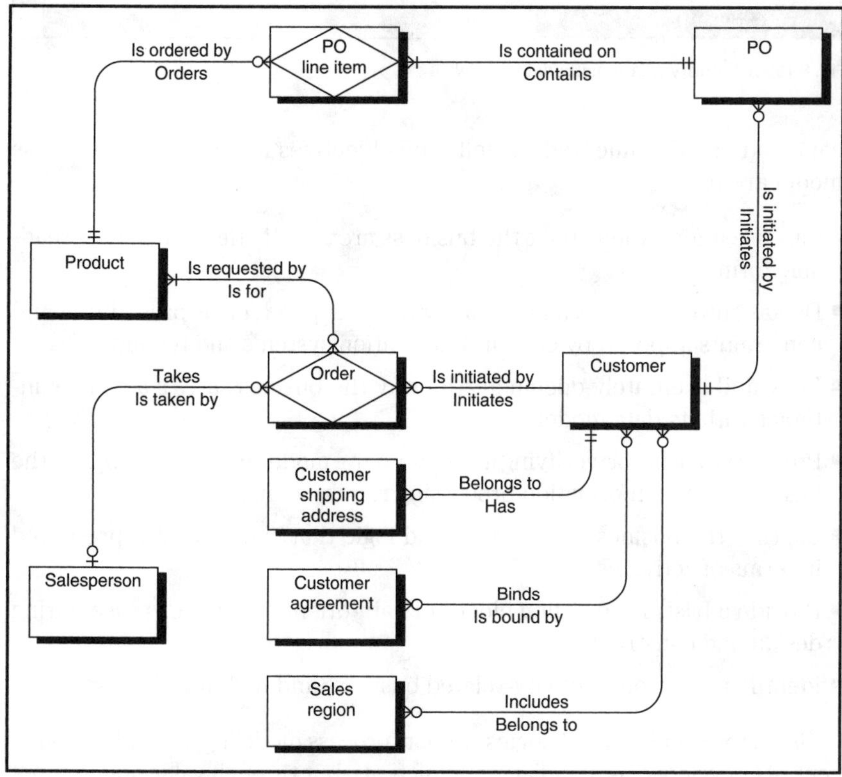


**Fig. 8.9** ADW entity relationship data model.

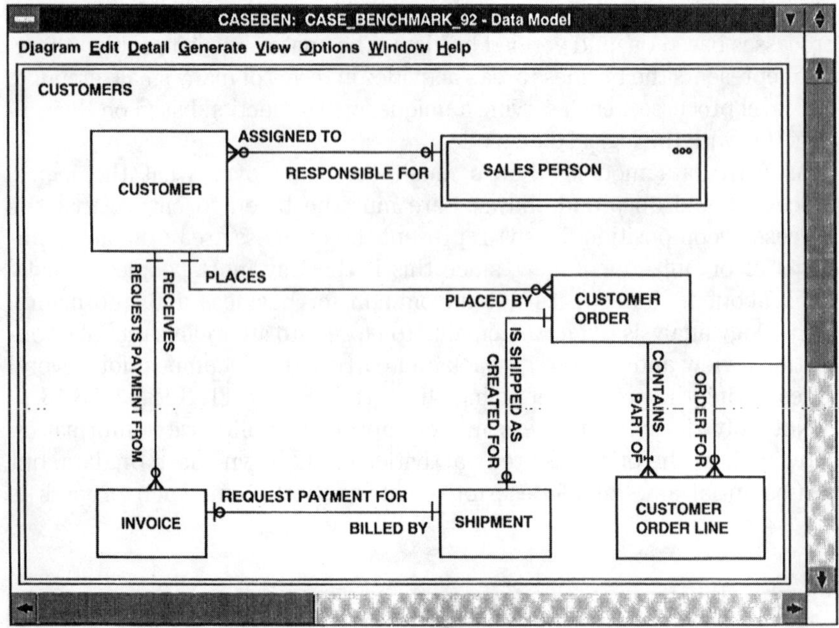


**Fig. 8.10** IEF entity relationship data model.

captured and documented as well. The objectives in building the process model are to:

- Capture information about the business area's activities in machine readable form.
- Document the business area's activities independent of procedures and constraints imposed by current information systems and technologies.
- Fully and accurately document the way the business area's activities interact with its data model.
- Provide a basis for verifying that the data model can fully support the business area's information processing requirements.
- Capture the business area's rules and logic that can be best represented in terms of activities.
- Provide a basis for defining blocks of data-oriented logic for reuse during design and construction.
- Identify and resolve activity-related business and technical issues.

CASE tools and methodologies support process modeling, not only through central encyclopedias and diagramming tools, but through value added functionality. Matrix processors, for example, can be used to develop a C-R-U-D

| Functional decomposition | Shows | Doesn't show |
|---|---|---|
| Detailed activities in the business area | x | |
| Activity-based business rules and logic | x | |
| How the detailed activities break out based on the data model | x | |
| How the detailed activities are carried out | | x |
| When the detailed activities are carried out | | x |
| Where the activities are carried out | | x |
| How the business area is automated | | x |
| The organization of the business area | | x |

**Fig. 8.11** What a functional decomposition shows.

matrix, similar to the planning C-R-U-D matrix, but at the leaf-level process and normalized entity type level. This low-level C-R-U-D matrix can be used to provide rough verification that the data and process models support each other by ensuring that each leaf-level process impacts at least one normalized entity type, and that each entity type in the data model is impacted by at least one leaf-level process. Finer, and more rigorous, verification that the data and

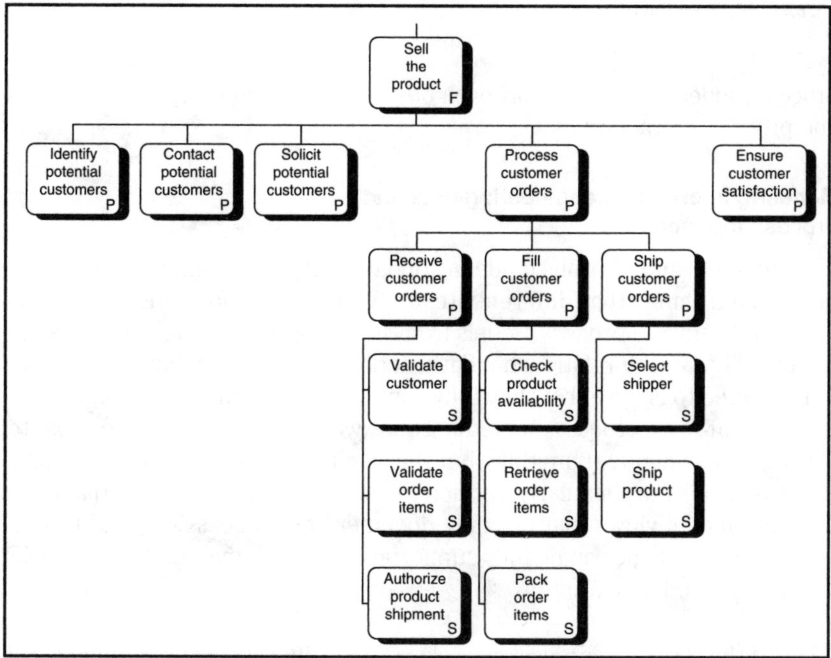


**Fig. 8.12** ADW functional decomposition.

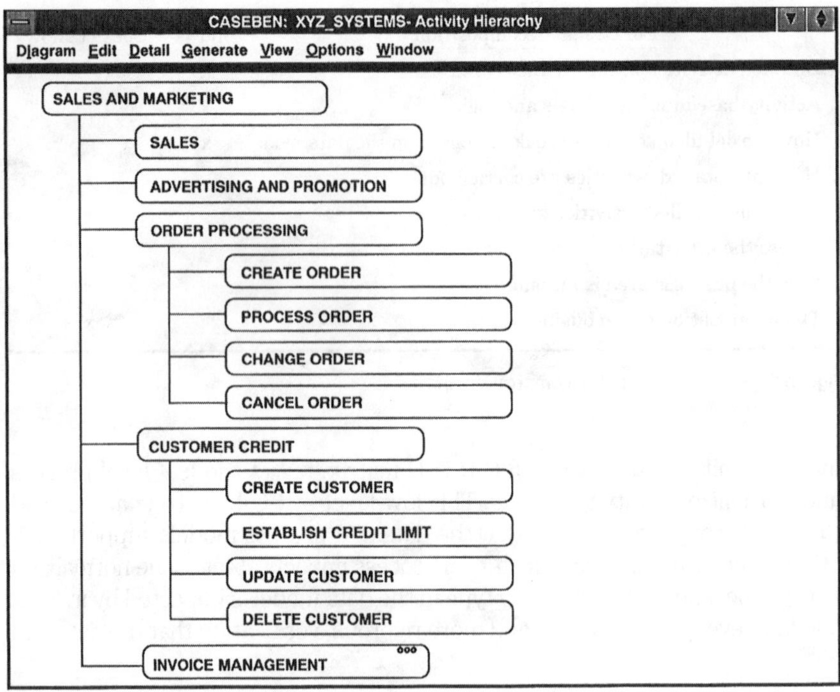


**Fig. 8.13** IEF functional decomposition.

process models indeed support each other is developed while modeling data and process interactions.

## Modeling information engineering data and process interactions

The complete and rigorous modeling of data and process interactions is one of the main things that differentiates ADW and IEF information-engineering-based data and process models from similar-looking models produced in the past. The entity relationship data models, for example, have been carefully verified to ensure that they fully support the information requirements of each leaf-level process, something that would be close to impossible to accomplish by hand for anything but the smallest and simplest applications. Process models are similarly verified in terms of detailed action diagrams and data model views that not only document the process's logic, but also ensure that the logic can be fully supported. The objectives of ADW and IEF interaction modeling are to:

- Verify the data and process models so that differences are resolved and the models completely support each other.

- Stabilize the data model so that it will not need to undergo costly changes during design and construction.
- Verify that the decomposition is data oriented, rather than organizationally or operationally oriented.
- Develop data-access-related business rules and logic for each granular process in reusable, machine-readable format.
- Document the access paths through which each leaf-level process accesses the data model.

Although interaction modeling is supported by ADW and IEF, the support is implemented by these tools in different ways. ADW supports interaction modeling primarily through data flow diagrams (DFDs) and secondarily through action diagrams, or mini-specs. IEF interaction modeling is accomplished through process action diagrams (PADs).

ADW uses data flow diagrams to track data flowing into and out of an application through the decomposition into each leaf-level (sequential) process. Since ADW data flows are tightly coupled to specific entity types and attributes in the data model, the sequential processes that are the origins and terminations of data flows are tightly coupled to the data model as well. This coupling, along with data-flow-oriented value added consistency checks, helps to ensure that the data model fully supports each ADW sequential process. Data flow diagrams are also useful in illustrating data dependencies between an application and other systems as well as among the processes in the decomposition. Timing, location, and physical storage, however, are not shown. (See Fig. 8.14.)

The rules and logic with which each sequential process accesses the data model are developed and documented in ADW using action diagrams,

| Data flow diagram | Shows | Doesn't show |
|---|---|---|
| How portions of the data model support each process | x | |
| How each process interacts with the rest of the enterprise | x | |
| How each process interacts with databases and files | | x |
| Information exchanged between processes in the decomposition | x | |
| Data dependencies among business processes | x | |
| Location of information flowing between processes and to business | | x |
| Timing of information flowing between processes and to business | | x |

**Fig. 8.14** What an ADW data flow diagram shows.

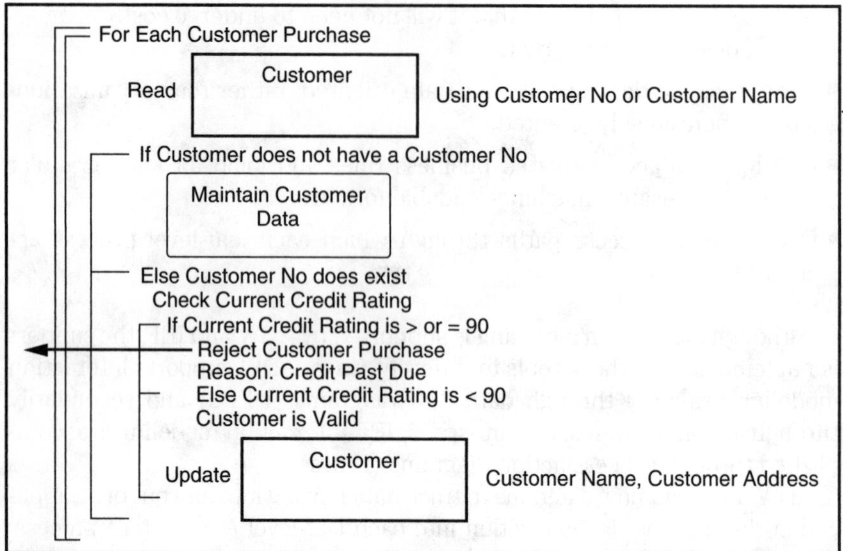
For Each Customer Purchase
Read
Customer
Using Customer No or Customer Name
If Customer does not have a Customer No
Maintain Customer Data
Else Customer No does exist
Check Current Credit Rating
If Current Credit Rating is > or = 90
Reject Customer Purchase
Reason: Credit Past Due
Else Current Credit Rating is < 90
Customer is Valid
Update
Customer
Customer Name, Customer Address

**Fig. 8.15** ADW mini-spec for a sequential process.

sometimes referred to as "mini-specs." The ADW action diagrammer ensures that the action diagrams are syntactically consistent. Correctness must be verified via business user participants and current systems analysis. (See Fig. 8.15.)

IEF verifies the data model and documents leaf-level (elementary) process data-oriented logic via action diagrams called process action diagrams ("PADs"), which are rigorously tied to specific data model entity types and attributes. PADs are extremely rigorous and specific in terms of both logic and the entity actions. Entity types, for example, can't be accessed unless the entity type is included in the PAD's "view" of the data model and the PAD includes a valid access path (or "selection criterion") that's valid for the entity type being accessed. Variable names must be completely consistent with those in the data model.

The extreme rigor and specificity associated with IEF PADs not only provide detailed data access specifications for each elementary process and validate the data model, but also allow the PADs to be used during design and construction as machine-readable input for the IEF code generator.[11] Correctness, as with ADW mini-specs, must be verified via business user participants and current systems analysis. (See Figs. 8.16 and 8.17.)

---

[11]IEF PADs form input to IEF code generators via PAD logic being used in IEF procedure action diagrams (PrADs). It's the PrADs that form the actual code generator input.

| Action diagram | Shows | Doesn't show |
|---|---|---|
| Elementary processes creates, reads, updates and deletes of entity types | x | |
| Elementary processes data access related logic | x | |
| Paths through which entity types are accessed | x | |
| Operational logic | | x |
| Anything to do with screens and reports | | x |

**Fig. 8.16** What IEF process action diagrams show.

## How Much Analysis Is Required?

Although methodologies and CASE tool documentation provide guidelines for how to model a business area, few provide guidance regarding how little or how much of the business area to analyze, or how much data, process, and interaction modeling to do. Although ADW and IEF, through rules and value added consistency checks, ensure that the analysis models are consistent at whatever level of detail they're developed, neither tool imposes a specific level of detail on its users. There are no checks, for example, to ensure that the data model is in third normal form. Neither tool checks the scope of a functional decomposition's leaf-level processes, and neither tool enforces a specific amount of action diagramming.

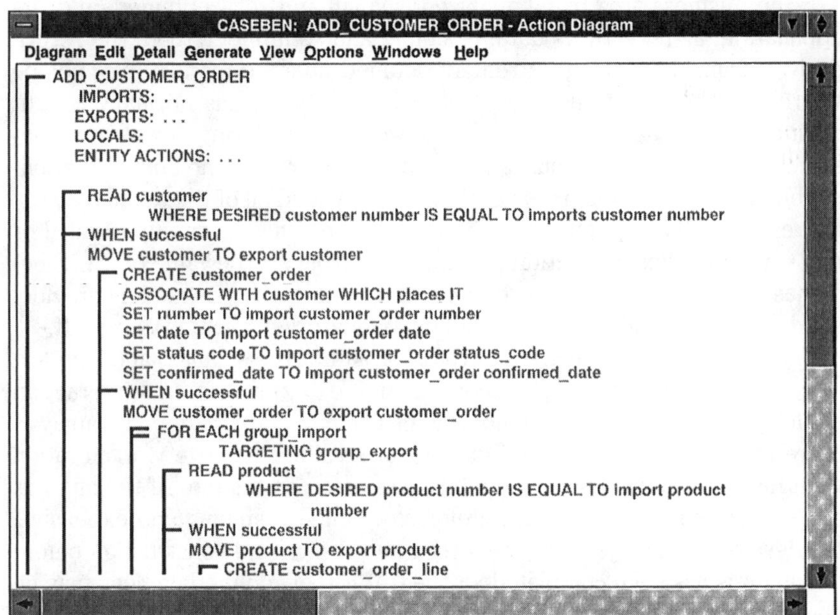


**Fig. 8.17** IEF process action diagram for an elementary process.

| Amount of detail | 0–6 months Simple | 6–12 months Avg complexity | Over 1 year Very complex |
|---|---|---|---|
| Low rigor Few details | High | Medium | Low |
| Moderate rigor and detail | Medium | High | Medium |
| Extremely detailed & rigorous | Low | High | High |

(Column heading: Size and complexity of application)

**Fig. 8.18** Return on analysis and modeling investment for business areas and applications of varying size and complexity.

The correct amount of analysis, and the correct amount of rigor and detail with which the analysis models are constructed, represent trade-offs between the size and complexity of the business area being analyzed, the effort available to be expended, the payback during design and construction, and the organization's tolerance for analysis. (See Fig. 8.18.)

If the business area being analyzed is small and self-contained, and the application, along with its data, is simple and well understood, the return derived from developing extremely detailed analysis models may not be worth the effort. For such projects, many of the details normally sought during analysis may be just as quickly worked out during design and construction. As application size and complexity increase, the ability of application development teams to get their arms around all of the details rapidly decreases, and a rigorous, detailed analysis becomes more important. For large and complex application development projects, the value of CASE becomes very dependent on the detail and rigor that analysis models provide, making detailed and rigorous modeling mandatory if CASE is to pay off.

The general rule for analysis is that, for all but the smallest and simplest projects, time and effort spent constructing data, process, and interaction models is paid back severalfold during design and construction. So, analysis represents a good investment. But there are real limits in every organization governing how much analysis the business area can tolerate. If the analysis models are too rigorous, and therefore too time-consuming and expensive, the development project may be forced into design and construction before the analysis has been completed, or the CASE tool and methodology may be abandoned altogether. Either way, much of the benefits that CASE can provide will be lost.

## The Six CSFs for CASE-Based Analysis

Successfully using ADW and IEF for analysis, so that the benefits of using CASE can be realized during design and construction, is far from automatic. The CSFs shown in Fig. 8.19, once achieved, will provide a sound basis for making a CASE-based analysis a success.

### Clear objectives and a reasonable scope

One of the most important CSFs for traditional application development is to clearly define, and stick to, the application's objectives and scope. Indeed, there are few better ways to thwart an application development effort than to start developing the application without clear and stable definitions of what the application should and should not address. The same CSF holds true for CASE-based analysis projects, but with the following twists. The first is that the business functions and data that define the BAA's scope should have a high affinity with each other in terms of the way they interact. If they don't, the process and data models will not be useful in verifying one another, and the process interaction model will be impossible to construct. For BAAs that are preceded by a CASE-based tactical plan, a high level of affinity will be achieved automatically, as a result of the C-R-U-D analysis. Analysis projects that are large and complex and don't follow a CASE-based tactical planning effort should therefore be postponed while the three-week to six-week tactical planning effort is completed.

The second twist is that the size of the business area being analyzed is more critical with CASE. The combination of CASE-based projects being front loaded with much of the loading showing up in analysis, and the high degree of detail and rigor required to make large application analysis pay off, dictates that analysis project scope be more carefully controlled for CASE. A good rule of thumb is that if the analysis project requires more than six months to complete, the business area being analyzed is too big or complex. Such projects should be broken down into two or more smaller BAAs (via a tactical planning effort) so that the six-month guideline is met.

1. Clear objectives and a reasonable scope
2. A balanced team with ample user participation
3. Balancing data and process
4. Taking a practical approach
5. Resolving business issues
6. Adequate facilities and support

**Fig. 8.19** Six CSFs for CASE-based analysis.

### A balanced team with ample user participation

The detail and rigor required to produce viable data, process, and interaction models of a business area, and the business orientation of the models themselves, require far greater user participation than traditional analysis does. I have never seen a successful analysis of a business area that didn't thoroughly and intimately involve the business users in developing the models and verifying the models, once they're produced. Analysis models that don't represent a balanced product of both information technology and business user involvement and verification are likely to be flawed and incomplete, a fact that may not surface until design and construction, when action diagrams have to be rewritten and the physical database continually regenerated. (See Fig. 8.20.)

Ample user participation means that the analysis needs to include business users as part of the team. This doesn't imply that the users have to move in with the analysis team and spend each and every work day modeling their business area, although for large and complex applications, doing so is not a bad idea. It does imply that business users must be available to the team in a relatively unrestricted manner.

Users who participate in CASE-based analysis should have (and have access to) detailed knowledge about their business area, knowledge that goes beyond the business procedures and rules—to the objectives, ideas, and reasoning behind the procedures. They should also have access to the working-level users in each business area who will be affected by the system. This is especially important if the analysis covers a large geographic area.

For the analysis to be successful, the users will have to understand something about the purpose and approach of the CASE-based analysis, and they will need to understand, and buy into, the business models that are the product of the analysis. Although the users have to be able to navigate and read the models, as some of the models will, in all likelihood, be too techni-

| | Business user participation: High | Business user participation: Low |
|---|---|---|
| High IT participation | Good analysis | Flawed analysis |
| Low IT participation | Flawed analysis | No analysis |

**Fig. 8.20** Importance of information technology and user participation during analysis.

cal for most users to be comfortable with, they will at a minimum have to understand the business implications. For complex applications, achieving this transition may require a translation of the models into work products that are more user oriented.

### Balancing data and process modeling

ADW and IEF, along with most of the information engineering derivative methodologies that support them, attach equal importance to data and process modeling. So interdependent are the data and process models that, once the analysis modeling effort has been substantially completed, it's often difficult to change one without making a corresponding change in the other.

The information engineering data to process balance and interdependence, however well supported by CASE tools and methodologies, doesn't always carry over to the business and information technology people who construct the models. Many modelers, particularly those who are new to CASE and information engineering concepts, are a lot more comfortable modeling one than they are modeling the other, and not surprisingly, the models that they produce can reflect their preference.

When staffing analysis projects, particular care should therefore be taken to ensure that each team reflects a balanced data and process modeling skills and preferences. Balancing data and process modeling should be explicitly stated as an analysis objective, and the models produced by each team should be measured against its achievement.

### Taking a practical approach

When developing the logical data, process, and interaction models demanded by CASE-based analysis, questions inevitably surface regarding how logical (i.e., how implementation independent) the analysis models should be. To what extent, for example, should the logical process and data models reflect the physical dispersion of the data, the technologies that the application will be used for implementing, or the way the application will be used? The answer to this question is simple; to achieve implementation independence, the logical models should be independent of all of these things.

When viewed from an analysis perspective, this answer is indeed correct. But CASE is bigger than analysis. It includes design and construction, and to be successful, it must produce a functioning application as its product. When viewed in terms of broader objectives such as increasing productivity, keeping development technology options open, and ensuring acceptable application performance, the answer to our question becomes less obvious. Including "redundant" entity types in a data model to store processed information which, although represented elsewhere in the model, would require substantial processing to become useful, can have a very positive impact on applications such as decision support systems, for which quick retrieval of the processed information is important. Capturing location-dependent information along with analysis entity types and leaf-level processes can provide valuable design information for applications being developed for a client/server environment. Although these are physical, rather than logical, considerations, and could be developed during design and construction, doing so can require substantially more work than developing them during analysis, with a resultant productivity decrease.

The proper answer to the question of how logical to make the analysis models should be to take a practical approach that emphasizes logical modeling, but that also takes physical and logical implications into account.

### A mechanism to resolve issues

The business and technical issues raised by CASE-based analysis can often impact the analysis project as well as the business area and the technologies that are harnessed to support it. The use of a single claims payment process, in our insurance example, impacted not only the decomposition, as more leaf-level processes were required to serve a broader range of functionality, but the data model as well, since it has to incorporate several sets of business rules required to pay different types of claims. The selection of database and reporting environment can impact the way data are modeled, as can data collection systems that not only collect, but also preprocess the application's data. The impact on the analysis models can be substantial, and it's not uncommon for issues such as these to bring an analysis project to a complete halt until they're resolved.

The successful completion of a CASE-based analysis is therefore dependent on the ability of the organization to quickly resolve both kinds of issues. For large applications, which must function in large and complex organizations, a formal mechanism will be required for resolving the business and technical issues that the analysis project will generate. Although the structure of such a mechanism is culturally dependent, and will therefore vary from company to company, the issue resolution mechanism should:

- Be empowered to make business and technical decisions for the business area.
- Provide representation of the application's major stake holders.
- Be capable of convening and acting quickly to address issues as they come up.

### Adequate facilities and support

The ways in which facilities and work environment can impact traditional application development have been well documented,[12] even if they're not always taken into account. Although the same requirement holds true for CASE-based analysis projects, there are a number of facilities and support requirements that are unique to CASE. The interdependence of the analysis models, along with the high user involvement requirement, create a need for better user access along with more conference space than is generally required for traditional analysis projects. The need for several business and information technology team members to work together on the creation or modification of a model can't be fully satisfied if sufficient conference space, tables, and white boards are not available. Also required for many CASE projects are fast workstations with good graphic support for CASE tools, and consulting support for methodologies and modeling techniques. The high dependence that CASE analysis projects have on this kind of specialized support make it a CSF, without which a successful analysis project is difficult to execute.

[12]J. Brady, "A Theory Of Productivity In The Creative Process," IEEE Computer Graphics And Applications, May 1986. Also see T. DeMarco and T. Lister, *Peopleware, Productive Projects and Teams,* Dorset House, 1987.

Chapter

# 9

# Using CASE for Design & Construction

Design and construction using ADW and IEF are among the easiest uses of CASE for people to understand. It's during these phases that CASE-developed applications can be viewed from an operational perspective—the same way they're looked upon and thought of by traditional users and developers. Compilable code, the principal end product of ADW- and IEF-based design and construction, can be viewed and evaluated against a familiar frame of reference. The databases, menus, screens, prototypes, and reports that these phases produce also represent work products that users are comfortable and familiar with. Design and construction is also the place in the information engineering CASE-based application development cycle where the productivity and quality gains associated with CASE begin to show up.

Yet, in spite of its familiar perspective and comfortable work products, ADW- and IEF-based design and construction is just as new and unfamiliar as CASE-based planning and analysis—and often just as misunderstood. For CASE-based design and construction to be successful, dependencies on work products developed during analysis, CASE tool leverage points, design envelopes, and new and very different roles for seemingly familiar products must be understood and addressed. Before they can be of use, intriguing design and construction technologies, such as component reuse and reverse engineering, must be understood along with their requirements, limitations, and CSFs.

Design and construction represent much more than two necessary steps in the end game of the integrated CASE application development cycle. They build upon the products of analysis, using and adding value to them, to produce the databases and compilable code that make up the application.

## What ADW and IEF Design and Construction Do

Design and construction turn the detailed and rigorous logical models, developed during analysis, into one or more functioning applications for a business area. The normalized entity types and leaf-level processes are clustered into applications to be designed and constructed. The business area's logical data model becomes the basis for developing a physical data model representing a database design for the application, and the physical data model is used to generate the application's database.

The ADW modules and IEF procedures, which represent the application operational structure, are developed. Action diagrams, along with data access rules and logic, are produced for each module or procedure, using the data-oriented PADs and based on mini-specs that were defined during analysis for each leaf-level process. Menus, windows, screens, and reports, along with screen- and report-oriented rules and logic, are added to the application's modules or procedures. These design models, in the form of ADW modules or IEF procedures, along with their screens, windows, reports, calls, dialog flows, and action diagrams, become input to the code generator, which produces the COBOL or C code for compilation.[1] (See Figs. 9.1 and 9.2.)

The compiled code is then tested and debugged, not by correcting the code itself, as in conventional design and construction, but by correcting the analysis and design models—the menus, screens, reports, and detailed action diagrams that comprise the code generator's input. This is the basic design and construction paradigm employed by both ADW and IEF.[2]

---

[1]Although the terminology for design and construction objects differs for ADW and IEF, the functions that they perform are substantially the same. Strictly speaking, ADW design and construction objects include modules, calls, screens, reports, and module action diagrams, and IEF design and construction objects include screens, procedures, dialogue flows, and procedure action diagrams.

[2]For an in-depth view of the ADW and IEF paradigms for design and construction, see: Dennis Minium, *A Guide To Information Engineering Using The IEF*, Texas Instruments, 1990. Also see Rick Mapier, *Information Engineering & Application Development Using KnowledgeWare's CASE Tool Set*, Prentice Hall, 1991.

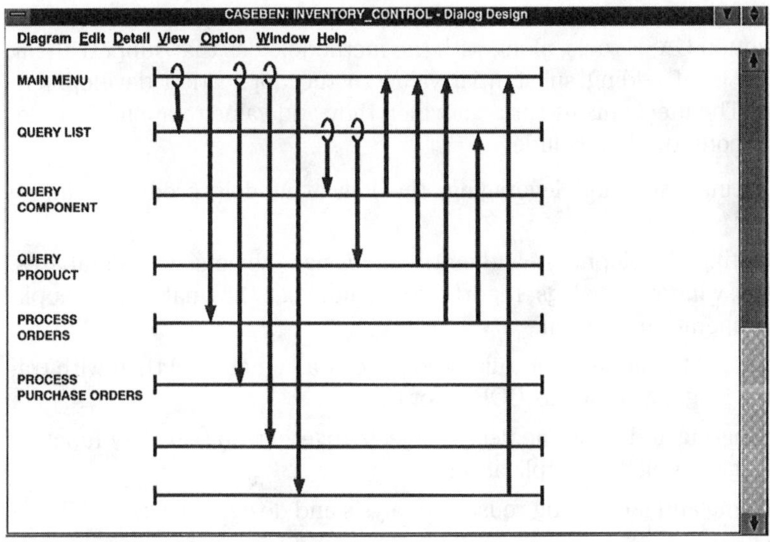


**Fig. 9.1** IEF dialog flow diagram.

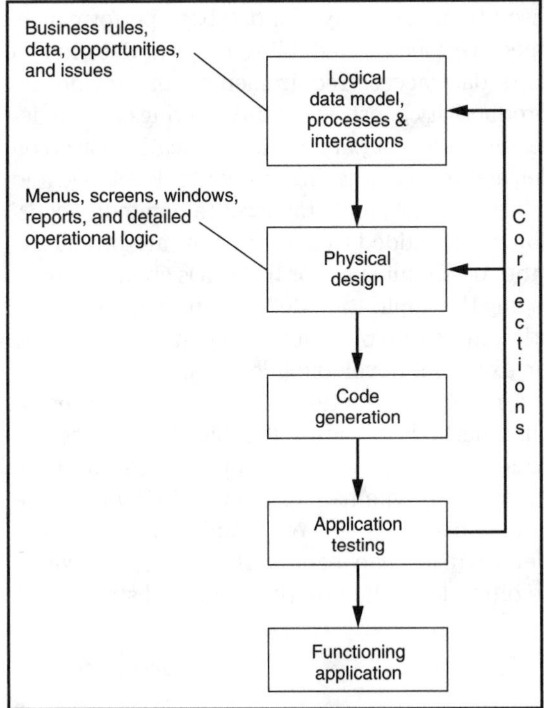


**Fig. 9.2** How CASE-based analysis, design, and construction interact to produce a functioning application.

As with planning and analysis, the ADW and IEF integrated design and construction CASE tools, along with the methodologies that support them, are capable of adding substantial value to the application development process. The mechanisms through which they add value to application design and construction include:

- Integrating with, and leveraging, the logical models produced during analysis.
- Facilitating development and entry of design objects, the databases, screens, windows, dialogs, reports, rules, and logic that make up an application operational design.
- Addressing the application rules and logic at a higher level than with traditional languages such as COBOL or C.
- Coordinating and tying the design objects together, so that they function as a single, integrated application.
- Promoting and facilitating reuse of analysis and design objects.

Both ADW and IEF use the logical data model, designed during analysis, as a basis for developing the application's physical database. Although design-specific data may be added to the logical data model, and its third normal form may be compromised to achieve physical database performance, starting with a fully developed, verified, and stabilized logical data model that supports the application's data access requirements can provide designers with an impressive productivity boost. Substantial savings can be derived from developing and testing different parts of the application based on a single, common, data model, and from not having to rewrite developed and tested programs as the database changes and stabilizes (a common occurrence with traditional development). Added to these savings are productivity gains derived from using the ADW mini-specs or IEF PADs created during analysis as a basis for developing the application detailed rules and logic.

Design productivity is further increased by facilities that are built into the CASE tools themselves. For example, developing screens, using ADW or IEF screen-painting facilities, requires a fraction of the effort required to code screens using traditional methods. Creating graphically oriented action diagrams by selecting actions from CASE-tool action menus is far more productive than using a text editor to type handcrafted COBOL or C code into a workstation. Action diagrams are also more graphic, more consistently structured, and easier to read than handcrafted code, for which structure and readability are often dependent on the whim and style of the programmers who write it.[3]

---

[3]James Martin, *Information Engineering* Book III, Prentice Hall, 1990, Appendix A. Also see James Martin, *Recommended Diagramming Standards For Analysts And Programmers: A Basis For Automation*, Prentice Hall, 1987.

The combination of menus, screens, and reports, which are painted instead of coded, and the level of the action diagramming languages themselves, work together to allow rules and logic to be expressed at a higher level than would be possible if the same logic were programmed using traditional languages. The high level achieved through screen painting and action diagramming is augmented by built-in functions such as ADW/CWS macros for handling screens or IEF implicit scrolling, which provides basic forward and backward scrolling without the need to write and debug complex scrolling code, statement by statement.

Consistency between design objects is ensured through CASE-tool coordination of the design models with each other. Fields, for example, can't be painted on screens unless they're represented in, and fully consistent with, the data model.[4] The same thing holds true for data that are created, read, updated, or deleted by module or procedure action diagrams. Productivity gains can be substantial, resulting from the automatic coordination of these design objects over conventional design and coding, in which their coordination is a manual and error-prone process.

Where libraries and subroutines enable conventional programmers to reuse certain objects, ADW and IEF CASE tools promote reuse to a far greater extent. The object-oriented ADW/RAD tool, for example, actively encourages the reuse of screen designs by ensuring that each screen inherits the characteristics of its parent screens. When you also consider reuse of analysis work products and design objects such as library modules, action blocks, and data model and IEF PrAD templates, the enormous potential of CASE-based reuse begins to emerge. Large parts of applications don't have to be coded at all.

Although each of these productivity-enhancing features can be found in certain conventional design and construction products, it's the combination of all of these features, along with their coordination and graphical implementation, that form the basis for the large productivity gains that can be achieved through Lower CASE.[5]

## Where ADW- and IEF-Based Design and Construction Fit In

ADW and IEF design and construction phases are executed following analysis, at the end of the CASE-based application development cycle, with

---

[4]ADW assures data model compatibility through screen data structures that are based on the implementable data model. IEF achieves the same result through procedure import and export views that are expressed in terms of implementable data model objects.

[5]Gordon B. Davis, "Productivity Gains From Computer Aided Software Engineering?," *Accounting Horizons*, June 1988. Also see James Martin, *Rapid Application Development*, MacMillan, 1991.

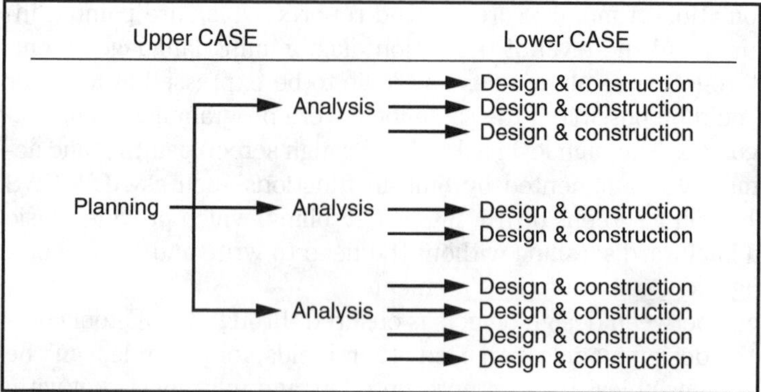


**Fig. 9.3** How design and construction fit into the CASE-based application development cycle.

a single BAA often resulting in several design-and-construction implementation projects. (See Fig. 9.3.)

The primary reason why a single BAA often leads to more than one implementation project is that it's a good way to control scope, so that functioning applications can be delivered sooner, and with reduced risk. A popular vehicle for scoping implementation projects is the C-R-U-D matrix—this time operating not using planning-level functions and subject areas, but us-

CASEBEN: ELEMENTARY_PROCESS/ENTITY_TYPE - Matrix

Diagram Edit Detail View Options Window

Cell Value:
= No reference
C = Create
D = Delete
U = Update
R = Read only

| Elementary Process / Entity Type | CUSTOMER | INVOICE | SALES PERSON | SHIPMENT | CUSTOMER ORDER | CUSTOMER ORDER LINE | PRODUCT | FINISHED GOOD STOCK | COMPONENT USAGE | COMPONENT | SUPPLIER | PURCHASE ORDER | PURCHASE ORDER LINE | COMPONENT STOCK |
|---|---|---|---|---|---|---|---|---|---|---|---|---|---|---|
| LIST INVOICE | | R | | | | | | | | | | | | |
| READ INVOICE | | R | | | | | | | | | | | | |
| DELETE INVOICE | | D | | | | | | | | | | | | |
| UPDATE INVOICE | | U | | | | | | | | | | | | |
| CREATE INVOICE | U | C | | U | | | | | | | | | | |
| CREATE ORDER | R | | | | C | C | R | | | | | | | |
| PROCESS ORDER | R | | | | U | U | R | U | | | | | | |
| CREATE CUSTOMER | C | | | | | | | | | | | | | |
| UPDATE CUSTOMER | U | | | | | | | | | | | | | |
| DELETE CUSTOMER | D | | | | | | | | | | | | | |

**Fig. 9.4** IEF elementary process and entity-type C-R-U-D matrix.

- Less time and effort are expended
- Higher dependency on analysis
- More graphical, higher-level rules and logic
- Less flexibility
- The generated code plays a much smaller role

**Fig. 9.5** Major design and construction differences between traditional application development and CASE.

ing the granular leaf-level processes and fully normalizedentity types developed during analysis. By defining projects based on leaf-level processes and entity types that interact heavily within implementation projects, but lightly across implementation projects, the C-R-U-D matrix can be useful in limiting interproject contention and simplifying model management. By identifying interproject dependencies, the C-R-U-D matrix can also provide valuable insights into the consequences of scheduling implementation projects in different orders. (See Fig. 9.4.)

## Differences between CASE-Based and Traditional Design and Construction

Although there are many differences between ADW and IEF integrated CASE and traditional design and construction, the major differences fall into the five categories listed in Fig. 9.5.

### Less time and effort are expended

Design and construction are the application development phases during which the productivity gains associated with CASE begin to show up, and the extra effort expended during analysis begins to pay off. Although the productivity gains realized from CASE are dependent on many factors, and can vary widely from project to project, savings of over 50% are achievable on both relative and absolute construction costs, compared to traditional construction.[6] (See Fig. 9.6.) But these savings in time and effort, however impressive, are not necessarily visible to the rest of the company. The problem is that, unlike the higher relative costs associated with CASE-based analysis, which are highly visible, the cost reductions associated with CASE-based design and construction are often seen only within the information technology organization.

---

[6]Donald L. Burkhard, "Implementing CASE Tools," *Journal of System Management*, May 1989.

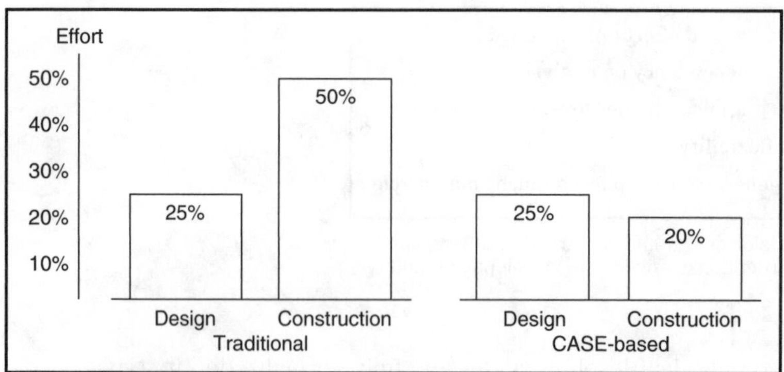


**Fig. 9-6.** CASE-based design and construction requires substantially less effort than traditional design and construction.

The same mechanisms that shield the rest of a company from the all too common construction overruns associated with traditional application development, can do an equally effective job of shielding the rest of the organization from the payback resulting from CASE.

Yet another difference between traditional development and CASE is the dependence of design and construction projects on the quality and completeness of the CASE-based analysis. The stable database and leveraged process logic, upon which design and productivity gains largely depend, will be useful during design and construction only to the extent that they're stable and correct. If the data model, for example, has not been verified through ADW data flow diagrams or IEF PADs, the module and procedure logic, created during design, may have to be rewritten over and over again, just like their traditional counterparts. Quality control in an integrated CASE environment must therefore begin not during construction, but during planning and analysis.

### More graphical, higher-level rules and logic

Representation of design rules and logic as a series of high-level, graphic models, rather than as code in programs, requires that the designers and coders express their ideas in new and different ways. Indeed, because of the high dependence of CASE-based design and construction on models developed during analysis, many traditional design prerogatives will already have been defined before an application even reaches the design phase. Even debugging is accomplished by modifying the analysis and design models instead of the code.

### Less flexibility

If CASE is to have a positive impact on productivity, designers of CASE-based applications will have less flexibility than designers of handcrafted systems. This is the result of:

- Working at a higher level.
- Reusing objects developed during analysis and through previous designs.
- CASE tool design envelopes.
- Predefined ways of doing things.

The ADW/RAD tool, for example, is most effective after screens, from which characteristics can be inherited, have already been designed. Efficient use of the ADW/CWS is highly dependent on leveraging predefined macros. Reuse of IEF PrAD templates and action blocks is effective only to the extent that designers are willing to use the screen handling, logic, and data accesses that they represent.

### The generated code plays a much smaller role

The final, and often the most baffling, departure from hand-coded systems, especially for experienced implementers, is the diminished role that the generated source code plays in CASE-based application development and maintenance. The focal point of CASE-based design and construction is the analysis and design models, which form the input to the code generators, not the generated code that they produce. Business requirements are developed, and errors are corrected, by working with the models that are created during analysis and design. It's only after the corrected models are once again processed into generated code, and the generated code is compiled and bound into the application, that the changes can be seen. The generated code, in the ADW and IEF integrated CASE paradigm for application development, represents nothing other than data that's produced by the code generator and that can be read by a compiler.

## Productivity, Generated Code, and Why No One Should Look at It

From the standpoint of where in the programming process the productivity gains afforded by CASE show up, the potential productivity gains can be generally classed into three areas: screen development, accessing data, and program logic.

Compared to what it might take a typical programmer in a COBOL, DB2, and CICS environment to code by hand, most of today's Lower CASE tools, including ADW and IEF, do well in the area of screen development. This result is not unexpected, as the information required for screen development is well bounded and easily defined, and because screen development, using COBOL and CICS, can be an extremely labor-intensive process. The same holds for screens developed for a GUI environment.

Productivity gains associated with database access are more complicated—and more mixed. Here, each code generator data manipulation language (DML) needs to be compared with SQL, the powerful, versatile, and high-level DML that is available to any programmer using relational databases. Although DMLs for some older code generators, which may have been highly productive in a nonrelational database environment, are not as productive as SQL, IEF PADs and CWS SQL statements can be every bit as productive, and just as easy to use. The data access related productivity gains associated with CASE therefore don't generally come from design and construction at all. They come from analysis. Productivity gains associated with program logic depend on a combination of the level of the code generator action diagramming logic and the ability of designers to make use of built-in functions and reusable objects. Although many of today's traditional programming environments can provide productivity gains over programming from scratch, it's the unique combination of reusable objects, high-level, and built-in functions of CASE-based design tools that provides the substantial productivity gains afforded by CASE-based design and construction.

While the productivity of modern Lower CASE tools is generally high, the productivity gains over hand-coding are variable. Their magnitude depends on a combination of factors, and can vary considerably, depending on the part of the program being generated. (See Fig. 9.7.)

Regardless of the potential or realized productivity that code generators provide, the ability to display and review the source code that they generate has obvious appeal, especially to people, such as myself, who used to write programs. But aside from satisfying a natural curiosity about the style and structure of the code that construction tools generate, why would you want to look at generated source code—and what would you do with the source code once you did look at it?

The evolution of compilers can provide some insight into these questions. When compilers were first introduced, everyone scrutinized the assembler code that they generated. Some enterprising individuals even sought to "fix" it, responding to the poor structure, and still poorer efficiency, of the generated assembler code. Although such fixes corrected bugs and often did make the generated programs run more efficiently, they didn't do much for productivity and maintainability, which were the primary reasons why compilers were introduced. Concern over the source code produced by

| | Traditional | CASE |
|---|---|---|
| Screen development | Low | High |
| Database access | High | High |
| Program rules and logic | Moderate | High |

**Fig. 9.7** Lower CASE productivity compared with that of handwritten code.

code generators doesn't do much for the productivity and maintainability gains sought through CASE tools either, and taken to an extreme, interest in the generated source code can introduce problems of its own.

When an east-coast financial services company that had a comprehensive and strictly enforced set of COBOL standards for their IBM mainframe environment acquired the ADW/CWS code generator, the first thing they did was to test the generated code against their coding standards to see how it measured up. Although the generated code compiled without errors or warnings, and flawlessly executed the logic expressed in their models, the code structure, naming conventions, and spacial relationships met less than 30% of their hand-coding standards. The evaluators, who were also the developers and enforcers of the company COBOL standards, didn't need to look any further. They never measured the code generator productivity, integration with their design tool, or the efficiency of the code that it produced. They simply threw the code generator out, and with it, all of the potential productivity gains from Lower CASE.

The point is that we shouldn't be concerned with what the generated source code might look like or (within reason) how efficiently it executes, any more than we worry about the looks of the assembler code that a new COBOL compiler generates, or how efficiently (not very, by assembler standards) it might execute. Both should be given the same degree of attention; they're just about as important.

## CASE-Based Component Reuse

The concept of designing computer applications to be constructed from standard reusable components is at once intriguing and misunderstood. Most hard goods, from automobile engines to televisions to the computer hardware that the applications run on, are constructed from reusable components. There are potentially immense productivity gains to be derived from building large-scale applications out of reused components and capitalizing the components as a reusable resource so that their cost can be amortized over many applications. These gains would be realized not only from application development, but also from maintenance.[7] But the idea of software factories and mass-produced software components, which goes back over twenty years, has thus far yielded neither positive nor consistent results.[8]

---

[7]Peter Wagner, "Varieties Of Reusability," ITT Proceedings of The Workshop on Reusability in Programming, 1983. Also see Ellis Horowitz and John B. Munson, "An Expansive View Of Reusable Software," IEEE Transactions On Software Engineering, Volume SE-10, Number 5, September 1984.

[8]Ted Biggerstaff and Charles Richer, "Reusability Framework, Assessment And Directions," IEEE Software, July 1987.

Information engineering and integrated CASE tools such as ADW and IEF, which actively promote software component reuse, hold the promise of making reuse a reality. ADW and IEF data models, which are consistent throughout an entire enterprise and reside in central, accessible, encyclopedias, are prime reuse candidates, as are BAA-developed PADs, and design-developed screens, modules, procedures, and templates.[9]

CASE-based reuse is also actively promoted by CASE-tool manufacturers. KnowledgeWare promotes reuse of screens via their ADW/RAD tool, as well as modules and macros from their design and construction workstations. Texas Instruments markets reusable IEF components, from basic screen and procedure templates to entire applications—models and all. I have seen companies purchase, and successfully employ, IEF-based applications, simply to reuse their modeling approaches as a means for speeding up analysis and design.

One would think that with methodologies, CASE tools, and CASE tool vendors all firmly behind the reuse bandwagon, and with individual reuse successes underscoring the concept's viability, that CASE-based component reuse would be commonplace. Yet it's not. Widespread reuse of CASE-based components in constructing large-scale applications remains an elusive goal that most companies can't achieve. The problem is that designing and constructing large-scale applications from reusable components requires a great deal more than methodologies, techniques, CASE tools, and vendors promoting and supporting reuse.

Although much has been written concerning the problems inherent in software component reuse, little has been written concerning how to achieve reuse using information engineering, ADW, and IEF. In my experience, the six CSFs listed in Fig. 9.8 represent the basic administrative and cultural framework that's required if significant and repeatable reuse is to be achieved using these CASE tools.[10]

### A rich library of CASE-based reusable components

Little benefit will be derived from ADW- or IEF-based reuse without a library containing reusable components that are capable of adding value to an organization's application development process. Entity types, attributes,

---

[9]James Martin, *Information Engineering*, Book III, Prentice Hall, 1990, chapters 3 and 19.

[10]The following tutorials by Freeman and Tracz, along with the *Information Engineering* trilogy and *Rapid Application Development* by James Martin, represent a reasonable survey of current literature on reuse. Note that most of the CSFs that I present for ADW and IEF reuse have also been observed by the authors of these works: Peter Freeman, *Tutorial: Software Reusability,* IEEE Computer Society Press, 1987; Will Tracz, *Software Reuse: Emerging Technology,* IEEE Computer Society Press, 1988.

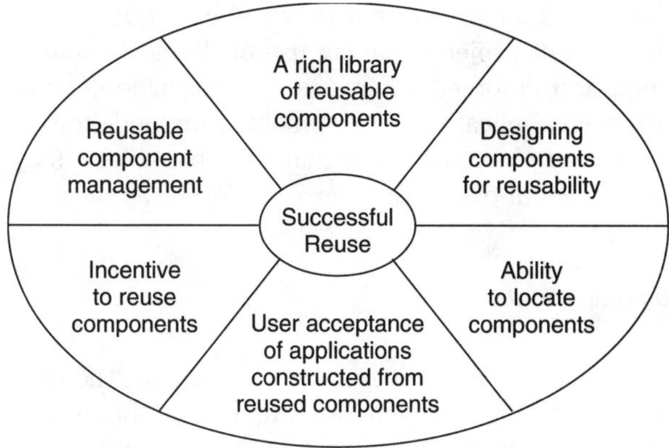


**Fig. 9.8** The six CSFs for successful reuse.

processes, action blocks, and screen templates will be reusable only to the extent that they support the organization's information system requirements, and are capable of functioning together, as parts of new applications. PADs and mini-specs, for example, will be reusable only in the context of the logical data model views for which they were created. They're not reusable alone. Module and procedure action diagrams are often associated with particular screens for entering and displaying the information that their modules and procedures process.

Creating a library that's rich in reusable objects takes time, and if it's to be used productively, the library must be carefully planned and built.[11] Information system requirements will have to be identified, articulated, and documented in the form of guidelines for the creation of each class of reusable object to be supported by the CASE tool and methodology. As the organization's business area is modeled and applications are developed, analysis, design, and construction projects will have to be monitored to ensure that the guidelines are followed, that viable reusable objects are generated, and that the generated objects are used to seed the library.

### Reusable component management

But seeding a library with viable reusable objects will not support reuse over more than a few closely knit projects, unless the library is managed and maintained. For a library of reusable objects to provide value to applications being developed by different teams, locations, and organizations, governance and maintenance issues have to be addressed. An administration will have to be set up to ensure that reusable components from analy-

[11]Issues involved with carefully planning and building a library of reusable software hold true for purchased, as well as developed, reusable objects.

sis and design models are maintained, and that they will continue to support all application development projects making use of them. Standards will have to be developed and enforced to ensure that reusable components are consistent with each application development team modeling effort. Timing conflicts will have to be resolved so that reusable objects stay constant long enough to be useful over a number of different application development efforts.

### Designing CASE-based components for reusability

Although designing components for reusability is easy to imagine, the concept can be tricky to implement. Developing model components that will be useful over a variety of different projects requires extra time and effort. Many library modules and action blocks will be reusable only if they're data-model driven rather than hard-coded, and all model components, supporting a reuse environment, will have to be very clearly documented.

The catch is that as long as application developers are measured and evaluated based on their ability to deliver functioning applications on time, and within budget, the extra time and effort required to make model components reusable will generally not be expended. Unless the fruits of reuse are shared, in direct and meaningful ways, by those who develop reusable models and model components, as well as by those who reuse them, truly reusable objects will not be generated in sufficient quantities to make the concept pay off.

### Incentive to reuse

Constructing applications by reusing someone else's work is not a welcome part of our collective applications development culture. Our propensity to design applications from scratch stems from:

- A natural desire, and in many information technology organizations, a traditional right, to fully exercise our prerogatives and creativity.
- Failed attempts to derive significant benefit from reusing application components in traditional environments.

Developers who use CASE tools and methodologies will not be exempt from these perceptions and beliefs simply because their CASE-based development environment promotes and facilitates reuse. Developers who are in a position to reuse objects will require meaningful and direct incentives, just as much as those who create the objects.

### Ability to locate reusable components

Even with everyone given proper incentives, a CASE environment that supports reuse, and a repository rich in reusable objects, the concept still will not work unless modelers can quickly and easily locate the reusable objects that they seek. Although both ADW and IEF provide convenient windows that display objects for potential reuse, neither tool does a lot to help its users find the reusable objects that are most appropriate for their immediate needs.

For large organizations with many application development projects, additional help in locating objects will be required if significant reuse, especially across different development projects, is to become a reality. Achieving CASE-based reuse in all but the smallest organizations will require location aids, such as publications, catalogues, indices, and keyword search capabilities to be developed, put in place, and made accessible to application development teams.

### User acceptance of applications built from reused components

CASE-based applications, which are the products of reused components, can impact users differently than equivalent applications that are custom-developed solely to meet their specific needs. Reuse implies compromise, often between meeting a precise need and deriving significant benefit from reuse. Reusing module or procedure action diagrams, along with the screens that they support, can affect the way an application behaves, as can reused entity types or data structures. Consider an ADW module or IEF procedure that was designed to display customer information for one application, but that doesn't display all of the customer information required by a second application in which it's reused. Since both of these CASE tools have excellent action diagramming facilities, changing the module or procedure action diagrams to accommodate the new requirement shouldn't be a problem. But it might be a problem if the new functionality requires significantly different data accesses to an altered data model, since the effort involved in altering the data model and the action diagram could easily exceed that required to develop new models from scratch!

These formidable problems can be aggravated by information system users who have grown used to applications that were totally custom built to suit their needs, and who may not be fully prepared to make the compromises that will be required for reuse to pay off. Houses, cars, clothing, and computers have all been compromised because of the prefabricated components from which they were manufactured. If reuse begins to work and becomes widely used, then businesspeople will begin to see similar compromises in their information systems.

## Reverse Engineering Older Applications into CASE-Based Models

It is indeed an intriguing concept to load old, expensive, and difficult-to-maintain applications into modern CASE tools, where their graphically oriented models can be more easily worked on, or even reengineered into new applications. This concept and the enormous potential for savings in terms of time, development, and maintenance costs if legacy information systems could really be recycled, has generated considerable interest in CASE technology. A consequence of this heightened interest is that many of today's CASE tools, including ADW and IEF, have developed at least some reverse engineering capabilities.[12]

A number of companies have met with some success in reverse engineering data, creating data models from physical databases, and reengineering older applications for newer databases. But reverse engineering activities that contain old and poorly coded COBOL programs, for example, into clean action diagrams, and eventually into analysis tool-based logical procedures and models models, has remained elusive. The contrast between data and process reverse engineering experiences is the result of fundamental differences between human and machine-readable information and their relative abundance in data and activity representations.

Consider the different ways in which information about data can be represented. Data information, in the form of databases and files, has a high machine-information content and can be directly read by executable programs. The same databases and files, however, have a low human-information content. They're not meaningful to people unless viewed through a higher level of abstraction, such as a data dictionary or COBOL file description (FD). Once that level of abstraction is reached, the same data information becomes highly readable, and therefore very useful to humans, and remains so regardless of the abstractness of the models or the CASE tools that facilitate them. In terms of human readability, further abstraction doesn't help very much. (See Fig. 9.9.)

Reading the data information inherent in a COBOL FD or data dictionary into a CASE tool such as ADW or IEF, where it can be displayed in convenient graphical form, improved upon, and used to design and generate new database, is therefore a doable task. This is why reengineering of data has been successful. (See Fig. 9.10.)

| Data representation | Level of abstraction | Human information | Machine information |
|---|---|---|---|
| Analysis tool data models | Very high | Very high | Medium |
| Design tool data models | Medium | Very high | Medium |
| Data dictionaries | Medium | Very high | Medium |
| Databases and files | Low | Low | High |

**Fig. 9.9** Human and machine information in data representations.

[12]"Reverse-engineering Tools," *Computerworld*, April 1990.

| Activity representation | Level of abstraction | Human information | Machine information |
|---|---|---|---|
| Analysis tool activity models | Very high | Very high | Very low |
| Design tool activity models | High | High | Low |
| COBOL programs | Medium | Medium | Medium |
| Assembler code | Low | Low | High |

**Fig. 9.10** Human and machine information in activity.

Reverse engineering of activity information, the inference of function from code, is quite different.[13] Each step in the reverse engineering of an application to higher levels of human readability and abstraction, from assembler code, to COBOL programs, to physical design models, and finally to the logical models addressed by analysis tools, requires more human information. The amount of human information that must be added in order to reverse engineer each step can be significant, as can the manual effort required to research and enter the data. Although knowledge-based technology may someday provide the means for making the addition of human information to activities easier, reverse engineering old programs into design and analysis CASE tools remains a very labor-intensive process.

## CSFs for ADW and IEF-Based Design and Construction

There are many factors that contribute to successful use of Lower CASE for design and construction of information systems, when it's used alone and when it's used in conjunction with Upper CASE as part of an integrated CASE environment. Figure 9.11 lists the five CSFs that must be achieved, over and above those associated with traditional design and development,

1. Integration with a high-quality and fully verified analysis
2. Continuity of personnel from analysis
3. Design and construction tool compatibility
4. Designing for the construction tool design envelope
5. Target technology expertise

**Fig. 9.11** The five CSFs for CASE-based design and construction.

[13]Jerry Huchzemeier, "What Can We Expect From Reengineering?," CEC Rapid Exchange, Computer Engineering Consultants, Ltd., Winter 1991.

for successful design and construction using integrated CASE tools such as ADW and IEF.

#### Integration with a high-quality and fully verified analysis

The magnitude of the productivity gains realized from design and construction is directly proportional to the quality and completeness with which the CASE-based analysis was executed. The combination of this dependence, which far exceeds the dependence of traditional design and construction on analysis, and the extra time, effort, and user involvement demanded by a CASE-based analysis, has made this design and construction CSF the most poorly understood and least-often achieved.

Productivity gains derived from incorporating logic into design-based procedures and modules depends on the quality of the ADW mini-specs and IEF PADs developed during analysis:

- The level of detail with which the mini-specs and PADs were created.
- The degree to which they were verified.

The advantages derived from developing and testing programs based on a single, common, data model, and from not having to rewrite the developed and tested programs as the database changes and stabilizes, are highly dependent on the care and quality with which the data model was developed and verified during analysis.

#### Continuity of personnel from analysis

Even with the most detailed, rigorous, and carefully verified analysis, questions concerning the analysis models are likely to come up during design and construction. It's not uncommon for design teams to alter and add to the analysis models in response to requirements that surface as the application is analyzed and developed from an operational viewpoint. Operational data, required for menus, screens, lists and reports, will have to be added to the logical data model, and the enhanced data model will have to be made implementable in the form of a database. Compromises, for example, may have to be worked out for attributes that were correctly analyzed, but that may not fit on a screen. PADs and mini-specs may have to be enhanced so that defaults and error conditions are fully and properly addressed.

These modifications and enhancements, if they're to be executed correctly so that the analysis models remain consistent and usable in design and construction, can be made most efficiently with the active participation of the business and technical people who created them. It doesn't work to to take the results of a CASE-based analysis and throw them "over the wall" for a totally new design and construction team to use as a basis for developing an operational application.

### Design and construction tool compatibility

Because the design models represent the input to the 4GL or code generator used for construction, total compatibility between the CASE tools used for design and construction is essential. Design-to-construction tool integration, while assured for integrated CASE tools such as ADW and IEF, can be problematic when design and construction tools are the products of different vendors.

While information can be transported from design to construction tools via common formats such as ESF, the completed design models may not represent 100% of the construction-tool requirements, and differences in approach, such as procedural-to-nonprocedural representations of program logic, may not be fully resolved. These kinds of inconsistencies can seriously compromise the productivity gains realized from either tool. If errors in screens, data access, or logic are not corrected by altering the analysis and design tool models, reverse integration, which depends on the design and analysis models being fully consistent with the generated application, can also be jeopardized, and with it, many of the benefits of Upper CASE.

### Designing for the construction tool envelope

Latitude in developing a design to implement the functional requirements developed during analysis is restricted not only by the business area operational goals and constraints, but also by the construction-tool design envelope as well. While most desired functionality can usually be achieved, if Lower CASE is to be productive, the functionality must be achieved consistently with the construction tool design.

When IEF is used, the tool's help template should be used, even if it lacks some desirable features. If ADW/CWS will be the code generator, the CWS macros should be defined at the beginning of the design process, so that the application can be designed to leverage the macros to the fullest possible extent.

Designers who take into account the close coupling between design and construction tools, along with their strengths and weaknesses, will be in a position to derive significant productivity benefits from Lower CASE. Those who don't will meet with much frustration.

### Target technology expertise

Although using design and construction tools to implement applications allows the designers to work at a very high level, leverage work done during analysis, paint screens, and make use of built-in functions and leverage points, CASE doesn't insulate developers from the target technologies in which the application will function. Target technologies are evolving at an extremely rapid pace, and as CASE tool vendors struggle to support new and desirable technologies, their implementations will be imperfect. Significant gaps in functionality and performance will exist, and expertise will be needed to help bridge the gaps.

Design and construction teams, especially where evolving technologies are employed, should therefore include expertise in each target hardware, system software, and telecommunications technology that's employed.

Part

# 3

# Strategies & Techniques for Success with CASE

Chapter

# 10

# CASE-Related Risk

Change is almost always accompanied by risk. This is as true for application development technologies as it is for the new target technologies that the developed applications will run on. CASE, and CASE tools in particular, are agents of change for both.

ADW or IEF, for example, can't be successfully adopted for information system development without incorporating the techniques that they support into a company's application development process and culture. CASE-enabled techniques require changes to the methodology with which application development is approached, and along with these altered approaches, changes to the ways in which information technology personnel, business users, and management interact with application development. CASE tools also affect target technologies by limiting choices to technologies that CASE tools support, and by defining the ways in which each technology can be used. CASE can therefore potentially impact the way the entire organization interacts with its information systems. These changes, whether explicitly acknowledged and managed, or simply allowed to occur, are inevitably accompanied by increased risk.

## Risk and the CASE Technology Life Cycle

CASE, as with almost any new information technology, will follow a life cycle during which it's introduced, becomes mature, and is eventually replaced with newer and more advanced technology. While the nature of the life cycle that CASE technology will follow can't be forecast with great certainty, it is possible to explore the types and relative magnitudes of the risks and benefits that accompany CASE during different portions of the CASE technology life cycle.

Companies that adopted CASE during the late 1980s, when the technology was in an early portion of its life cycle, experienced a combination of low benefits and high risk. CASE tools, laboring under a combination of DOS-imposed memory restrictions and the need to get something to the market quickly, were conditionally stable and lacked basic functionality such as prototyping, tight integration, and efficient model management. Integrated code generators for ADW and IEF barely worked, and the target technologies that they supported, such as DB2, were themselves immature and sensitive to variations in design approaches that were too subtle for the 1980s CASE technology to cope with. Information-engineering-based methodologies to support the early versions of ADW and IEF were poorly understood, and not widely available. Experienced personnel were scarce.

Companies adopting CASE during the 1990s, as the technology moves through the middle portion of its maturity curve, are deriving a lot more benefit from the technology than did its early adopters. They're also experiencing significantly reduced risk.[1] (See Fig. 10.1.)

Unlike their predecessors, the CASE tools of the 1990s work—almost unconditionally. They're also becoming vehicles for bringing the benefits of 1990s advances, such as knowledge-based technology, client-server environments and object-oriented designs, successfully to bear on application development. As CASE methodologies become ubiquitous, well supported, and understood, the risks associated with their adoption will diminish. Many of the most capable information technology professionals are making the transition to CASE, just as they did to the structured analysis, relational, and workstation technologies during the 1980s. As the 1990s complete, I believe that business users and management will become comfortable with the CASE paradigm, and its cultural impact will gradually be absorbed into many company cultures. CASE, in short, will have come of age.

Today's rapid, and at times chaotic, advances in information technology make it difficult and far from certain to predict when CASE will enter the later stages of its technology life cycle. What is certain is that when CASE technology does reach the later part of its maturity curve, its relative benefits will decrease, and the risks associated with CASE will once again go up. The most competent information systems professionals will, in all likelihood, have moved on to newer technologies, leaving their less capable CASE-oriented brethren behind. Companies that develop and support leading-edge technologies will lose their incentive to integrate with CASE. Application development methodologies (or whatever replaces them) will be optimized to support technologies that are newer and more powerful than CASE, just as today's methodologies no longer support the labor-intensive hand-coding-based technologies that preceded CASE.

---

[1]Richard Barton, "Justifying CASE," *CASE Trends*, May/June 1990. Also see Alan S. Fisher, *CASE: Using Software Development Tools*, John Wiley & Sons, 1991, Chapter 17.

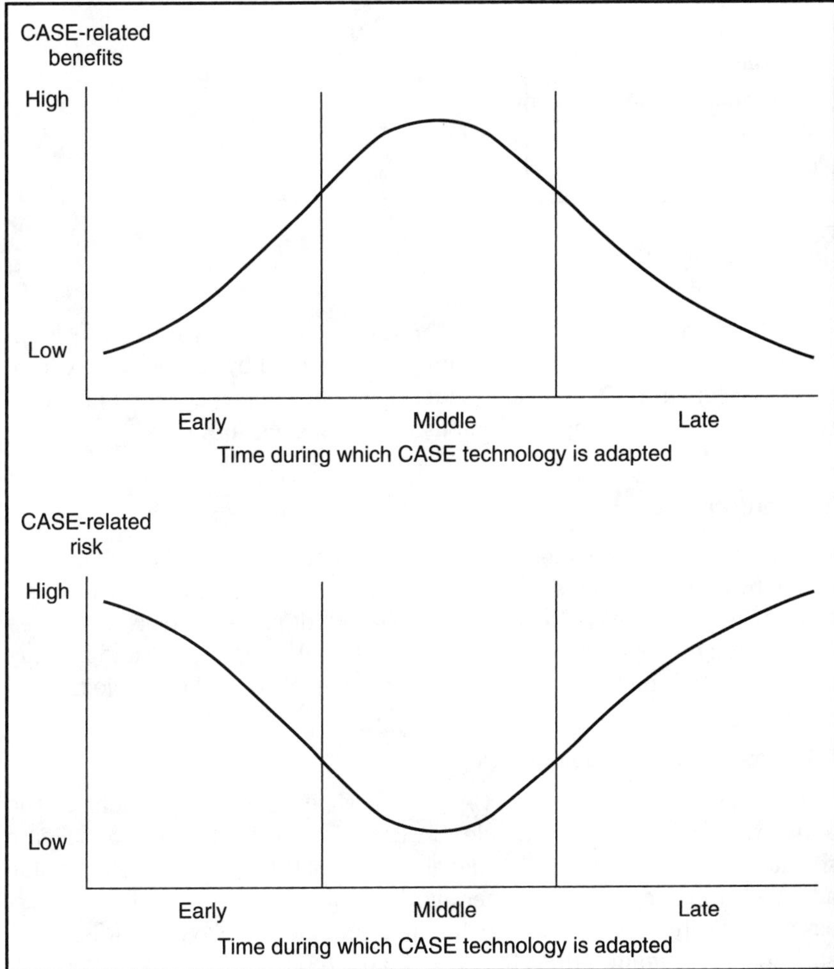


**Fig. 10.1** How CASE-related benefits and risks change the CASE technology life cycle phase.

Although we're entering the middle portion of the risk and benefit curves, where CASE-related risk is significantly reduced, the reduction is relative. CASE still comes along with substantial risk.

### Classes of CASE-related risk

The 1990s risks that accompany the use of CASE for application development are ubiquitous and diverse. They can affect not only those who deal directly with CASE technologies, but also an entire company, even its ability to compete. (See Fig. 10.2.)

- Technology risks
- Business risks
- Coordination risks
- Project risks
- People risks

**Fig. 10.2** The five classes of risk that accompany CASE.

The five classifications addressed in this book are not based on technology, the risk's origin, or even who might be affected by the risk. They have been developed solely to facilitate identification and management of CASE-related risk so that companies can use CASE successfully.[2]

## Technology Risk

CASE tools and methodologies, along with the target technologies on which CASE-based applications execute, present a well-defined set of risks for those who adopt CASE. Technology risks include not only risks associated with the technologies themselves, but additional compatibility and interaction risks resulting from the use of multiple CASE-related technologies.

### CASE tool and methodology risk

The risk associated with using CASE tools is very much dependent on the added value the tools can provide. CASE tools that don't tightly coordinate the models that they're used to develop, and that don't provide many value added consistency checks, generally don't present substantial risk. Risks associated with adopting new techniques, and methodologies that leverage such tools are minimized. As they can be adapted to support a variety of traditional software engineering—even manual—approaches and techniques, their use often requires only moderate change on the part of those associated with application development.

As the value that CASE tools provides increases, and technique and methodology options associated with the tools narrow, the applicability of traditional approaches and techniques decreases as well. Adoption of such tools must almost always be accompanied by new methodologies, and with the new methodologies, changes in the way information technology users and management interact with their applications development function.

[2]This chapter addresses risk from an ADW and IEF context. For a more general discussion of software development risk and its identification and management, see Robert N. Charette, *Application Strategies For Risk Analysis*, McGraw-Hill, 1990.

The changes that adoption of such tools requires can be great, and so can the risk. (See Fig. 10.3.)

As most CASE tools fall somewhere in between these points on the value-risk curve, the trade-offs between added value and risk become more subtle and harder to deal with. ADW and IEF, for example, both provide high value to their users, and both therefore also provide substantial risk. IEF, however, can provide slightly higher value because it's more tightly integrated than ADW, and because it provides tighter value added consistency checks. ADW, while still providing substantial value, is more tolerant in terms of techniques and approach, and therefore represents slightly lower risk.

CASE tools, along with the methodologies that they support, are evolving at a rapid rate, with new versions often brought to market in immature states—sometimes only a few months apart. While the rapid development of CASE technology provides a continuous stream of new, and often valuable, features, new tools and methodologies can also be a source of risk to those who use them for their application development. New CASE tools can require a shift in user workstation technology, and along with the workstation shift, a shift in the ways that application developers interact with their tools. Even after CASE has been successfully adopted and its cultural changes and risks successfully managed, new methodology techniques such as Rapid Application Development (RAD), and new CASE tools such as ADW/RAD that support them, can introduce additional risk by changing the way users and management interacts with application development. In general, changes to methodology are associated with higher risk because they impact more parts of companies than do changes to CASE tools.

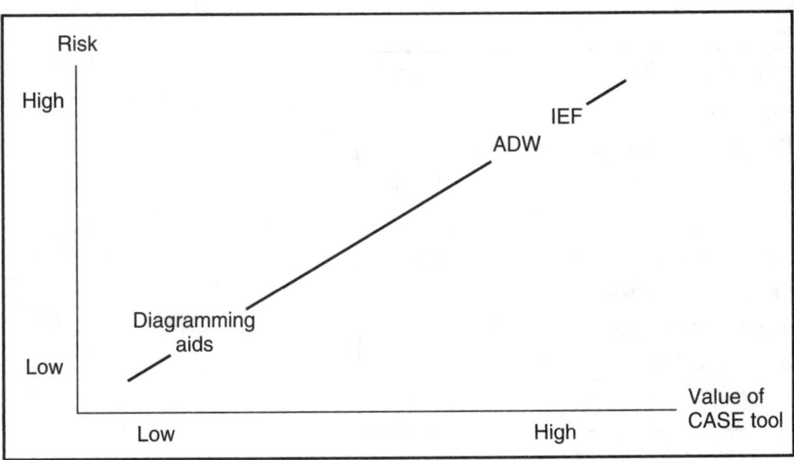


**Fig. 10.3** Risk as a function of value added by CASE.

### CASE tool and methodology compatibility risk

Additional CASE-related risk is introduced when compatible CASE tools and methodologies are not used for each phase of the application development process. (See Fig. 10.4.)

Use of different methodologies for planning and analysis can be accomplished with relatively low risk, provided that the methodologies view information systems development in roughly the same way. Navigator and IEM, for example, can be used almost interchangeably between planning and analysis since both are based on information engineering principals, and both model activities, data, and interactions in a compatible way. The use of different CASE tools for planning and analysis, however, can be more problematic, since deriving ongoing benefit from the enterprise models that are produced during planning requires that the enterprise models be kept totally consistent with the analysis models, which almost always change as result of the analysis process. Managing planning-to-analysis tool compatibility risk therefore requires that the tools be compatible, and that models be transferable back and forth between these phases.

Analysis-to-design compatibility becomes more critical, since many methodologies and tools use analysis objects such as IEF PADs and ADW mini-specs in the design process. Although moderate differences in analysis and design methodologies can often be tolerated without introducing unacceptable risk, maintaining consistency among analysis and design models makes the use of different analysis and design tools a much riskier proposition. Where different design tools are used to develop code generator input, compatibility between design and construction tools is mandatory. The risks associated with using different tools or methodologies for design and construction are therefore both high.

| Compatibility | Risk |
|---|---|
| Planning to analysis: | |
| Planning methodology | Low |
| Planning CASE tool | Medium |
| Analysis to design: | |
| Analysis methodology | High |
| Analysis CASE tool | Medium |
| Design to construction: | |
| Design methodology | High |
| Design CASE tool | High |

**Fig. 10.4** Vertical development cycle compatibility risks.

Integration of different tools and methodologies for use in different parts of the CASE application development cycle can also lead to new technology use risks. There are few guarantees that different vendors will evolve their products in compatible directions, or that any vendor will adhere to its current CASE development paradigm. Use of a design tool with a good bidirectional interface to the ADW/AWS analysis tool, for example, may preclude the use of the ADW/RAD tool, which uses partially populated AWS models as input, adds value by defining the application's user interface, and populates portions of the ADW/DWS design tool.

### CASE tool target technology risk

The manual technologies traditionally used for developing large-scale information systems tend to be flexible in terms of the target technologies that they can support. These manual technologies have also remained relatively stable for many organizations, even though target technologies have evolved. The traditional paradigm for developing applications has therefore placed minimal constraints on the target technologies that could be employed, leaving information system architects relatively free to configure new technologies independently of development-imposed constraints. Adoption of CASE for application development puts development technology on a curve similar to that of target technologies, and like the evolving target technologies that it supports, CASE comes with constraints that must be taken into account. It can therefore lead to additional risk if there is a failure to engineer a CASE-based application's target technology architecture concurrently with its development architecture.

The risks associated with developing information system architectures without taking CASE technology into account can take a number of different forms. For example, a company that requires a fault-tolerant architecture to achieve seven-day-per-week, twenty-four-hour-per-day availability for a critical application will have to develop that architecture around Tandem hardware if their CASE tool is IEF, since that's the only fault-tolerant hardware platform that IEF currently supports. Resolving the incompatibility problem by developing the application manually, or by using an alternate CASE tool such as HPS, which supports alternate (Stratus) fault-tolerant hardware, may produce the application, but it will leave the company without an automated mechanism for ensuring that the IEF-based enterprise models and the new non-IEF application remain consistent. Pressures to develop and maintain applications in most companies are more than sufficient to ensure that without such a mechanism for maintaining consistency, the models will soon diverge. The major risk, in this case, is not that the application may not work, or be developed in the most productive manner, but that information used and produced by the application may not be able to leveraged by the company for competitive advantage.

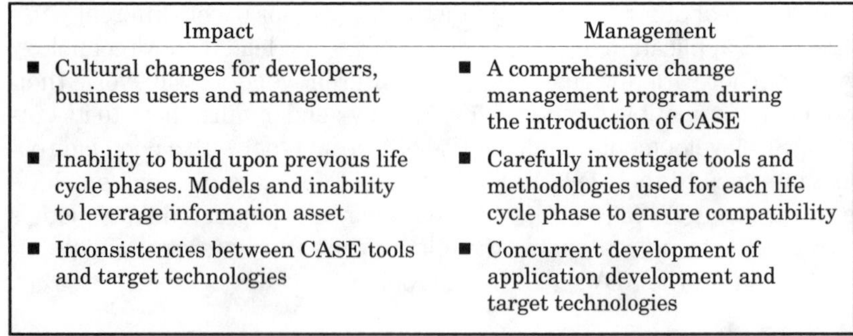

| Impact | Management |
|---|---|
| ■ Cultural changes for developers, business users and management | ■ A comprehensive change management program during the introduction of CASE |
| ■ Inability to build upon previous life cycle phases. Models and inability to leverage information asset | ■ Carefully investigate tools and methodologies used for each life cycle phase to ensure compatibility |
| ■ Inconsistencies between CASE tools and target technologies | ■ Concurrent development of application development and target technologies |

**Fig. 10.5** Impact and management of CASE-related technology risk.

Development and target technology compatibility risks are not limited to hardware platforms. They include operating systems, database management systems, LANs, teleprocessors, even GUIs, since CASE tools impose their own constraints on the ways in which CASE-developed GUIs may function. In each instance, the risks resulting from engineering target and development technologies separately can go far beyond the application being developed. They can affect the entire company, along with its ability to effectively compete. (See Fig. 10.5.)

## Modeling and Coordination Risk

In the CASE paradigm for application development, a considerable amount of risk is associated with the models themselves. CASE-based analysis models, for example, that don't accurately reflect the business, can lead to a flawed application much more directly than a poor traditional analysis would. This is a direct result of the:

- Heavy dependence that CASE-generated systems have on the models produced during analysis.
- The difficulty that users have in verifying models that do not represent an operational view of their business.
- The absence of a robust design phase during which a faulty analysis, no matter how flawed, can be corrected.

Analysis design errors, once modeled, tend to propagate into the generated system, negating many of the potential benefits of CASE. CASE-based models must therefore be carefully verified and checked.

For large organizations in which analysis models will be developed by many different, geographically dispersed organizations, ability to use Upper CASE models as a vehicle for administering and leveraging the organization's information can also be at risk. Unless each business area is modeled according to the same standards, and each model is consistent with common enterprise (planning) models, the ability to integrate the models, and the ability to reuse parts of models in building applications, can be lost. A model administration function is needed to manage this risk by developing and enforcing modeling standards, and to ensure that planning, analysis, and design models remain consistent with each other as applications are developed.

### Vertical integration risk

Model inconsistencies can also be classed as vertical and horizontal. Inconsistencies between planning models, analysis models, design models, and source code can be described as vertical, while horizontal inconsistencies include incompatibilities between activity and data models during any phase of the CASE-based application development cycle. Horizontal consistency, confined to a single CASE tool, can usually be achieved through the tool's consistency checks. Vertical inconsistencies, however, address differences across CASE tools where integration and tool-to-tool consistency checks are more variable. Achievement of vertical integration therefore tends to be more problematic.

Since company strategic parameters are modeled using planning tools, and applications are developed with analysis and design tools, planning-to-analysis model inconsistencies can lead to applications that don't support the company strategically. If the analysis data models for each application are not fully consistent with a stable, planning-tool-based enterprise data model, disparities in the way different applications view common data can develop. These vertical disparities can seriously compromise a company's ability to integrate applications and leverage its information asset. (See Fig. 10.6.)

Vertical inconsistencies between analysis and design models contribute to application, rather than strategic, risk. Regardless of the quality or veracity of an analysis, the degree to which the CASE-developed applications will support the business area will be at risk if the application's design models are not consistent with the models produced during analysis. As design models evolve to support the application's inputs, outputs, menus, screens, reports, and new functional requirements, the new design models will have to be checked against the analysis models to ensure that business requirements, modeled during analysis, are not compromised. Failure to resolve design-to-analysis model inconsistencies can not only lead to productivity loss, as time and effort are expended to bring the applications into conformance with the business area's real needs, but also to maintenance productivity loss, since the analysis models will lose their utility in helping to analyze the consequence of changes and modifications.

The very different role that source code plays in CASE-based applications can lead to additional vertical risk. Operational standards, such as safekeeping of source code and recompiling the source when applications are moved, no

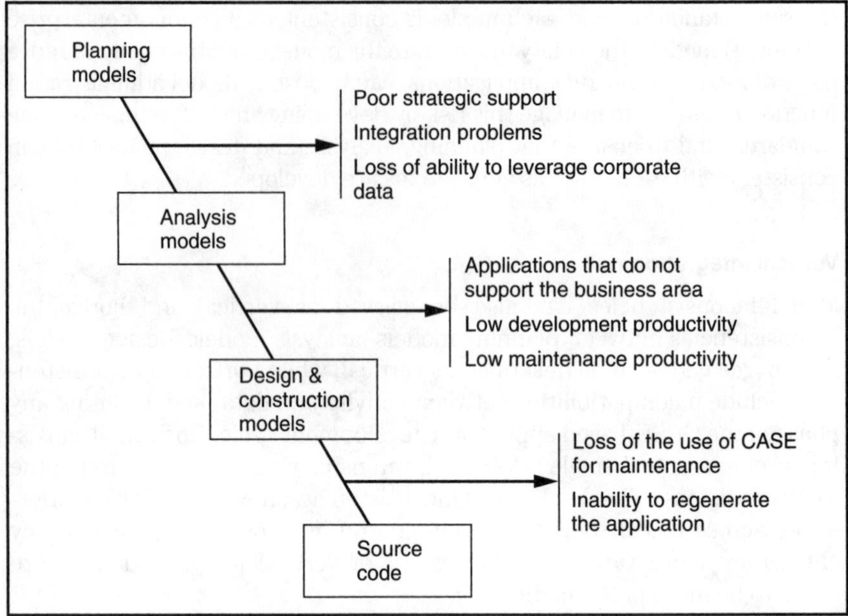


**Fig. 10.6** Risks due to vertical model inconsistencies.

longer lower risk in a CASE environment. The ability to regenerate an application by recompiling the application's source doesn't guarantee that the application can be maintained, as it would with handcrafted source, since much of the coding standards and associated documentation will not exist for source code generated through CASE. Indeed, modifying or enhancing CASE-generated source code can *create* new risk, since the application and its models will no longer be consistent with each other. For such systems, modifications and enhancements made to the models, which is the way CASE-based applications should be maintained, can't be accomplished without the risk of overwriting modifications and fixes imbedded in the modified source code.

A final risk resulting from inconsistencies between the models and the source code is that the models can lose their utility in regenerating the application in new or different target technologies.

### Timing and bridging risk

The small size of (properly scoped) CASE-developed applications, coupled with the short amounts of time required to generate them, can substantially increase the number of applications that are implemented at the same time. For large-scale application development efforts, the source of CASE-related timing and bridging risk is the coordination required to manage the concurrent implementation of a substantially increased number of applications and pieces of applications.

It was a daunting but usually manageable task to develop software bridges between large, traditionally developed applications, which tended to be implemented slowly, one at a time. It can be much more challenging to create similar bridges between many rapidly emerging parts of new applications, portions of the old applications that are being replaced, and different parts of the new applications themselves. Not only do a much larger number of bridges have to be developed, but the timing of the implementations themselves has to be carefully coordinated to ensure that sufficient time is available to fully test each implication and each of its bridges.

Rapid implementation of many small CASE-based applications can also affect the way development projects interact with the company's database administration (DBA) function. DBA support is likely to be required on a continuous, rather than discrete, basis, as many small applications are rapidly designed and tested. Companies that adopt CASE for their application development, but fail to address the higher intensity of their DBA support requirements, are therefore at risk of losing much of the productivity gains from Lower CASE. (See Fig. 10.7.)

## CASE-Related Business Risk

A significant difference between CASE and other information technologies is that the risks associated with adopting CASE are not limited to technology, or even to information technology management. CASE risks can impact the business, sometimes in very direct ways.

### CASE investment risks

The most straightforward of the CASE-related business risks are those associated with investment. Although the cost of acquiring CASE is technology and quantity sensitive, and can therefore vary widely from installation to installation, the cost of a single CASE workstation with one or more CASE tools,

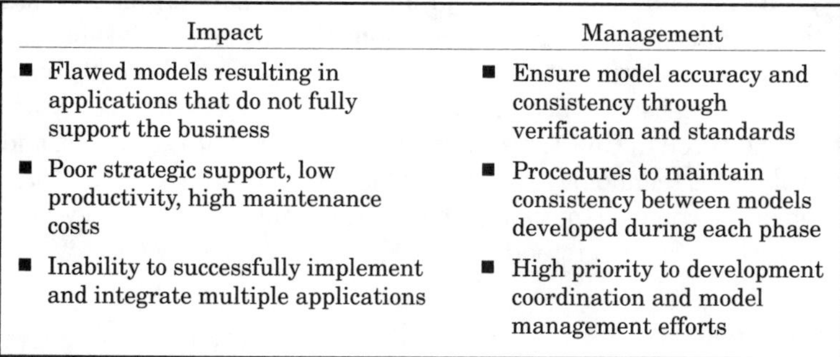

| Impact | Management |
|---|---|
| ■ Flawed models resulting in applications that do not fully support the business | ■ Ensure model accuracy and consistency through verification and standards |
| ■ Poor strategic support, low productivity, high maintenance costs | ■ Procedures to maintain consistency between models developed during each phase |
| ■ Inability to successfully implement and integrate multiple applications | ■ High priority to development coordination and model management efforts |

**Fig. 10.7** Impact and management of CASE-related modeling and coordination risk.

a suitably fast PC with a printer, and a copy of a CASE-based methodology can easily add up to $20,000 or more.

The initial investment required to successfully adopt CASE technology must also include the costs of developing CASE-knowledgeable human resources. Training to give information technology and business user staffs a head start on methodology and related planning, analysis, or design techniques, if purchased from an outside vendor, can come to $10,000 or more for a three-to-five-day class for up to twenty people. The training, no matter how successful, will almost certainly need to be supplemented through outside consulting services for advice on implementing CASE and in successfully completing initial CASE-based projects. These charges can exceed non-CASE consulting rates by as much as 100%. Employees who have difficulty making the transition to CASE may leave, adding turnover costs to the required investment.

Ongoing investments in CASE will include the direct cost of business employees from the user community, whose participation on CASE-based planning and analysis projects can greatly exceed traditional project user requirements. Staffing a CASE-based BAA with equal quantities of user and information technology personnel, for example, is not an uncommon practice. Added to this direct investment are the costs of keeping the business operations running with reduced staffing levels while the CASE projects are completed. Additional investment in target hardware, telecommunications, and system software may be required as a result of using CASE. Since not all technologies will be supported by every CASE methodology and tool, the low-cost technology solution to a business problem may have to be modified to take CASE support into account. The result might well include increased technology costs.

### CASE expectation risk

Optimistic expectations for development of CASE-based applications often lead to additional business risk. Since many of today's businesses are planned around, and ultimately depend on, the information systems that support them, application delivery expectations that are not achievable can put entire business programs at risk. Controlling this potentially costly business risk involves realistic expectations concerning productivity gains that can be achieved through CASE, proper management of CASE projects, and ensuring that CASE technology is not used on critical business projects until the company becomes experienced with CASE and the technology's capabilities and risks are understood.

### Critical project risk

Choosing a business-critical project as a basis for a company's initial experience with CASE is not uncommon. The reason for choosing such a

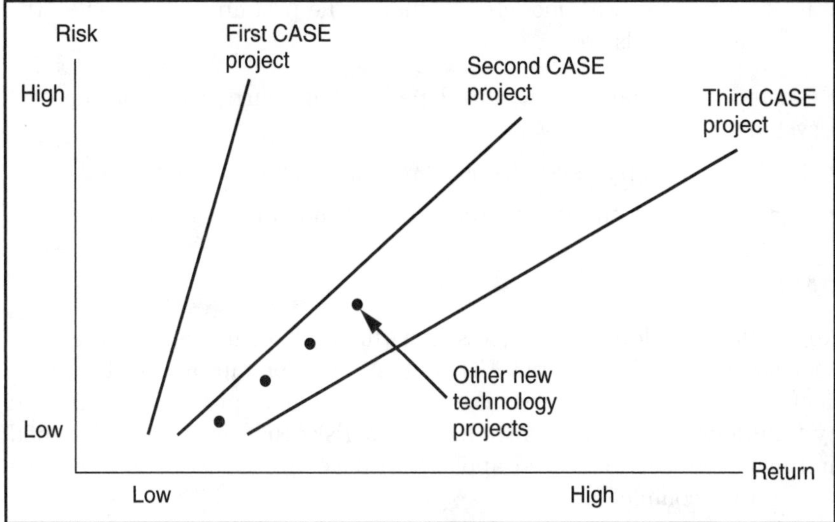


**Fig. 10.8** Risk versus return for initial projects utilizing CASE and other information technologies.

project is, of course, temptation. Huge potential benefits can be derived from using CASE to develop a mission-critical business project. The problem, however, is that because CASE involves so many fundamental changes to the way applications are developed, the risks associated with using CASE are far greater for the initial projects than they would be with other new technologies. Experience with several CASE development projects is often required before CASE-related risk begins to approach the risks associated with other information technologies. (See Fig. 10.8.)

An obvious strategy for controlling critical-project risk is to develop familiarity and competence with CASE early, so that the company develops enough CASE experience to take advantage of critical project opportunity without having to take on additional CASE-related risk.

### Model orientation risk

Since CASE-developed applications reflect models developed during planning, analysis, and design, these applications will support the business's future requirements in new and innovative ways only to the extent that the models address the future. CASE-based models that are legacies of past systems, business practices and constraints can throttle much of the innovation enabled by CASE. The business risks associated with modeling past and current, instead of future, business requirements are therefore risks of lost opportunity.

Risks associated with models oriented to the past are highest when the CASE-based models are:

- Created by the people who developed and are currently using the past systems.
- Developed from past systems using reverse-engineering techniques.
- Verified primarily through current systems and practices. (See Fig. 10.9.)

## CASE Project Risk

Application development projects, regardless of technology, have always been associated with high risk.[3] This situation is not improved by the introduction of CASE. CASE alters the way development projects are affected by traditional risks, and it introduces new risks that must be understood and managed if CASE-based application development projects are to be successfully completed.

### CASE project scoping risk

Although large application development projects have always been riskier than small projects, this is especially true with CASE. Indeed, defining projects that are too large to manage with acceptable risk probably ranks among the most common reasons why CASE projects fail.

| Impact | Management |
|---|---|
| ■ Loss of investment in CASE tools, workstations, methodology, and training | ■ An implementation program that introduces CASE gradually, on successively larger and larger projects |
| ■ Business operations may degrade due to loss of key individuals while they participate on CASE projects | ■ Techniques, such as JAD, to leverage business user participation. Location of development teams in user areas |
| ■ Loss of business opportunities and initiatives due to failed or late CASE projects | ■ Realistic expectations for CASE. Avoidance of CASE for business-critical projects until CASE is understood |
| ■ Loss of innovation and new approaches enabled by new technologies or circumstance | ■ Deliberate measures to ensure that CASE models represent the future and are not constrained by the current or the past |

**Fig. 10.9** Impact and management of CASE-related business risk.

[3]Robert N. Charette, *Software Engineering Risk Analysis And Management*, McGraw-Hill, 1989.

Analysis and design models are more difficult to manage on large projects due to contention between different teams who need to work on and update the same model objects at the same time. Entity types and attributes, which are central to more than one BAA team's analysis, can theoretically be shared among the different teams as long as only one team can update each attribute and entity type. But, the reality is that more than one team will often find that it can't effectively work with the entity type or attribute unless it can also change or update it. Although there are a number of techniques for dealing with this problem, including checking out small pieces of the model, checking them out for short periods of time, and manually resolving the inconsistencies, each method involves additional risk either to the integrity of the models or to the timely completion of the project.

For projects that are geographically dispersed, it can be even more problematic to ensure that models developed by teams in different locations are developed with compatible standards and modeling approaches. Disagreements develop over how to model time-dependent accounting information, or over whether to model inventory parts or inventory part characteristics. These disputes can take substantial time to resolve, putting the project at risk.

If large projects are not broken down into smaller projects, the large amounts of time and effort that must be spent on CASE-based analysis can become an additional source of risk since there are limits to the amount of analysis that any company will tolerate. This risk is exacerbated by the CASE tools themselves, which can become slow and cumbersome to operate as models become large.

### Project estimating risk

An additional risk associated with information-engineering-based CASE projects involves the inability of development project teams and their management to accurately estimate project time and costs until partway through analysis. Because of the newness of CASE technology to many organizations, and the very different application development paradigm that CASE represents, reliance on past experience and judgment as yardsticks for estimating application development costs may not be appropriate for CASE. This problem is often compounded by additional CASE-related unknowns such as vertical integration problems, access to business users, methodology impact, and inappropriate expectations. Traditional function point factors such as inputs, outputs, inquiries, data files, and interfaces are also problematic because these factors are not addressed in ADW and IEF information-engineering-based development projects until well into the development effort's design phase. Although some companies such as Texas Instruments have developed promising estimation models based on planning and analysis metrics such as num-

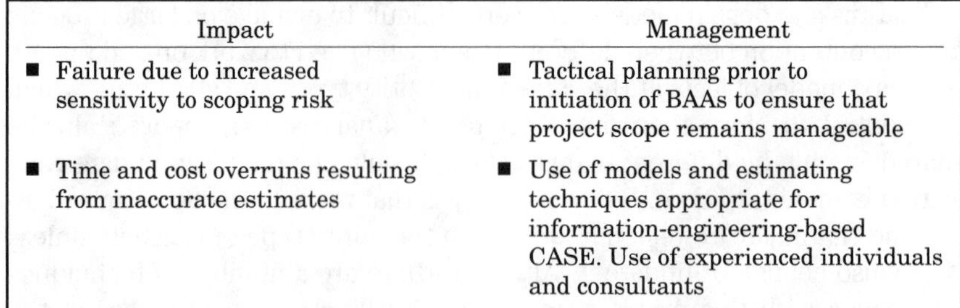

| Impact | Management |
|---|---|
| ■ Failure due to increased sensitivity to scoping risk | ■ Tactical planning prior to initiation of BAAs to ensure that project scope remains manageable |
| ■ Time and cost overruns resulting from inaccurate estimates | ■ Use of models and estimating techniques appropriate for information-engineering-based CASE. Use of experienced individuals and consultants |

**Fig. 10.10** Impact and management of CASE-related project risk.

bers of functions, processes, and entity types, this technology is new and can be tricky to use. (See Fig. 10.10.)

## CASE-Related People Risk

Sources of people-related risk include the substantial changes to information technology, management, and business user cultures that accompany the introduction of CASE. Before these risks can be managed, each must be understood in terms of the personnel and cultures that it affects.

The high demand for information technology professionals who understand CASE, combined with the relatively small number of individuals who are experienced with the technology, have made maintenance of adequate staffing levels a problem, even for small CASE projects. This is especially true for information technology organizations that can't easily adjust their pay scales to reflect the seller's market created by the advent and acceptance of CASE.

CASE projects, even when fully staffed with competent and experienced information technology resources, may still experience significant staffing risk since different individuals are likely to have come from diverse CASE backgrounds and experiences. It's certainly not an easy task, but it is feasible to develop a unified approach, train everyone in the approach, and ensure that the unified approach is implemented.

An additional set of challenges and risks is developing CASE-knowledgeable human resources from an existing information technology staff that has been carefully optimized over many years to support traditional applications development. Systems analysts and managers, who were brought up to make systems run efficiently in the physical world of programs, teleprocessors, and databases, can have a difficult time following CASE methodologies that emphasize logical analysis throughout much of the application development cycle. The risk is that such people can be tempted to approach CASE based on their traditional frames of reference, losing much of the benefit that CASE can provide. The insidious aspect of this risk is that many don't even see what they're losing until it's too late.

Consider the common temptation among many traditional analysts to denormalize the logical data model because they feel they can see (intuitively) that denormalization will cause the system to run efficiently under their relational database. What they may not see is the loss of granularity that the fully normalized data model provides, and with it, the way the granularity can be used to optimize the database design, not based on intuition and insights, but based on a careful analysis and understanding of how the data model will be called upon to support the leaf-level processes involved with each key business event.

Management can fall into similarly insidious traps when they try to manage CASE projects. For example, if the cultural shift in objectives from speed to quality is not implemented in the management process, substantial risk can result. This happened when the manager of a large-scale IEF project used time-box techniques to manage the project's initial BAA modeling to a tight deadline. While her techniques worked, and the initial data and activity modeling efforts were finished ahead of schedule, the models that they produced were incomplete and not fully verified. When the time came to write PADs, the project teams discovered that many of the PADs could not be completed without making (sometimes substantial) changes to the incomplete data model. Since the project was managed in lock step, with all three BAA teams writing PADs and changing the data model at the same time, serious data model contention developed, and progress ground to a dead halt.

### Businesspeople risks

CASE requires businesspeople to learn new ways of interacting with and participating in an information system development process that may bear little resemblance to the way it may have worked in the past. The combination of the:

- New set of tasks that require levels of abstract and conceptual thinking that they may not be trained in or used to.
- New, and seemingly backward, order in which the tasks are approached.
- Almost endless evolution of work products that they feel should have been done.
- Close working relationships with information system people, on their turf, using their terminology.

All of these can make the new process into a difficult and frustrating experience. The risk is that frustration levels can become so high that the business users lose confidence in the CASE application development process that counts on them to be key participants. If the business users on the development team lose confidence and interest in their CASE-based analysis, seriously flawed models and little benefit from CASE are the inevitable results. Care must therefore be taken to ensure that the business users who participate in CASE-based application development understand and remain comfortable with the process.

### Business and information technology competency risk

Business users, who become too comfortable with the CASE-based application development process and add substantial value to the CASE projects in which they participate, face a different risk. High levels of participation over a long period of time on information system development projects can cause them to lose currency in the business expertise that they have. This risk is aggravated by the increasingly fast pace at that which business practices are evolving. A quick scan of the companies that are looking into, or engaged in, reengineering their business processes will provide insight into the considerable speed and breadth of business change. In many sectors of the economy, participation in two to three back-to-back application development projects can put even the most competent and knowledgeable business users at some risk. (See Fig. 10.11.)

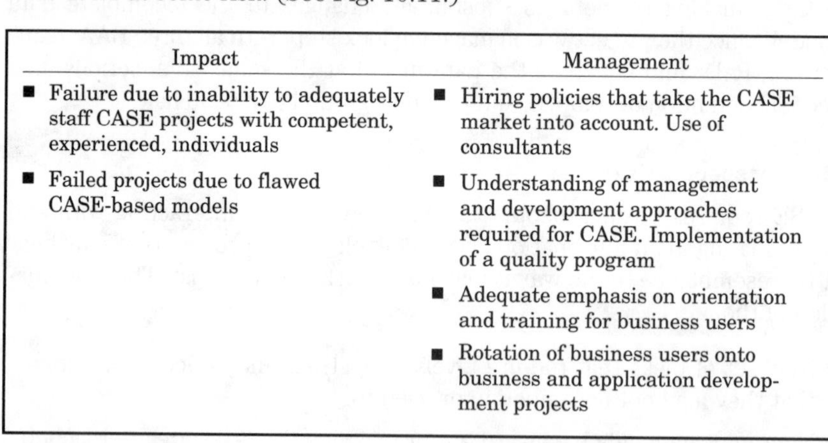

| Impact | Management |
|---|---|
| ■ Failure due to inability to adequately staff CASE projects with competent, experienced, individuals<br>■ Failed projects due to flawed CASE-based models | ■ Hiring policies that take the CASE market into account. Use of consultants<br>■ Understanding of management and development approaches required for CASE. Implementation of a quality program<br>■ Adequate emphasis on orientation and training for business users<br>■ Rotation of business users onto business and application development projects |

**Fig. 10.11** Impact and management of CASE-related project risk.

Chapter

# 11

# Managing a CASE-Based Project

The V.P. of Application Development and her staff stared at each other in disbelief. Of their first five CASE-based development projects, three were totally out of control, and of the two remaining "good projects," one was beginning to look pretty shaky. The problems facing the V.P. seemed particularly disturbing because her investment in CASE, which was supposed to add quality and consistency to her application development process, seemed to be doing just the opposite. The troubled projects had even been assigned to her best and most seasoned managers.

Successful management of large-scale application development projects has always been a challenge, even for experienced managers using tools and techniques that are familiar and well understood. CASE adds significantly to this already formidable challenge, impacting not only the most seasoned development project managers, but also the analysts, programmers, and business users who are associated with their projects.

With the introduction of CASE, application development managers find themselves faced not only with managing a set of new and very different phases and tasks, but also with rethinking the management of seemingly familiar tasks. CASE-based projects require unique inputs, and they produce new work products in a totally different order than do traditional projects. They're sensitive to new problems that sometimes occur in the most unexpected places, and as if to add insult to injury, well-run CASE-based projects can produce a completely new set of signals to their business users and management, adding confusion to a management process that is not universally understood, even for traditional projects.

- Phase sensitivity
- Project consistency and support
- User participation
- Project deliverables
- Meaning of project signals

**Fig. 11.1** How CASE impacts application development project management.

The growing number of impressive achievements using CASE indicates that CASE-based development projects can be successfully managed, and that the issues and challenges that they present can be effectively addressed.[1] Successful management of CASE projects does, however, require that these differences, and their management implications, be thoroughly understood, and that specific techniques to address them be incorporated into the application development project management process.

## Fundamental Differences and Management Implications

Although CASE-based application development differs significantly from traditional development, for developers, business users, and information technology management, not all are affected equally, or even in the same ways. Figure 11.1 shows the major differences in the way CASE impacts application development project management.

### Phase sensitivity

ADW- and IEF-based CASE projects are extremely sensitive to what happens in early application development cycle phases—during tactical planning and business area analysis. While planning and scoping are important for most application development projects, they're particularly important for ADW and IEF projects because they:

- Help to focus attention on relevant topics during the very detailed information-engineering-based analysis.
- Minimize contention between different development teams over shared business model objects.
- Limit the size of analysis effort, which can be time-consuming, costly, and difficult for companies to tolerate.

[1]Consulting experience and conversations with KnowledgeWare and Texas Instruments CASE tool users. Also, conversations with KnowledgeWare and Texas Instruments consultants.

Successful CASE project management requires not only that special attention be paid to tactical planning and scoping, but also that the development project not be started until tactical planning and scoping efforts have been completed.

Business area analysis assumes increased importance for information engineering-based CASE projects because it:

- Ensures that the application will meet the business's requirements upon initial delivery, a major potential benefit of integrated CASE.
- Stabilizes the data model so that high productivity can be achieved during the design and construction phases that follow.
- Verifies the leaf-level processes.
- Develops code generator input.[2]

This sensitivity can present a formidable challenge to project management, who must ensure adequate interest and participation in an exercise that is detailed, frustrating, time-consuming, and that may not seem relevant to operationally oriented business-user project participants. The importance of meeting this challenge is underscored by the fact that a thorough, high-quality analysis is part of the fundamental basis upon which integrated CASE design and construction tools are built. It's not easy, economic, or sometimes even possible to make up for a poorly executed analysis via redoubled integrated CASE design and construction efforts, as it sometimes is for traditional projects. Special care must therefore be taken to ensure that these early phases in the information-engineering-based application development cycle get the emphasis and attention they require, and that they yield high-quality models.

### Project consistency and support

CASE projects also require more coordination and support than traditional projects. Attaining high productivity from CASE requires that entity types, processes, screen templates, and action blocks be consistent and sharable, and that compatibility issues over the way they're modeled by different teams and projects be identified and quickly resolved. Timely and efficient resolution of modeling object inconsistencies is achievable, provided that management:

- Develops and enforces standards and conventions, not only for object names and structure, but also for modeling approaches.
- Ensures that mechanisms are in place to identify and quickly resolve significant differences and inconsistencies.

---

[2]James Martin, *Information Engineering,* Book II, Prentice Hall, 1990, Appendix VI. Also see Dennis Minium, *A Guide To Information Engineering Using The IEF,* Second Edition, Texas Instruments, 1990, chapter 20.

While standards and resolution mechanisms are easy to conceive and have easily understandable benefits, they tend to be difficult for management to put into practice because of conflicting project goals, varied backgrounds of project participants, and perceived infringements on creativity.

In addition to CASE tool, methodology, and modeling technique support, which CASE projects require to help them cope with the very new and different technology that CASE represents, CASE projects also require changes in support. Data administration, if it doesn't understand and buy into information engineering principles, can interfere with, rather than help, the CASE-based modeling process. Model coordination and management can not only be a full time job for each CASE project, but also can require significant mainframe, server, and communications support. Greater, and more continuous, DBA and testing support are also likely to be required.

The problem, and the support challenge for management, is that because the need for these kinds of support can increase sharply as CASE projects progress through their life cycle, the magnitude of the need may not be fully apparent until late in the development process when not enough time is left to procure the required support. Assignment of continuous, full- or part-time DBA and testing resources to each CASE project, especially during design and construction, and careful attention to CASE tool model management and development coordination will help ensure adequate support, and with it, a manageable project.

### User participation

The amount and intensity of user participation demanded by CASE projects far exceeds that required for traditional projects.[3] For most companies, the increased participation can represent a significant, and sometimes unwelcome, shift in the way the company deals with its application development projects, a shift that also presents a new set of challenges to project management. To make its ADW or IEF projects successful, management will have to ensure that:

- Adequate numbers of quality, knowledgeable, conceptually oriented business users are available to the project.
- Communication channels to the line managers and operations staff, who will interact with the application, are open and available to resolve issues and clarify requirements.

Having made users available to participate in the CASE-based application development process, management is faced with the additional challenge of

[3]Jessica Keyes, "How Software Is Developed Undergoing Basic Changes," quotes from Clive Finkelstein, *Software Magazine*, January 1992.

ensuring that their participation is meaningful and that the development project benefits from it. Having achieved adequate levels of user participation, management must therefore:

- Help users and information technology personnel communicate effectively with one another.
- Ensure that each understands the process in which he or she will participate, so that their communication will be meaningful and helpful to the project.

#### Project deliverables

The deliverables produced by a CASE project can present a particularly nettlesome set of problems for the project's manager. In determining an integrated CASE project's success, perhaps the most important of all deliverables are the BAA deliverables, which are:

- Models that are neither tangible nor representable in a form that is easy to understand.
- Presented in an order that is almost opposite to the order in which traditional deliverables are produced.
- Apt to evolve and change, sometimes significantly, during the analysis process.

Armed with these deliverables, CASE project managers are faced with identifying problems, measuring progress so that the project can be completed on schedule, and with mollifying a justifiably skeptical set of user, information technology, and corporate managers.

#### Meaning of project signals

CASE project managers must cope not only with the demanding set of problems resulting from the seemingly backwards and difficult-to-understand deliverables that their projects produce, but also with an equally perverse and seemingly backward set of signals that their projects send out. Consider the speed with which an integrated CASE-based analysis is completed.

In almost everything encountered in business, "speed" is synonymous with "good." Faster service means satisfied customers; faster production means lower costs and higher profits; fast procurement indicates that the purchasing department is doing a good job. But when building ADW or IEF models, "fast" can just as easily mean "bad." Indeed, one of the most common CASE problems is for applications development teams to produce poor-quality models too quickly. There are three principal reasons why this happens.

The first is cultural. Application development teams, composed of people who are used to traditional applications development, are predisposed to move through the process as quickly as possible. They have, of course, been carefully trained to do this. The second reason is a direct result of the power of ADW and IEF to produce large, complex, and impressive-looking models very quickly and with a modest amount of effort. The third reason why poor models tend to be produced too quickly is that the quality of the models can be elusive and difficult to measure for the applications developers who produce them, and for their management. For instance, ADW and IEF value added consistency checks can ensure that a model is complete, consistent, and compatible with other models in the tool's repository, but they can't ensure that the models correctly represent: the true needs of the business area, the future as opposed to the past, or the strategic initiatives of the organization. Achievement of these modeling objectives is largely dependent on user and management participation and on the way the project is managed.

## CASE Project Management Begins Before the Project Starts

Good practices dictate that management of even the most traditional application development projects should begin early, ideally before the project even starts. But in many companies, the combination of scarce resources, high workloads, business exigencies, tight schedules, and inadequate development planning make this ideal the exception rather than the rule. The reality is that management of most application development projects starts sometime after the project begins.

Many traditional development projects are relatively tolerant of management and environmental deficiencies; the sensitivities and risks are understood, and projects are successful despite inadequacies in preproject management. However, this doesn't hold true for integrated CASE, in which each phase of the application development life cycle is dependent on a carefully orchestrated combination of models built during previous phases. These models can require an unusually high degree of user involvement and project support. For information-engineering-based integrated CASE to provide a substantial return on investment, analysis and design phases must be carefully managed from the beginning. Let's take a closer look.

### Before starting an ADW or IEF BAA project

Although information-engineering-based analysis projects (BAAs) can be challenging to manage and to keep on track, the place where management first loses control often occurs before the project even starts. The reason is that BAA projects don't exist in isolation—they're built on foundations, in the form of models, objectives, and scope, which are the products of information-engineering-based strategic and tactical planning projects. Their

- Clearly articulated, and accepted, business objectives
- Quality, methodology-compatible planning models
- Reasonable scope
- CASE tool and methodology-knowledgeable resources
- Knowledgeable, conceptually-oriented business users
- Mechanisms to resolve business and technical issues
- Adequate facilities

**Fig. 11.2** Checklist for beginning a BAA project.

sensitivity to the foundations upon which they're built far exceeds what it would be for traditional projects.

For a BAA to be successfully completed, its management should therefore not begin with managing the first BAA modeling task, or with a detailed project plan, although both are necessary. It should begin instead with project-oriented tasks designed to ensure that the project has a viable foundation, in terms of goals, scope, resources, and deliverables—the products of previous (planning project) modeling efforts. The checklist in Fig. 11.2 shows the minimum foundation and project infrastructure required to launch a successful BAA. If one or more of the checklist's elements are not in place, the project's management should carefully consider sparing their company's shareholders a needless expense, and their company's management the embarrassment of a failed project, by postponing the start of the BAA until the deficiency is corrected.

**Clearly articulated and accepted business objectives.** The requirement that the business objectives for the application be articulated and clearly understood by all who are involved with the analysis project is certainly a key traditional project requirement. Indeed, failure to agree upon what an application is to accomplish is among the prime reasons for failure of both traditional and CASE projects.[4] The introduction of CASE, however, makes this requirement even more critical because:

- The amount of time, effort, and political capital that a BAA consumes means that more is at risk if the objectives are found to be wrong and have to be corrected partway through the analysis.
- The dependence of design and construction phases on the analysis models make it extremely difficult and expensive to change what the application is to accomplish once the BAA has been completed.

[4]Robert N. Charette, *Software Engineering Risk Analysis And Management,* McGraw-Hill, 1989, Pages 31-33.

A joint application development (JAD) session to develop and verify the project's objectives, with the analysis project's business and technical sponsors and stakeholders as participants, should therefore be one of the first activities for a BAA project.

**Quality, methodology-compatible planning models.** The planning data and activity models represent the foundation upon which BAA models are built. For the planning model business functions to be decomposable into ADW or IEF processes, and for its high-level entity types and subject areas to be broken into ADW or IEF fully normalized entity types, both must not only exist, but each must also have been modeled using a methodology that is compatible with the information-engineering-based methodology used for analysis. Beginning a BAA without the foundation provided by these models exposes the analysis project to constructing analysis models that:

- Are not fully compatible with those of other BAAs and that may require expensive and time-consuming rework before compatibility is achieved.
- May have to be developed based on current systems (the most convenient modeling source in many organizations) and therefore fail to incorporate a future logical view of the business area being analyzed.

Time invested in verifying, becoming acquainted with, and internalizing the planning models (or reconstructing them if they're old, flawed or don't exist), therefore represents a sound project management investment.

**Reasonable scope.** Although BAA scope is typically defined during tactical planning, this doesn't guarantee that each BAA has a viable scope when viewed from application development and implementation perspectives. Since it's the BAA (and later, the design and construction) team that has the responsibility for delivering the working application on time and within budget, it's imperative that the BAA team verify and buy into their project's scope. Although there are checkpoints during a BAA at which the entire development project's scope can be reevaluated and narrowed, defining scope early, at the beginning of the BAA, affords the project's management the greatest opportunity for impacting the time and cost of the BAA. It's also the time during which the BAA's scope can be narrowed with minimal throwaway cost and wasted political capital.

**CASE tool and methodology-knowledgeable resources.** Competent and experienced CASE tool and methodology-knowledgeable resources can be scarce and difficult to hire. Whether acquired as employees or consultants, surprising amounts of time may elapse before an analysis project is fully staffed. It's therefore imperative that, to the extent that tool and methodology resources can't be identified and allocated to the project:

- Sufficient time be incorporated in the project plan to procure needed resources.
- Analysis and modeling schedules be adjusted to reflect the additional time.

Based on current experience, it's usually sufficient to allow six to eight weeks to acquire high-quality ADW or IEF resources. However, if more time is be required, due to local circumstances, such time should be spent if a successful project is important. CASE is a new and complex technology; high-quality expertise will be required. Its acquisition should not be compromised.

**Knowledgeable, conceptually oriented business users.** Business users who are knowledgeable and conceptually oriented can be just as hard for the BAA project to procure as its CASE tool and methodology resources, especially in many of today's flatter, downsized business organizations. The difference is that the project's business resources can't be hired; they must be borrowed from the business's operations. To the analysis project manager, borrowing business users from the company's line operations can be problematic, since:

- Line managers may not be enthusiastic about parting with their best people.
- Agreed-upon and actual availability may not be sufficient to satisfy the project's requirements.
- The individual(s) allocated to the project may not be sufficiently deep in each area within the project's scope to supply the informational needs that the BAA will generate.

An arrangement for business user procurement that sometimes works is to assign conceptual users at a managerial level to the project on a full-time (or close to full-time) basis until the project's analysts and modelers become acquainted with the business area and initial models have been developed. The full-time business users are then returned to their operation's responsibilities, where they coordinate and facilitate the access to line managers and operations personnel that the BAA will require as its models are developed to a more detailed level. The once full-time business users continue to participate in model reviews.

**Mechanisms to resolve business and technical issues.** Almost all BAAs spawn business and technical issues, many of them nettlesome, political, and complex. The challenge to the BAA's management is that progress on the analysis project can be held up pending resolution of such issues. For all but the smallest organizations, dealing with this potentially catastrophic problem requires that formal mechanisms be put in place in the form of individuals and committees empowered to deal with and quickly resolve these problems. From the BAA project's perspective, these mechanisms should be set up in parallel with the other items on the checklist, before work on the BAA begins, so that they will be in place and ready to serve the BAA when they're needed.

**Adequate facilities.** Although adequate facilities are needed for any analysis project, if it's to be completed successfully and on a timely basis, this requirement assumes greater importance for CASE-based BAAs. The reason is that facilities that would be expensive and frivolous expenditures for traditional projects are necessary for CASE. For example, automatic white boards can allow much of the detailed modeling to be done outside of the CASE tool; this not only speeds up the modeling effort, but also reduces the time frame during which models that may share common objects with other BAAs have to be checked out of the common repository—a real time waster on many BAA projects. Very fast workstations can greatly speed up the portion of the modeling that is done on CASE tools, which can execute slowly, even on today's most powerful PCs. Enhanced meeting spaces are often needed to facilitate a human interaction-based business modeling process.

### Before starting a CASE-based design and construction project

ADW- and IEF-based design and construction projects, like the BAAs that precede them, are difficult, if not impossible, to manage to a successful outcome unless a minimal set of foundation elements are in place at the project's start. The checklist presented in Fig. 11.3 should be useful to design and construction project managers and their peers in helping to identify and understand each element so that it can be achieved and set in place prior to the start of their projects.

**A well-defined target technology architecture.** While a BAA can be executed relatively independently of the application's target technology architecture, design and construction projects cannot. They're very technology

- A well-defined technology architecture
- High-quality analysis models
- A reasonable scope
- Continuity of personnel from analysis
- Methodology, CASE-tool, and target technology expertise

**Fig. 11.3** Design and construction checklist.

dependent. The hardware, telecommunications, and system software technologies in which the system will be implemented must therefore be defined prior to the beginning of the design and construction project. It's important that this be done, not only to ensure that the project has a fixed target and purpose, but also so that the project's manager can ensure that:

- The target technology is supportable with design and construction CASE tools being used.
- Expertise in each target technology will be available to the project in sufficient quantities and on a timely basis.

To the extent that these conditions can't be fully met, use of alternate CASE or target technologies should be investigated. However, new CASE and target technology intersections, which are not yet field-proven, should be pursued only if all stakeholders understand the risks that such unproven target and development technology intersections pose to development projects. A viable strategy in such situations can be to develop the system using proven target technology, and regenerate it in the future, when the new development or target technology is stable and well understood. The reduced risk achieved by this strategy may well be worth its added expense in terms of hardware, software, and training throwaway costs.

**Quality analysis models.** The dependence of design and construction projects on the quality of the analysis models can't be overemphasized, for it's during the design and construction phase that analysis shortcuts pay their perpetrators back. Deficient analysis modeling is a pervasive problem due to the large amount of additional time required to create high-quality analysis models, pressure to complete a time-consuming analysis on schedule, and the fact that the consequences of not developing high-quality models don't show up until the next phase.

Analysis models that were not constructed by the design and construction team should therefore be carefully reviewed to ensure that they will form a good foundation for the design and construction project before the project proceeds. In addition to helping to manage this real and pervasive project risk, the review will help the design and construction team to internalize and buy into the models that they will be using.

**Reasonable scope.** The beginning of the design and construction phase represents the second, and last, place in the integrated CASE-based application development cycle at which application delivery scope can be narrowed without encumbering the project with excessive political or "throwaway" costs. Although there may certainly be times when an application's entire BAA functionality has to be delivered all at once, there are many more times when it can be delivered and absorbed a little at a time, and some instances when certain functionality developed as part of the analysis may not have to be delivered at all.

It's therefore almost always a good idea to precede the start of a design and construction project with a system delivery scoping effort, which breaks a large design and construction project into several smaller projects. Executing several smaller design construction projects instead of a single large project:

- Makes the design and construction phase more manageable.
- Helps reduce overruns.
- Produces initial deliverables more quickly, which helps maintain management confidence in CASE.
- For certain projects, can make the business's absorption of the new system into a more manageable task.

**Continuity of analysis participants.** The deliverables produced by traditional analysis can form a suitable, and often self-sufficient, basis for traditional design and construction. Once an information system's external design is set in terms of menus, screens, dialogue, reports, and interfaces, execution of the system's internal design and eventual construction in the specified target technologies can often be handled by a separate design and construction team. If the traditional analysis was sound, and if the design and construction team is good and follows acceptable practices, a viable information system will often result.

This scenario doesn't work with CASE. The reason is that, although a properly executed CASE-based analysis is far more detailed, rigorous, and deep than its traditional counterpart, it's data oriented, and doesn't fully address the application's operational requirements.[5] It's therefore difficult, if not impossible, for a design and construction team to develop sufficient understanding of the information system's operational needs purely from the analysis. To close this gap, it's essential to have continuity of personnel who participated in the analysis. Carrying key analysis personnel into the design and construction team will help the project produce a viable application by:

- Providing operational knowledge that was acquired and documented, but not modeled, during the analysis.
- Interpreting and explaining modeling approaches that may not be obvious.
- Providing a consistent project interface to business and information tech-

---

[5]The data orientation of an information engineering analysis should not be confused with the equal emphasis that the methodology places on modeling data and activities. Analysis activities, in the form of information engineering processes, are data oriented in that they create, update, delete, and sometimes read the data model's entity types.

nology contacts, who provided their knowledge and expertise to the analysis project and whose knowledge and expertise will also be needed by the design and construction project.

**Methodology, CASE tool, and target technology expertise.** Two common, yet paradoxical, errors made when starting up design and construction projects are to assume that:

- Because design and construction are familiar concepts, large quantities of methodology and CASE tool expertise will not be needed.
- Because the CASE tools and methodology remove and isolate the project from the application's target technologies, large quantities of technological expertise will not be needed either.

Neither of these assumptions is true. While Lower CASE can certainly help project teams leverage their design and construction efforts, it can't totally isolate the project from the application's target technologies. Methodology and CASE tool expertise will also be required to derive value from the logical data model and process logic developed during analysis, and to fully leverage the capabilities of the design tool and code generator. When planning a CASE-based design and construction project, care should therefore be taken to ensure that each of these types of expertise will be available to the project.

## Management Issues and Strategies for ADW and IEF Projects

In addition to starting the management process early—before the project begins, and the standard set of good management techniques that are just as applicable to integrated CASE as they are to traditional application development projects, there are a number of integrated CASE-specific issues and management strategies for addressing these issues. These strategies will help ensure that ADW and IEF projects produce consistent and successful results. Although there are many good practices and techniques for managing integrated CASE projects, Fig. 11.4 shows some of the more significant, yet least understood, project issues and strategies for successfully managing application development using ADW and IEF.

### Ensuring quality in CASE-based models

Modeling is an intrinsic part of ADW- and IEF-based application development. Not only do logical business models form the principal products of analysis, but operational models, based on the analysis models and developed during design and construction, form the principal input to the code generators that generate the applications. Indeed, more integrated CASE

- Managing model development
- Ensuring that quality models are produced
- Managing user participation
- The matrix processor as a management tool
- Prototyping as a management tool
- Coordinating development and modeling efforts
- Estimating project time and effort

**Fig. 11.4** Management issues and strategies for ADW and IEF integrated projects.

development effort is probably expended on developing models than on anything else. For ADW or IEF to be productively used for application development, and for a company to derive high value from CASE, the modeling processes must yield models that are:

- Accurate, faithfully capturing the business's needs.
- Comprehensive and detailed, so that no parts of the application are left to chance.
- Appropriate for the specific methodology and CASE tool, so that each can be effectively used.
- Consistent, so that the modeling approaches used to develop each part of the application work the same way.

In short, success with CASE is highly dependent on the quality of the models, and just as in hard-goods manufacturing,[6] there's an inverse relationship between quality and cost—in this case, the higher the quality of the models, the lower the application development cost. (See Fig. 11.5.)

Assurance that CASE-based application development projects yield high-quality models, however, is far from certain. Nor is it easy to achieve. The alacrity with which ADW and IEF can be used to generate impressive-looking models, coupled with the conceptual nature of models and the newness of the technology, can make model quality difficult to define, measure, and control. Developing quality models requires careful attention by management throughout the entire CASE-based application development process. Managers of CASE projects can help ensure quality by:

[6]John J. Heldt and Daniel J. Costa, *Quality Pays,* Hitchcock Publishing Company, 1988. Also see David A. Garvin, *Managing Quality: The Strategic And Competitive Edge,* The Free Press, New York, 1988.

- Emphasizing quality; making it important (if the company has a quality program, it should be extended to include CASE).
- Using and paying careful attention to methodology and CASE tool consistency checks.
- Conducting external model reviews at key points during the development process.
- Making sure that the application's users fully participate in the modeling and model review processes and that they are aware of the importance of understanding and verifying the models being produced.

A good place to start is underscoring the need for producing quality models, the reasoning behind the need, and the quality costs that will be incurred if quality models are not achieved for all CASE project participants. It's important to make sure that the business users, analysts, and modelers understand the importance of getting the models right and the emphasis that model quality will be given by management.

But, putting out the message will not yield acceptable results unless each of the project's participants understands that progress will be measured on the bases of quality, speed, and quantity—not quantity and speed alone. This is not an easy concept to convey or to enforce, since it runs counter to many information technology, indeed many company, cultures. Expected time and efforts to complete each modeling task, the criteria that will be used to evaluate the task's work products, and the controls used to ensure that the evaluation is accurate will begin to drive home the message, and to ensure that quality in models is achieved.

Although ADW and IEF both support extensive value added consistency checks, quality models will not be produced unless the consistency check results are heeded. For instance, if an error resulting from an ADW data

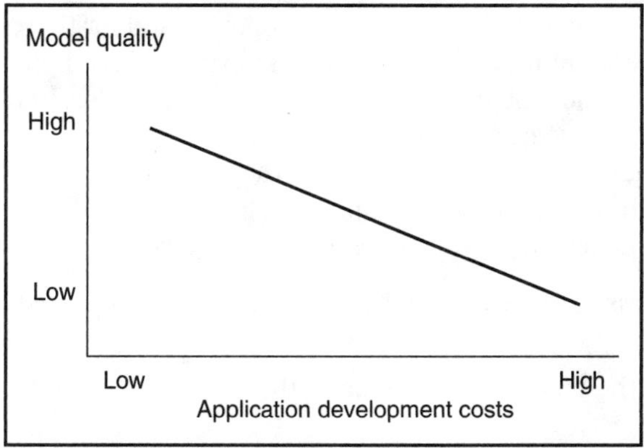


**Fig. 11.5** Model quality versus application development cost.

conservation analysis is ignored, a logical data model that doesn't fully support each of the application's requirements may result. When the logical data model is translated into a data structure (a model of the application's physical database), and eventually into a database, the database will not support all of the processing required by the application. Although the flawed database design can be corrected, and the required functionality can be developed during construction and testing, the corrections are likely to be expensive—many times as expensive as correcting the original error. CASE tool and methodology consistency checks are important and each should be fully understood before a modeling effort is considered complete.

Model reviews at key stages in analysis and design phases, conducted by people who were not directly involved in the modeling process, can provide additional and valuable checks on model consistency and quality. Omissions and inconsistencies in modeling approach, which might slip through CASE tool consistency checks, can be often caught in this way. Good candidates for this task are DAs, DBAs, outside consultants and methodology and tool experts from other (noncompetitive) projects and departments. The major criteria for external review participants are deep CASE tool and methodology expertise and familiarity with the business area.

Users can provide projects with a valuable, and possibly the most important, means for verifying the accuracy and completeness of CASE-based models. Involvement of users who are on the project and those who are external to the project but have a stake in the system, should be encouraged, and their input should be taken seriously. There's probably no better way to ensure model completeness and accuracy than through high-quality user participation in the model review process.

### Managing user participation

Managing user participation, however, can be challenging and tricky. The CASE paradigm for application development can require considerable reorientation for users who are new to application development and for those who have been involved with traditional development efforts. For CASE development to be successful, new objectives, tasks, order, deliverables, and responsibilities will have to be learned, understood, and accepted.

Although users and their needs vary widely, and there are many techniques for achieving high-quality user participation on integrated CASE projects, successful user involvement will almost always require:

- Abundant and continuous user involvement throughout the entire modeling process.
- User understanding of the modeling process and the models that are its products.

Lots of user participation in the modeling process, starting with the initial modeling sessions and ending with construction, is a key requirement for ensuring that high-quality models will be produced. Depending on availability, orientation, and conceptual ability, user involvement can take a number of different, but equally viable, forms. Users can participate jointly via facilitated sessions, individually through direct interviews, or, if they're inclined and able to do so, they can work with the modelers and participate directly in the modeling process. The idea is to be sure that business users are constantly involved in the modeling process, and that their involvement is based on real understanding so that they can make meaningful contributions.

For users to contribute, they will need to understand what's happening, why it's happening, and what their responsibilities are at each point in the modeling process. Time should therefore be spent at the beginning of each user session to orient and focus the users on the BAA so that they understand how it fits into the big picture, the models and issues that will be discussed, and the responsibilities of all participants. Business and modeling issues raised during previous sessions should be included, along with their resolutions. It's also helpful to use visual aids such as an ISP function hierarchy diagram, a C-R-U-D matrix showing how the BAA fits in, or even a large-scale data model showing entity types that are in other BAAs but that may be referred to during the session.

The use of a C-R-U-D matrix in a modeling session paid dividends for a vice president at a national service company when he became concerned about whether or not a BAA team fully understood all of his business area's interactions with the rest of the business. The team supplied him with a C-R-U-D matrix and instructions to place an "X" in any cell in which he felt that an unforeseen dependency might exist. At the follow-up meeting held a week later, each "X" was analyzed, and where appropriate, converted to C-R-U-D notation. The result was the identification and correction of several unforeseen dependencies, much better user buy-in and higher senior-management confidence in the BAA process.

Consider working with users in layers, so that they will not be intimidated by their bosses or their subordinates. There are few things as quiet as a user who is concerned about asking a silly question in front of his or her boss, or a supervisor who is afraid of appearing ignorant in front of his or her subordinates. Users with their own agendas, regardless of the agenda or the reason why they have it, will have trouble making meaningful contributions to the modeling effort, so going to extra lengths to make them comfortable with the modeling process is almost always a good thing to do.

Best modeling results are achieved when everyone involved in the modeling process understands that the models represent evolving deliverables and that they may change many times, sometimes significantly, during the process. This is likely to be a foreign and uncomfortable concept, not only for operationally oriented users in line positions, whose business life revolves around completed tasks, but also for information technology participants. A DBA, for example, participating on an IEF project at a large insurance company recently refused to help the BAA team create an implementable data model prior to writing PADs because she felt that "there might be changes to the logical model that could require a redesign of the database." For meaningful participation in the modeling process, and for high-quality models to result, evolution of deliverables must be viewed as a good, rather than bad, sign, since it indicates that progress is being made.

### The matrix processor as a management tool

The CASE tool matrix processor, which is used extensively in strategic and tactical planning, to verify data and activity models, can also be used to clarify the models for BAA participants. The technique involves using CASE-tool-supported matrices to associate business requirements, concerns, issues, problems, even manual procedures, to objects in the data and activity models. The matrices can be easily maintainable and populated with processes and entity types that can help modeling participants better understand their models by enabling them to track the multiple functions supported by each model. Association matrices can be especially useful in helping to clarify how business rules are embedded in the data model, as this is not always obvious to all project participants.

### Prototyping as a management tool

Prototyping during the BAA modeling process can be an excellent way to ensure user understanding and to verify the activity and data models from an operational perspective. This can easily be accomplished using the ADW/RAD tool, which helps transform the models into menus and screens. For projects using the IEF, an equivalent result can be achieved by extending the BAA to include the initial portion of design in which preliminary procedures, screens, and dialog flow are defined and the BAA models prototyped using IEF "autoflows". In either case, the modest amount of extra effort expended in developing an operational view of the BAA models prior to investing heavily in a physical design can pay the application delivery project back manyfold. Prototyping during an information engineering analysis can be especially useful in:

- Verification of the application's scope at a time when scope changes can be resolved with minimal project impact.
- Ensuring that each of the project's participants develops a good understanding of how the analysis models impact the application.
- Identification of data model attributes, which become obvious to users when the application is viewed operationally.

- Identification of functional requirements such as inquiries and controls, which can be overlooked during analysis.
- Correction of analysis errors stemming from misconceptions of how the application will operate.[7]

As the application enters its design and construction phase, prototyping can once again be employed to aid in operational design.

### Coordinating development and modeling efforts

Coordination of modeling efforts should be a prime consideration when managing all but the smallest and most isolated CASE projects. Where multiple teams will be developing models that share information or activities common to the same project or across different projects, common objects will exist in the models that each team develops. For the projects to be successful and productive, the common objects, and the analysis and development efforts that create them and determine their use, will have to be coordinated and managed. Model and development coordination for CASE projects should include:

- Stewardship of sharable objects.
- Development of common, reusable modeling approaches.

Model objects that are sharable across teams and projects can include processes, action diagrams, templates, attributes, and entity types. Although attributes and entity types must be sharable across all modeling efforts that access common data, sharing screen templates is a good way to ensure that the generated systems will have a consistent user interface, and sharable processes and action blocks will help enable object reuse. For an application development project to share objects successfully, so that they will be consistent, reflect each team's needs, not change unexpectedly, and be available for access when needed:

- Strict standards must be disseminated and enforced for each sharable object.
- Stewardship must be assigned so that everyone understands which team can modify each object.
- Mechanisms must be set up to identify object inconsistencies and to resolve conflicting requirements.

---

[7]Although prototyping, as part of analysis, is not consistent with all interpretations of information engineering, I have found it to be a very effective tool for ensuring that the analysis is accurate and complete. A number of ADW and IEF users have successfully incorporated prototyping during analysis into their information-engineering-based methodologies.

To achieve maximum productivity from CASE when multiple development projects are under way, administration of common modeling objects will generally not be sufficient. Equal attention will have to be allocated to developing standard modeling approaches to common business requirements so that each team doesn't have to spend its limited time and resources to solve each one independently. One company, for example, identified historical calendars, location hierarchies, customers, and inventory as the four most difficult modeling areas that would have to be addressed by almost every one of its development efforts. Each modeling area was assigned to a different team so that each could develop common data and activity models capable of serving the needs of the entire development effort. The results, in terms of consistency, reusability and reduced modeling efforts, saved the company substantial amounts of time and effort over the life of their development projects. The fact that their information systems have been developed using common and well-understood modeling constructs will save even greater amounts of time and efforts during maintenance.

### Estimating project time and effort

Estimating the time and effort required to develop an information engineering CASE-based application represents a management paradox. Function points, based on traditional parameters such as inputs, outputs, inquiries, files, and interfaces[8] are not useful for ADW and IEF development because these parameters are not addressed until the application reaches its design and construction stage. And by the time an ADW or IEF integrated CASE project does go into design and construction, most of the development effort will have already been expended and estimates, however accurate, will be less relevant. The problem is compounded by the newness of CASE technology, the lack of experience in estimating CASE projects, the speed with which the technology is evolving, and unrealistic expectations regarding CASE.

This paradox can be solved by developing estimates based on information engineering planning and analysis objects such as functions, processes, subject areas, and entity types. Texas Instruments has been able to estimate IEF projects by using counts of functions and subject areas or high-level entity types that are available at the beginning of an analysis project, and counts of elementary processes and entity types that are developed as the analysis proceeds. By taking additional factors such as project complexity and experience, which impact estimates, into account, surprisingly accurate estimates can be developed. I have seen similar techniques successfully used with ADW.

---

[8]Capers Jones, *Programming Productivity,* McGraw-Hill, New York, 1986, Pages 73-78

The important things to keep in mind when developing such estimates are that:

- The project should be reestimated at several points during the analysis process, as more becomes known about the application and the models become a better platform on which to base the estimates.
- Sufficient time and effort should be allocated to the steep learning curve that always accompanies the implementation of CASE.
- A company-specific database should show how analysis model objects affect project estimates.
- The estimates and the estimating process should be checked by people who are experienced with the CASE tool and the methodology.

In the absence of a way to use planning and analysis object counts, probably the best source of early development project estimates are traditional

| Symptom | Probable Causes |
|---|---|
| ■ Trouble getting started | Incompatible methodology<br>Insufficient methodology training<br>Insufficient CASE-tool training<br>Flawed strategic or tactical planning models |
| ■ Slow or halting progress | Insufficient business knowledge<br>Insufficient access to users<br>Inadequate support<br>Inadequate facilities |
| ■ Extremely rapid progress | Shallow or flawed analysis<br>Misunderstanding of methodology |
| ■ Unhappy business users | Insufficient model verification<br>Inadequate or inappropriate business user training<br>Wrong people selected as user participants |
| ■ Lack of business issues | Shallow or flawed analysis<br>Analysis models based on current, rather than future, system |
| ■ A stable data model | Shallow or flawed data modeling process<br>Analysis models based on current, rather than future, system<br>Flawed or missing interaction models |
| ■ Contention over model objects | Flawed C-R-U-D matrix or affinity analysis<br>Flawed or missing model management |

**Fig. 11.6** Troubleshooting guide for ADW and IEF analysis projects.

| Symptom | Probable causes |
| --- | --- |
| ■ Poor productivity | Failure to fully utilize procedure action blocks, library modules, or templates<br>Improper leveraging of construction-tool functions<br>Flawed analysis<br>Inadequate CASE tool or methodology training |
| ■ Highly customized screens and reports | Poor use of macros or procedure action blocks<br>Inadequate reuse of shared objects |
| ■ Long elapsed time before first deliverables | Failure to control scope prior to design<br>Flawed project plan |
| ■ High integration-testing failure rate | Flawed analysis data model<br>Inadequate model management<br>Inadequate standards |
| ■ High stress-testing failure rate | Flawed analysis data model<br>Inadequate access path analysis during analysis<br>Failure to convert logical analysis data model into a viable database design<br>Inadequate DBA support |

**Fig. 11.7** Troubleshooting guide for ADW and IEF design and construction projects.

estimates, augmented by the combined experience of a number of individuals who are experienced with the CASE tools and methodology.

## A troubleshooting guide for ADW and IEF projects

There are obviously many things that can potentially go wrong with an ADW- or IEF-based application development project. Many problems are intrinsic to the tools and the methodologies that they support, while others are company or culture specific. Figures 11.6 and 11.7, while certainly not a substitute for experience, and far from complete, show some of the most common symptoms for troubled analysis, design and construction projects, and the most probable causes for each.

Chapter

# 12

# Introducing CASE

The dizzying pace at which information technology has evolved during the past decade has turned the introduction of new application development technologies into a frequent and commonplace event. New databases, languages, development aids, and reporting environments appear—and often disappear—from the application development scene almost as frequently as the PC workstations on which many of them run. Although many of these products improve the application development process, few have a profound effect on the information technology organization, and still fewer have any effect on the rest of the company. Even relational databases such as DB2, RDB, or ORACLE, which represent a total departure from traditional data management technologies, are accessed via similar DMLs that can be executed from traditional programs written in COBOL or C. Although the programmers may have to learn a new DML, and the DBAs must master the vagaries of a new database, the rest of the information technology organization can remain largely unchanged, and the rest of the company doesn't have to know or care.

CASE is different. The introduction of information-engineering-based CASE represents "radical innovation" and causes nothing less than a reengineering of the way applications are conceived, developed, introduced, and maintained.[1] Every part of the company can be profoundly affected. What's needed, therefore, is not an introduction at all, but comprehensive change management—the same kind of change management that would accompany

[1]Wanda Orlikowski, "Radical And Incremental Innovations In Systems Development: An Empirical Investigation Of CASE Tools," Massachusetts Institute Of Technology CISR Working Paper No. 221, April 1991.

the reengineering of any of the company's other core business functions.[2] Although the general objectives and CSFs for managing change in organizations certainly apply to CASE, the 4 CSFs that are specific to introducing ADW- and IEF-based integrated CASE are presented in Fig.12.1.

## Understanding the People Issues and Their Impact

CASE, and the profound and sweeping changes that accompany it, can't be successfully assimilated into an organization unless the people who make up the organization accept and buy into CASE. Indeed, among the many issues that must be addressed and overcome to successfully implement CASE, those that are people related are at once the most crucial, and the least understood. A well-thought-out-and-executed change management plan is the obvious solution. But, for the change management plan to work, it must specifically address the fear, uncertainty, skepticism, frustration, confusion, and isolation that almost always accompany the introduction of CASE. (See Fig. 12.2.)

### Inertia

It's difficult for anyone, from the janitor to the chairman of the board, to walk away from a substantial investment, especially when the investment has been, and still is, paying off. Yet, this is precisely what companies introducing CASE are asking their information technology professionals to do. These professionals have invested heavily in developing facility with and expertise in traditional development technologies, and for many of them the investment has paid off handsomely in terms of lucrative and stable careers.

- **Understanding the people issues and their impact**
- **Communications and change management**
- **A viable CASE training program**
- **A pilot program with early, demonstrable success**

**Fig. 12.1** Four CSFs for a successful CASE ADW or IEF introduction.

[2]For a broader view of information technology and organization-based change management, see: Walter J. Utz, Jr., *Software Technology Transitions*, Prentice Hall, 1992; John F. Rockart and Debra Hofman, "Improving Systems Delivery: A Managerial Perspective," Massachusetts Institute Of Technology CISR Working Paper No. 223, June 1991; Colin A. Carnall, *Managing Change In Organizations*," Prentice Hall International (UK), 1990.

**Fig. 12.2** How the introduction of CASE affects people.

It's not realistic to expect that a company's information technology professionals will toss away years of hard-won expertise in conventional technology and eagerly go through the process all over again with CASE. The inertia that so often thwarts the introduction of CASE is founded on real concerns that have their origins in real investments. Information technology professionals can and do walk away from their traditional technology investments, but like the chairman of the board, they can't be expected to do so until they're convinced that there's no alternative.

### Fear

The introduction of any new technology will be accompanied by at least a moderate amount of fear, especially when self-esteem, reputations, and careers are at risk. If the new technology is a language, for example, new syntax and rules, along with a litany of hidden pitfalls, must be learned before an information technology professional can become proficient with the language. Once proficiency in the new language is attained, the fear subsides, and our information technology professional can get down to the task of leveraging his or her new-found technical expertise for job security and advancement.

When the technology being introduced is CASE, the challenges and the fear that accompany its introduction can be much more acute. The reason is that unlike the introduction of a conventional technology, such as our new language, the introduction of CASE often involves:

- Several new technologies such as data modeling, activity modeling, relational data management, GUI design, and a workstation-based CASE tool, many of which seemingly have to be mastered at once.
- A new methodology calling for unfamiliar deliverables to be produced in a new order by a CASE tool that is not fully understood.
- Working closely with business users and the acquisition of new, detailed, and often complex business knowledge.
- In some cases, new criteria for being evaluated.

It should not be surprising if the fear that accompanies any new technology turns to panic when the new technology is CASE, considering the amount of new and different competencies that CASE requires, the fact that the needs for competencies often overlap, requiring several to be mastered at the same time, and that hard-won careers can hang in the balance.

#### Uncertainty and skepticism

The uncertainty and skepticism that often accompany an information technology professional's initial introduction to CASE, stem from the:

- Perceived need to deliver a "working" application on time, even if it doesn't quite do what its users really need.
- Lengthy learning curve that he or she must traverse before CASE-based applications can be delivered as quickly or as assuredly as conventional applications.

For all but the smallest and simplest applications, several months can elapse before the developers begin to see and realize many of the benefits afforded by CASE. When combined with the rampant stories and rumors about problems and failures caused by CASE, this delay can confirm the uncertainty and vindicate the skeptics. Most information technology professionals need to go through the entire CASE-based application development cycle at least once before they begin to internalize CASE's benefits.

#### Frustration

Substantial frustration for information technology professionals, their users, and their management is an inevitable by-product of introducing CASE. For application developers and their business users, the frustration stems from:

- The CASE development paradigm, in which the path toward a deliverable application is not straightforward or obvious.
- CASE tool idiosyncrasies, rules, and consistency checks that ensure that their application development process conforms to a metamodel, which in most cases is neither well documented nor fully understood,
- The high involvement of business users in the application development process.
- The intransigence of CASE methodologies, and all too often, the lack of adequate methodology and CASE tool support.

The frustration that CASE introduction brings to business users stems from the combination of having to supply many more details about operations than were required in the past, and until the application is delivered, getting a lot less back in the form of understandable work products. For a justifiably skeptical information technology management, frustration comes from managing, and being responsible for, a vastly different applications development process and receiving an entirely different set of signals, neither of which is well understood.

### Isolation

The very detailed and precise analysis projects, which quickly follow the initial introduction of CASE, often require that the applications be developed jointly by teams composed of application developers and their business users. Where geographical dispersion permits, the joint teams are often colocated with the application's users. Although colocation provides valuable and distinct advantages to analysis teams in terms of accessibility and currency of the information that they must seek, it can also serve to isolate the team's information technology and business user participants.

For application developers, participation on colocated joint teams often means that they move into new surroundings, work with different people, and worry about different issues than their information technology peers. As a result, they may no longer receive departmental correspondence as quickly or be able to fully participate in all of their organization's meetings. Even casual contact with their information technology peers may be lost, and if space is particularly tight, they may (temporarily?) lose their offices as well. It should therefore not be surprising if such people feel abandoned—isolated—even by their information technology organization, nor should it be surprising if part of the blame for their isolation falls to CASE.[3]

---

[3]One information technology professional who was colocated (in the same building, but on another floor) with her business users felt this so acutely that for the eighteen-month duration of her IEF-based project, she refused to unpack the cartons containing papers and belongings that accompanied her "temporary" move from her old office.

The same thing can happen to a joint team's user participants. Businesspeople can feel isolated because they're removed from the line positions in which they had expertise, authority, and success. They then work with application developers in building information systems in a technology that businesspeople don't—and don't want to—understand. And if joint teams were not a part of the company's traditional application development culture, user participants might blame CASE.

### Confusion

The newness of the methodology and development tools that accompany CASE can lead to a great deal of confusion for the application developers who first begin to use them. Formal and informal application development conventions, which took years to sort out, and which work, may no longer be applicable to ADW or IEF development projects. The impact that the introduction of CASE has on the company's application development culture can cause confusion regarding:

- When and how development projects interface with application support organizations such as technology architecture, data administration, database administration, and information technology audit.
- How deliverables are supposed to be produced, and what they should look like.
- How far to go in each methodology step in terms of detail and correctness.
- How to tell a quality job from a poor one.

For the introduction of CASE to be successful, confusion over fundamental application development issues such as these must be revisited and sorted out.

## Communications and Change Management

A successful implementation of CASE can be achieved only to the extent that each of the major CASE-related people issues is effectively addressed. CASE can't be successfully implemented by management decree, nor can it be implemented solely on the basis of merit or grass-roots technical support. A well-orchestrated communications and change management plan is an absolute requisite for successfully implementing CASE in all but the smallest organizations.

The nature of the change management plan, and the specific issues that it must address, are culture dependent, and will therefore vary from company to company. But, regardless of the company's culture, size, or line of business, the communications and change management plan, to be successful, will have to assess the people-related issues, not only in a context of communications, to get the word out, but also in a context of:

- Unfreezing the status quo so that people become open to the new ideas that CASE represents.
- Listening, so that the real needs and concerns of the people who must buy into CASE can be identified and addressed.
- Demonstrating success, to make CASE real and to reinforce its benefits.
- Providing support so that the people who must learn to use CASE can develop the competencies that they will need.
- Solidifying the CASE paradigm for application development in place.[4]

### Overcoming inertia

The people who make up an information technology organization have a substantial investment in traditional technology, and overcoming their inertia must begin with shaking their comfort with their current investment. This doesn't imply that their investment was wrong or bad, but rather that the investment is no longer viable in any company that is introducing CASE, or perhaps even in the future job market. There are good statistics available to back this up.

In most companies, this message can be effectively communicated only if it comes directly from top corporate and information technology management. Depending on the corporate culture, the communication can take the form of an insert in a periodic newsletter, a memo, or a personnel letter to each employee. Whatever the medium, the message should be the same, and it should be crystal clear: CASE will be the basis for new application development. A good analogy that's sometimes useful is that of "a 'constitution,' which can be amended, but not overthrown, since it allows for flexibility without the possibility of reverting back to traditional development."[5] Without a clear and unambiguous commitment from top management, the skeptics who are intent on subverting the implementation of CASE will have a field day!

Although delivering the message is absolutely essential, ensuring that all who will be effected by CASE hear and internalize the message is just as important. If inertia is to be overcome, the change management plan will have

---

[4]Beverly Goldberg, "Manage Change—Not the Chaos Caused by Change," *Management Review*, November, 1992. Also see Ira Gregerman, "Introducing New Technologies Or Keeping Up With The Joneses," *CASE Trends*, January/February 1990.

[5]Interview with Beverly Goldberg, Vice President, Twentieth Century Fund and Principal of Siberg Associates, Inc.

to include a mechanism to carefully monitor the message's result, and to redeliver its content in alternate forms, until it sinks in.

### Dealing with fear

Since CASE will bring new methods, approaches, and technologies to bear on a company's application development process, some of the fear that accompanies its introduction will be justified. Application developers, and to a certain extent, their business users, will indeed have to develop competencies and new areas of expertise if they're to retain their careers.

Management's first defense against the paralyzing fear that accompanies CASE is to keep the introduction of CASE and other new technologies to a minimum, and to provide both the means and the time to master them. This introduction strategy was expertly executed by a midwest service company that introduced IEF for DB2 and CICS, both of which were already part of the company's repertoire of traditional technologies, even though they fully intended to move to a GUI and client-server target technology environment. Only after a number of projects successfully completed their IEF-based analysis and design, and a reasonable comfort level with their new CASE tool and methodology had begun to emerge, were client-server and GUI technologies introduced. In addition to holding the line on new technologies, the company made sure that each employee received substantial tool and methodology training, and that ample consulting expertise was available to the business and information technology personnel on each project. People who will be dealing with CASE need to understand that they will be given sufficient time, support, training, mentoring, and help in developing expertise in the technologies.

One astute young manager at a large East-coast insurance company took the concept a step further, employing their new, information-engineering-based methodology as a change agent. Their new methodology, which was developed to support traditional and CASE-based application development, allowed traditional developers to become comfortable with the information engineering paradigm before moving on to CASE.

Finally, application developers need to understand that CASE can be mastered, that they will be fully supported during their learning process, and that career advancement opportunities await those who do well with CASE. Positive reinforcement, in terms of management recognition and career advancement for application developers who successfully use CASE, will help allay fears and calm the uncertain and the skeptics.

### Overcoming uncertainty and skepticism

Much of the uncertainty and skepticism that accompany the introduction of CASE stems from a fundamental mismatch between what CASE does and what many application developers have become used to doing. If the goal is to deliver applications to their users on time, regardless of how well they serve their user's needs, and regardless of how much time and effort will have to be spent to correct them, the skeptics will be right. CASE will be of little practical use.

CASE becomes valuable, and the learning curve associated with mastering it becomes tolerable, only when the goal of application development is redefined to take the quality of the applications that are delivered into account. By redefining successful application development in terms of quality applications that meet users' basic needs upon initial delivery, the groundwork will be set for redirecting skepticism away from CASE and toward the technologies that preceded it.

Uncertainty and skepticism are also vulnerable to information technology and business peers who have personally experienced the benefits of CASE. Developing a core of credible peer "champions" who have successfully developed applications using CASE, can demonstrate that:

- CASE really does increase the quality and productivity with which applications can be delivered.
- The new technology can be mastered by the company's employees.

For peer champions to be useful in fighting the skepticism and uncertainty that accompanies the introduction of CASE, they will have to be developed quickly, cover all levels within the information technology and business organizations, and be propagated throughout new CASE projects. Peer champions who meet these criteria can be very effectively developed as by-products of CASE pilot programs, provided that bright, highly motivated achievers are chosen to participate in the CASE pilots. An interesting, and sometimes unwelcome, by-product of developing peer champions is that they can also become equally valuable assets to other companies that seek to make similar transitions to CASE. Care should be taken to ensure that peer champions' compensation and career paths reflect their newfound skills and achievements.

A third, and essential, principle in combating uncertainty and skepticism toward CASE is to provide application developers with the opportunity to develop their own personal comfort with the new technology. It's far easier to be skeptical of what management might tell you, what you might have read in a book, or something you were taught in a seminar, than of what you actually participated in and personally experienced. Participatory CASE workshops, in which small groups of peers can meet with others who have successfully made the transition and with experienced CASE experts, therefore represent a good vehicle for developing this kind of comfort. CASE workshops will provide developers with a nonthreatening environment in which they can vent their concerns and issues, and in which each one can be directly addressed.

CASE workshops can also be effective in giving application developers a chance to try CASE out and to develop a hands-on feel for how the technology really works. This is especially important for managers who are comfortable managing traditional development, in COBOL for example, because many were (and often still are) crack COBOL programmers. The idea is to give them the opportunity to become just as personally knowledgeable in CASE, to use CASE to develop models and generate applications, and to meet with peers and discuss CASE-related managerial issues and concerns. Only after they go through such a process can they begin to internalize the myriad of CASE-related managerial issues that they will have to deal with.

### Reducing frustration

Considerable frustration among application developers, users, and management can result from the introduction of the new and often poorly understood CASE paradigm for application development. This can't be entirely avoided, but it can be effectively addressed using a three-part approach that emphasizes:

- The way the CASE methodology leads to a deliverable application.
- The ideas and philosophy behind the CASE tool.
- Common application development team objectives.

The primary defense against frustration with CASE is to provide information technology, business user, and management personnel with a clear, understandable road map of how the CASE development paradigm works. CASE orientation sessions that are small and specifically developed for their audience are good vehicles for providing the basic understanding that each of these groups will require. To effectively address the frustration associated with the CASE application development paradigm, the workshops will have to cover the:

- Forces behind the evolution of CASE.
- Philosophy behind the new CASE methodology.
- Tasks that will be performed, and the signals and work products that they can be expected to produce.
- Responsibilities of each participant.
- Problems and issues that they may have to address.

Although CASE tool training is an obvious and common component of nearly every CASE introduction, the training is, almost without exception, limited to teaching application developers to be proficient "mouse drivers."

The way the CASE tool works, the metamodel upon which it's based, and the rules and consistency checks with which it adds value to the development process, are almost universally ignored. Yet, it's the CASE tool's metamodel, and its rules and consistency checks that govern the tool's use, that modelers must deal with on a day-to-day basis and that contribute to much of the tool-related frustration over idiosyncratic issues such as why ADW entity type identifiers sometimes spontaneously appear, or why checking a single IEF subject area out of the mainframe encyclopedia sometimes brings the entire data model in it. CASE tool training for application developers, covering the tool's metamodel and these kinds of issues, can markedly reduce frustrations related to the way the CASE tool works.

The unusually high level of user participation on CASE-based development projects can also add considerably to the frustration of the information technology and user team participants who don't share a common set of goals. When user and information technology development team participants belong to two or more different organizations, with different management structures and objectives, frustrations over a single team striving to achieve conflicting goals and objectives inevitably result. Care must therefore be taken to ensure that all who participate in the application development process internalize, and are measured against, the same criteria for success—the timely delivery of a high-quality, working CASE-based application that meets user and company needs.

### Addressing isolation

Isolation can be addressed through a series of simple but effective measures designed to ensure that joint team participants who are colocated with their users remain an integral and vital part of their organizations.

The same participatory peer workshops that are useful in helping to overcome uncertainty and skepticism can also provide a unique opportunity for keeping joint team participants fully integrated with their organizations. The key is to make their workshop attendance mandatory, flying them in and rescheduling the workshops if necessary to accommodate their restricted availability. While on-site, joint team participants should be given ample opportunity to actively participate in the CASE workshops so that they can share their frustrations and experiences, and to attend non-CASE meetings and workshops as well. This will not only ensure that they remain active information technology organization participants, but also will help allay concerns about not keeping up with other, non-CASE, emerging information technologies. The same principle applies to business user participants, who will need to keep up with emerging business practices and trends.

These extra measures to ensure participation should be supplemented by a simple yet effective measure that consulting firms, where employees spend much of their time on-site with clients, have learned to take long ago: don't give away their offices. Regardless of how sporadically it may be occupied, a person's work space is a powerful symbol of his or her home in an organization. The cost of maintaining the extra space will almost always be more than offset by the organizational unity that it brings.

### Heading off confusion

Much of the confusion resulting from the new CASE paradigm and methodology can be mitigated by supplying development teams with relevant examples of each deliverable that's called for in the methodology and produced by the CASE tool. Although ADW and IEF come with sample deliverables as part of their documentation, such deliverables are meant only to provide general guidance to the broad spectrum of CASE users that represents their market. Such samples are seldom inclusive or relevant enough to satisfy the needs of the confused application development teams who have to figure out how to produce quality deliverables that are specific to their company and their project. Taking the time to develop and document company-specific prototypes for each methodology and CASE tool deliverable that development teams must produce will close the gap and alleviate much of the confusion surrounding their production.

Confusion surrounding CASE project support, on the part of CASE project teams and the organizations that must support them, can be effectively dealt with by developing a detailed support road map that addresses each kind of support. (See Fig. 12.3.)

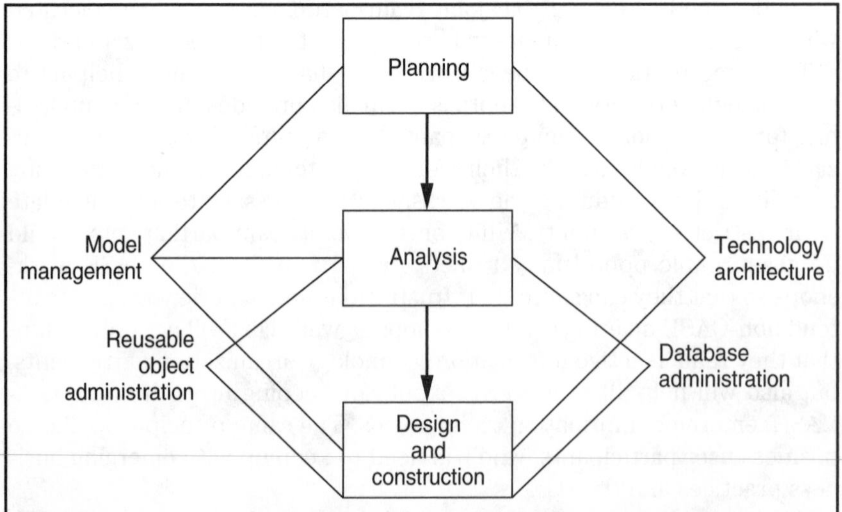


**Fig. 12.3** Kinds of support typically required by CASE-based application development.

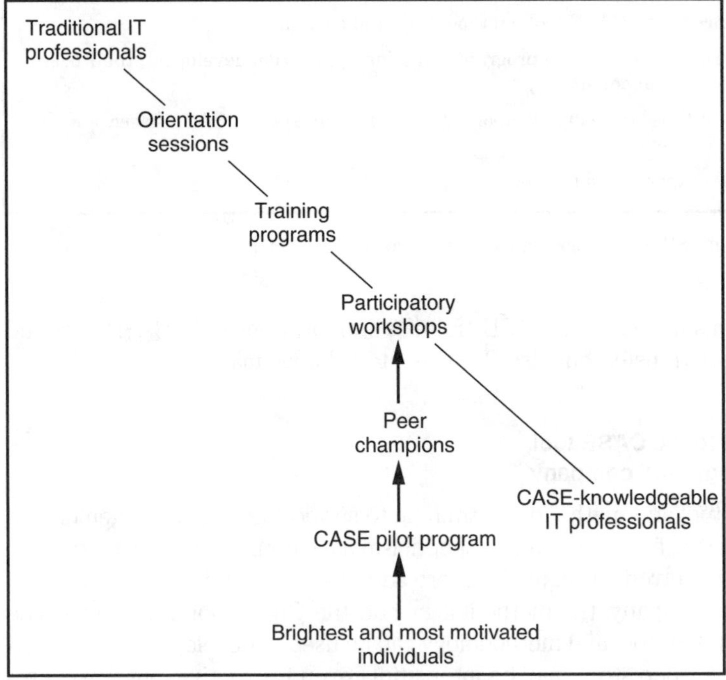


**Fig. 12.4** How pilot programs, orientation sessions, training programs, and participatory programs interact.

To be effective, the support road map will have to include specific responsibilities for the project team and each support organization, and objectives and sample deliverables for each kind of support. Although development of such a road map can involve heated exchanges over the nature of the deliverables and the governance issues that surround them, the time and effort spent in creating a single, comprehensive, understandable road map will be paid back many times in terms of smoothly and successfully executed CASE-based projects. (See Fig. 12.4.)

## A Viable CASE Training Program

Almost all CASE introductions include a CASE tool training component, and many include methodology training as well. There's little doubt that most CASE training programs succeed in transferring knowledge about CASE technologies. But, for the CASE implementation to succeed, the training program must accomplish more than CASE tool or methodology knowledge transfer. The training program must be an integral part of, and fully support, the comprehensive change management and application development reengineering that the introduction of CASE represents. The four CSFs shown in Fig. 12.5

- Relevance to the CASE tool, methodology, and company
- A comprehensive training program targeting application developers, their users, and their management
- A "just-in-time" refresher component for people engaged in CASE-based application development
- Credible, experienced trainers

**Fig. 12.5** Four CSFs for change-management-based CASE training.

will help ensure that the CASE training supports not only CASE tool and methodology transfer, but also CASE-related change management.

## Relevance to the CASE tool, methodology, and company

For CASE tool and methodology training to support change management, so that the inertia, fear, uncertainty, skepticism, isolation, and confusion that accompany the introduction of CASE are addressed, the training must be relevant to the company, the methodology, and the CASE tool being used. The fact that a CASE tool and methodology can be used to develop an information system for a video store may be interesting, even instructive, but it will provide little comfort to an application developer faced with automating trade processing for an investment bank, developing a nationwide reservation system, or controlling a just-in-time inventory system for a manufacturing company. Not only will such training fail to address CASE-related people problems, but it can also aggravate them by failing to cover significant, legitimate, and worrisome technical issues such as processing transactions in real time, dealing with constantly changing products, or efficiently handling relational tables with millions of rows.[6]

But, a training program that takes the company, methodology, and CASE tool into account is seldom sufficient. To be effective, the program will have to address the specific methodology as it will be used by the trainees as they develop applications, including all changes and adaptions. A course that emphasizes current system analysis as a means for verifying analysis models, for example, will not be credible or relevant to developers, users, or managers who are faced with extensive business process reengineering.

The same considerations also apply to CASE tool training, which will be relevant only to the extent that it addresses the way the CASE tool will actually be used. ADW training, which emphasizes the tool's extraordinary flexibility,

[6]Alice LaPlante, "Making A CASE For Better Training," *Computerworld*, February 25, 1991.

for example, will not be useful to developers who will be using the tool to support a formal methodology with a well-defined development approach. To be useful to application development participants and to fully address change management, the training program must specifically address the needs of the business and the methodology and CASE tools as they have been adapted for the company's use.

### Comprehensiveness

In addition to being relevant, CASE training must be comprehensive. To be effective, and to support change management, the training program must address the specific needs of business users and management. All are crucial to successful change management and a successful CASE implementation.[7]

Training for business users must, above all else, be geared to their business skill set, experience, and needs. User training must therefore be different from, and should not be confused with, the very technical training that's required by information technology personnel. User training should include the business philosophy and economic reasoning behind the CASE tool and methodology and how they will be used to benefit their part of the business. The business benefits can and should be supplemented with a road map clearly showing what will happen during the CASE-based application development cycle, when it will happen, and why. Business users will need to know how to approach CASE projects so that they get the most benefits for the business and from their application development dollars. User training might also contain an introduction to CASE-based models, and segments on how to read and interpret them. The user course might end with a segment on user participation and responsibilities as part of developing a quality CASE-based application process.

Application development line managers, who are responsible for, but who may not participate actively on application development teams, should receive specific training on:

- The CASE-based application development cycle.
- The pitfalls commonly encountered during each phase of CASE-based development.
- The signals that they should watch out for.

Training for top management should include a CASE overview so that they can develop a sense of what the new technology is all about and a sense of what they should expect (bad and good) from CASE-based projects.

---

[7]Jonathan S. Sayles, "Training and CASE—Strange Bedfellows?", *Data Training*, May 22, 1990.

### A "just-in-time" refresher component

The CASE-based application development team requirement for a just-in-time training component is an unavoidable consequence of:

- Experience often being required on several CASE projects before sufficient CASE development knowledge can be fully internalized.
- The fact that the CASE-based application development cycle typically exceeds the length of time during which the knowledge transferred during training can be retained.

Just-in-time refresher training can also be an effective vehicle for making the training totally relevant to each project's business, technical, and scheduling needs.[8] To be most effective, the just-in-time training should therefore be conducted on a team-by-team basis, whether just before or during the execution of specific CASE-related tasks. Interviewing, JAD, modeling, and tool-usage techniques can all be effectively covered in this environment. Team-based just-in-time refresher courses can also be a good mechanism for capturing feedback from teams who are beginning to use CASE.

### Credible, experienced trainers

To be fully credible, and to support ADW and IEF relevant change management, the training program will need to emphasize not only relevant examples, but also practical experience. The problem is that trainers with relevant planning and application development experience can be expensive—and sometimes difficult to find at any price. One way to effectively address this problem is to rotate employees and consultants, who have successfully used CASE in the company's pilot program, through the training program either as instructors or coaches who assist the instructors in supplying relevant examples, adding credibility, and keeping things on track.

## A Pilot Program with Early, Demonstrable Success

Although some companies have made a success of CASE by jumping in head first and implementing CASE on crucial projects, there are many advantages to having a well-executed pilot project program, in terms of a successful CASE implementation.[9] Pilot projects support the change management process by demonstrating that CASE works, and by supply-

[8]Alice LaPlante, "Making a CASE for Better Training," *Computerworld*, February 25, 1991.

[9]Paul Radding, "Searching For Success: How Companies Are Making CASE Work," *CASE Trends*, November/December, 1990.

ing the CASE implementation effort with the peer champions that will be required to help overcome the uncertainty and skepticism that so often accompany CASE's introduction. Pilot projects can also be an excellent source of CASE project veterans who have used the methodology and CASE tools to successfully develop applications within a company's business and information technology cultures. Such people, when deployed on strategic CASE projects, can be very effective in ensuring that the projects are successful.

For a pilot program to be successful in terms of implementation and change management, it will have to include a series of increasingly complex projects that are not political, and that provide a good framework for sorting out the myriad of issues and changes associated with CASE. Skipping over this important step in the CASE implementation process can tempt implementors by:

- Providing management with a quick solution that seems attractive because of the large potential for saving time and cost.
- Providing the information technology department with a convenient vehicle for justifying the introduction of CASE technologies that might otherwise be too costly.
- Harnessing a new technology to save a large-scale project that's already over budget and behind schedule.

These temptations can subvert the change management process and should therefore be avoided.

The pilot approach provides a vehicle for introducing CASE-related change with an initial well-defined, low-risk pilot project, and progressing in incremental steps to successively larger and more complex projects, using more complex combinations of CASE technologies.

The pilot approach can begin with a CASE-based tactical plan that creates a CASE environment, in terms of high-level models and well-defined BAAs, within which successive pilot projects can proceed. The first pilot project should be very limited in scope, with each successive pilot adding successive levels of complexity until large, division-level projects are reached. The central idea behind this approach is to build confidence in CASE while avoiding the introduction of too many changes in any one project and to provide sufficient time and opportunity for the change management process to work. New CASE technologies and complexities are added only as confidence builds and the changes introduced on previous pilots have been successfully assimilated.

There's no way to develop a single pilot program that will effectively serve every company's needs. Companies, and their CASE implementations, can differ substantially, and to be successful, the pilot program must be tailored to each company's specific needs and tolerance for change. The

| Project | Time frame | Result |
| --- | --- | --- |
| Planning | 2–3 Months | Pilot project definitions |
| 1st Pilot | 4–6 Months | Proof of concept<br>Confidence in CASE |
| 2nd Pilot | 6–12 Months | Useful system<br>Peer champions for change management<br>Veterans for CASE project deployment |
| 3rd Pilot | 12–24 Months | Mainstream core system<br>Foundation for follow-up CASE projects<br>Peer champions for change management<br>Veterans for CASE project deployment |

**Fig. 12.6** CASE introduction time frames based on successive incremental pilot projects.

sample pilot programs described in Fig.12.6 might support a conservative CASE implementation approach suitable for large corporations.

The objectives of the planning project, which precedes the first CASE pilot, are to:

- Develop company experience in, and demonstrate the benefits of, the CASE-based tactical planning process.
- Emphasize the concept that CASE-based application development projects should be executed as part of a CASE-based tactical plan, beginning with the company's first exposure to CASE.
- Define a series of pilot projects that can be successfully executed using CASE.

To facilitate learning and relieve pressure, the six to twelve weeks usually required to execute a tactical plan has been expanded to two to three months.

The objectives of the first CASE pilot are to prove the CASE concept and to begin developing confidence in the CASE process. Although the first project will be small, and may therefore be looked upon as insignificant by some skeptics, it's important to demonstrate that CASE works—that working applications can be developed without programming and without traditional analysis and design.

The second pilot begins to produce the peer champions that will be required by the change management process for combating the uncertainty and skepticism that come and the introduction of CASE. It can also be a valuable source of CASE project veterans who can be used to seed subsequent CASE projects with internally generated CASE expertise. Development and successful deployment of internal CASE expertise can be an important confidence builder for management, who may be concerned that many of the company's initial CASE projects are apt to rely too heavily on CASE-knowledgeable consultants to augment internal staff.

The third, and last, pilot in our example produces a core system upon which significant amounts of subsequent application development will depend. In addition to being an excellent source of peer champions and internal CASE expertise, using CASE to develop a core system will help to remove all doubts that CASE will be successfully used to develop the company's large-scale, mainstream, applications. It will catch top management's attention and will help to promote CASE by laying the foundation, in terms of CASE-based models and templates, for efficiently using CASE for developing each of the core system's subsequent applications.

Chapter

# 13

# What CASE Does & How to Measure It

CASE represents a lot more than another new information technology. In addition to the considerable time and effort spent on selecting, procuring, and learning to use CASE tools, techniques, and methodologies, successful implementation of CASE can cause substantial and wrenching changes to a company's application development culture. Indeed, every business function that produces or uses company information will ultimately feel the effects of CASE in terms of the way they interact with the information technology function, the information they work with, and the computer applications that they use.

In light of the substantial size and scope of the monetary and cultural investments that CASE represents, questions concerning the company's return on these investments are certainly legitimate. Claims that CASE has the capacity to increase application development productivity and the quality of the applications themselves, are, if not well substantiated, certainly ubiquitous. However, the following questions remain unanswered:

- How CASE increases productivity and quality.
- Where the increases show up.
- How to quantify CASE-related productivity and quality gains.
- How to measure CASE's impact on a business.

Questions concerning what CASE might do, aside from increasing productivity and quality, are often not even asked.

| Area | Change resulting from CASE |
|---|---|
| ■ Productivity | Initial decrease, followed by an increase |
| ■ Quality | Dramatic increase |

**Fig. 13.1** The two major quantifiable and measurable effects of CASE on a company's information systems and its business.

Although the implementation of CASE causes many changes, there are two major areas in which the effects of CASE can be quantified and measured: the effect that CASE has on a company's information technology and its business, and the way a company's information technology and business interact.

As Fig. 13.1 indicates, not all areas are impacted in the same manner, nor are the changes resulting from CASE affected in the same way by time. Application development productivity, as we shall see, will almost always dips before the much-sought-after increase begins to show up, and information system performance may not increase at all. Other areas in which CASE can have significant impact, such as strategic business support or responsiveness to a rapidly changing business environment, are often not even associated with CASE. Let's take a closer look at each of these areas, to explore the effects of CASE and the ways in which each of the effects might be measured.

## How CASE Affects Productivity

Developing even rough measures of the productivity gains resulting from CASE can be a tricky process, since many extraneous factors such as business knowledge, experience, geographic dispersion, target technologies, and access to reusable objects are all highly variable, and each can profoundly affect productivity. For instance, an experienced team developing a well-understood application in a stable and self-contained workstation environment with access to a rich and familiar library of reusable objects, may develop applications with many times the productivity of a second team developing a poorly understood application in a dispersed environment without a rich library of reusable objects. Such factors can easily outweigh the productivity effects of CASE. By the time CASE-related productivity factors such as learning curve, cultural changes, human resource development, and management differences are accounted for, the effect that CASE has on productivity can become murky and difficult to discern.

### The CASE productivity curve

Even with non-CASE productivity influencing factors such as business experience, development environment, application understanding, geographic dispersion, and target technology held constant, the introduction of ADW or IEF is likely to be accompanied by a substantial dip in productivity as the company absorbs an entirely new information-engineering-based approach to applications development, and an array of new CASE-based development projects proceeds through a protracted and costly analysis.[1] The productivity dip is often aggravated by a combination of having to overcome CASE tool, methodology, and target technology incompatibilities, and unrealistic expectations of immediate productivity gains. CASE-based productivity gains can therefore take twelve to eighteen months or longer—well after the initial adoption of CASE—to be realized.[2] (See Fig. 13.2.)

### Factoring maintenance into productivity measurements

The productivity gains afforded by ADW and IEF are real, and provided that the company has achieved the five CASE CSFs and stays with CASE long enough, the gains do show up after the initial dip. But they do not always show up where you would expect them to. The obvious results of a CASE-related productivity increase should include shorter amounts of time to develop applications and lower resource requirements (fewer staff days) consumed during the application development process—and these

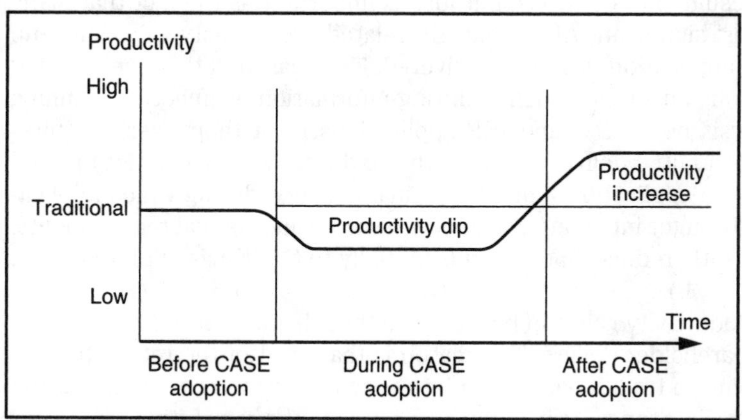


**Fig. 13.2** CASE adoption productivity curve.

[1]The dip in productivity that accompanies the introduction of ADW and IEF is a common phenomenon, and has been documented by many CASE practitioners and consultants. For an excellent article that contains additional references on this productivity dip, see: Cathleen Santousus, "The Fine Art Of Figuring CASE Payback," *Computerworld*, March 27, 1989.

[2]Kathy Spurr and Paul Layzell, *CASE On Trial*, John Wiley & Sons, West Sussex, England, 1990, Chapter 15—"Making CASE Work" by John Parkinson.

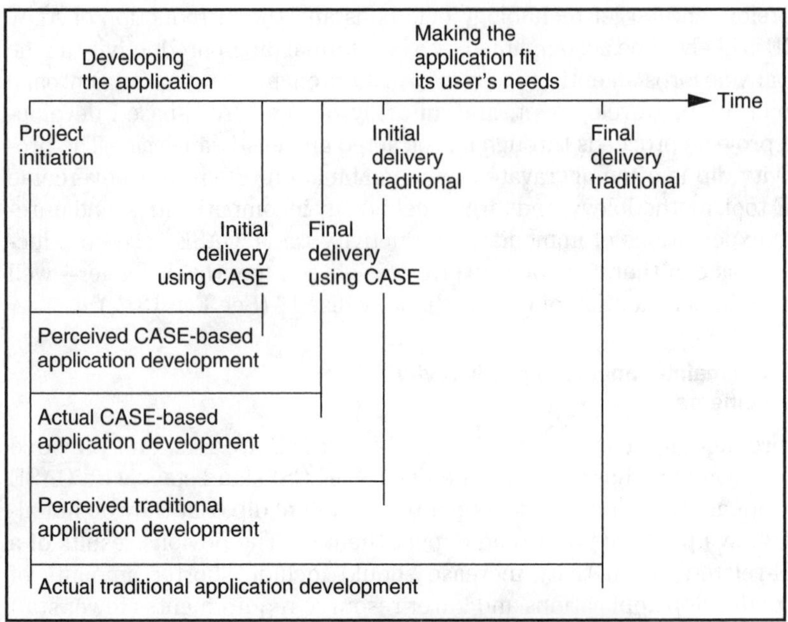


**Fig. 13.3** Where perceived and actual productivity gains show up.

are the results. Less obvious, but just as important, is the fact that many of the most significant ADW- and IEF-related productivity gains show up after the application has been delivered. The reason is that the detailed and rigorous business modeling during information engineering planning and analysis help ADW and IEF applications meet their user's requirements upon initial delivery. The costly (and totally unproductive) period between the application's initial and final delivery, during which applications are brought into conformance with the business's real requirements, is significantly reduced, adding substantially to CASE-based productivity. (See Fig. 13.3.)

This productivity gain can be elusive, although real in terms of contribution or shareholder dollars. The reason is that most of the retrofitting required to make traditional applications usable tends to be done under the guise of "maintenance," since doing so can take the retrofitting off the application development budget, making its cost more tolerable to the company. The result is that the perceived difference in time and effort required to develop CASE-based and traditional applications—measured from project initiation through initial delivery—can be small compared with the actual differences measured from project initiation through final delivery. To accurately assess the productivity gains from ADW and IEF integrated information-engineering-based CASE, the actual differences must be measured and taken into account.

### Measuring the effects of CASE on productivity

Measuring the differences between CASE-based and traditional application development productivity requires the use of productivity metrics—metrics that are capable of measuring productivity differences between two totally different paradigms for application development. The most ubiquitous metrics for measuring application development productivity include lines of code (LOC) or function points. Let's examine the suitability of each for traditional and CASE-based development so that we can gain insight into their applicability for measuring the productivity gains afforded by CASE.

**Using lines of code to measure productivity.** Lines of source code as a productivity metric has the obvious advantage of simplicity. Lines of code are easy to count, and productivity metrics derived from LOC are therefore easy to compile and measure. But since LOC is heavily dependent on language and coding style, it can represent a viable productivity metric only when the paradigm for generating the lines of code is constant.[3] Indeed, as Capers Jones points out, lines of code tend to go down as the level of programming languages and productivity goes up, resulting in a productivity measurement paradox![4] For ADW and IEF code generators, the lines of COBOL or C code generated to satisfy a business requirement have little correlation to CASE productivity. And lines of code generator input can be just as useless, since for ADW and IEF, the code generator input is just as likely to be diagrams.

**Utilizing function points to measure productivity.** Using function points to measure productivity with CASE is better than using lines of code[5], but there are still problems. Productivity, in terms of function points, usually takes the form of function points achieved per unit of effort.

The problem is that both function points and units of effort become blurred in a CASE environment for two reasons. The first is that function points do not provide a good metric for one of the major productivity benefits of CASE—the increased relevance and value of the function points produced to the information system's users and company. The second problem

$$\text{Productivity} = \frac{\text{Function points}}{\text{Units of efforts}}$$

---

[3]Chris F. Kemerer and Benjamin S. Porter, "Improving The Reliability Of Function Point Measurement: An Empirical Study," Massachusetts Institute Of Technology CISR Working Paper No. 229, October 1991.

[4]Capers Jones, "Measuring Software Productivity," *CASE Trends*, January/February 1990.

[5]Capers Jones, *Programming Productivity,* McGraw-Hill, 1986 Pages 42-82.

with using function points to evaluate CASE productivity is that many of the parameters upon which they're based are not constant, since they're developed during analysis and design as part of the information engineering discovery process. Function points, however, can provide a reasonable metric for measuring CASE-based productivity, provided that the effort is measured at final delivery, the point at which the application is fully accepted by its users as fully supporting their mission objectives.

$$\text{Productivity} = \frac{\text{Function points at final delivery}}{\text{Units of effort}}$$

Units of effort, for ADW or IEF integrated CASE, must include planning, analysis, design, construction, and maintenance up to final delivery. Including each ADW- or IEF-supported application development phase takes into account not only the extended and expensive planning and analysis phases, but also the quality with which they helped define the functionality that the business really needed. If each of these ADW and IEF phases are taken into account, differences between integrated CASE and traditional development productivity can be accurately measured as follows.

Productivity = Function points at final delivery / Total units of effort expended during:

Planning (amortized over development projects)
+Analysis
+Design
+Construction
+Maintenance (up to final delivery)

### Productivity Conclusions

There are two productivity-related conclusions that can be drawn from this. The first is that CASE-related productivity is difficult to measure and that it can take a long time to get past the productivity dip that accompanies the introduction of CASE. The second conclusion is that the impact of CASE on productivity can't be accurately measured or assessed until after final delivery. For large information systems, this may occur two or more years after the system is delivered, and five or more years after the initial introduction of CASE. A complicating factor is that the combination of application development politics and delivery-oriented (as opposed to quality-oriented) corporate cultures can work to ensure that initial delivery is the only point at which reliable productivity data exist. The implication is that, while individual and anecdotal productivity information abounds, abundant, objective, and reliable data on the productivity increases resulting from CASE are not yet available.

## What CASE Does to the Quality of Information Systems

With the possible exception of increasing productivity, an increase in information system quality is probably the most sought-after benefit from CASE.[6] Although few would argue with the need to develop high-quality information systems, what "high-quality information systems" actually means and exactly what benefits can be derived from them, is not always clear, or consistent. William Perry defines the most common software quality attributes as:

"■ Correctness—the extent to which a program satisfies its specifications and fulfills its user's mission objectives.
- Reliability—the extent to which a program can be expected to perform its intended function with required precision.
- Efficiency—the amount of computing resources and code required to perform a function.
- Integrity—the extent to which access to data by unauthorized individuals can be controlled.
- Usability—the effort required to learn, operate, prepare input for, and interpret output of a program.
- Maintainability—the effort required to locate and fix an error in an operational program.
- Testability—the effort required to test a program and ensure it performs to its intended function.
- Flexibility—the effort required to modify an operational program.
- Portability—the effort required to transfer a program from one hardware configuration to another.
- Reusability—the extent to which a program can be used in other applications related to the packaging and scope of the function that the programs perform.
- Interoperability—the effort required to couple one system with another."[7]

---

[6]"Leading Trends In Information Services," Deloitte & Touche Information Technology Consulting Services, Fourth Annual North American Survey, 1991, Page 5.

[7]William E. Perry, "Quality Concerns In Software Development," *Information Systems Management*, Spring 1992. A similar set of software quality attributes and definitions, which can be found in many software engineering publications, were first published fifteen years earlier by J. McCall, P. Richards, and G. Walters, "Factors In Software Quality,"3 volumes, NTIS AD-A049-014, 015, 055, November 1977.

While certainly desirable, and a good basic framework for exploring the quality-related effects of ADW and IEF, these classic software engineering quality attributes view information system quality from a programming, rather than business, perspective. To add a means for quantifying information system quality in terms meaningful to a business, we will borrow a concept from the manufacturing sector's current "total quality" thinking: quality costs.

*Quality costs* are defined by Ronald Fortuna as "those costs incurred because of poor quality—essentially those costs that would not have been incurred if a product or service were precisely correct the first time and every time thereafter."[8] In terms of information systems, quality costs can take on different meanings, depending on the perspective from which they're viewed. From an application development perspective, quality costs would include the cost of:

- Correcting errors due to misunderstanding the business requirements during analysis, design, coding, and testing, and maintenance—up to the application's final delivery.
- Correcting program bugs due to improper implementation of correctly understood requirements such as faulty logic, or inadequate edits. Viewed from the broader perspective of an information technology function or department, our definition of quality costs would expand to include the costs of:

  a. Altering or enhancing applications to support new and changing business requirements—after the application's final delivery.

  b. Effort required to integrate insufficiently documented and incompatible applications.

  c. Effort required to integrate information across applications in the face of unreliable, unknown, or inconsistent data.

  d. Additional data center capacity required due to inefficient application execution.

From a corporate or enterprise perspective, quality costs would include business-related costs, such as:

- The cost of low productivity operations attributable to information systems that are difficult and cumbersome to use and that provide less than adequate information.

---

[8]Ernest C. Hugh, Ed., *Total Quality: An Executive's Guide for the 1990s,* Dow Jones-Irwin, Illinois, 1990, Chapter 1 "The Quality Imperative," by Ronald M. Fortuna. For an in-depth treatment of quality costs, see John J. Heldt and Daniel J. Costa, *Quality Pays,* Hitchcock Publishing Company, 1988, Pages 1-24.

- Lost opportunity costs due to the information technology function's inability to deliver required functionality in time to support time-and-information-dependent business initiatives.
- The cost of negotiating and competing with less information than the company would have if all of the needed information could be delivered in a usable form, when and where it was needed.

Let's take a closer look at how ADW- and IEF-based integrated CASE affects each of our traditional software quality attributes and how CASE can affect application development, the information technology function, and indeed an entire company, through quality costs.

### How CASE affects correctness

CASE has a profound and positive effect on correctness, especially in terms of applications fulfilling their customer's mission objectives. While traditionally developed applications may meet their specifications, the specifications—and all too often the development team's interpretation of the specifications—on which the applications are based, don't always fully satisfy their user's objectives or intent. Applications that are based on specifications developed through rigorous and detailed ADW- or IEF-based analysis of a business area's problems and requirements tend to satisfy their user's mission objectives and intent with higher consistency and to a far greater extent that with traditional application development. When the application development cycle begins with ADW- or IEF-based planning, and the planning and development efforts are vertically integrated, the generated applications support not only their user's mission objectives, but also those of the company. (See Fig. 13.4.)

### How CASE affects reliability

If reliability is defined to include mean time to failure (MTTF), and mean time to repair (MTTR),[9] the effect of CASE on information system reliability

| Effect on correctness: SIGNIFICANT INCREASE |
|---|

**Fig. 13.4** How CASE affects correctness.

[9]This definition of information system reliability, which was suggested by Roger Pressman in *Software Engineering: A Practitioner's Approach,* Third Edition, McGraw-Hill, 1992, Page 582, is particularly useful when examining how CASE affects reliability because both mean time to failure and mean time to repair are effected by CASE. For an excellent discussion on the relationship of design, reliability, and quality, which is applicable to information systems, see J.M. Juran, *Juran On Quality By Design,* The Free Press, New York, 1992, Pages 1-115.

| Effect on reliability: SIGNIFICANT INCREASE |
|---|

**Fig. 13.5** How CASE affects reliability.

can be both positive and significant. A more thorough analysis, cleaner designs, generated code, and the added integrity afforded by implementing business rules in terms of data instead of process, tend to significantly increase MTTF for ADW- and IEF-developed applications. MTTR is reduced through: use of CASE-based analysis and design models to predict the unforeseen (and sometimes catastrophic) consequences of correcting software failures, and better division of application development projects resulting from CASE tool-enabled C-R-U-D entity-type-to-process affinity analysis. (See Fig. 13.5.)

### How CASE affects efficiency

CASE generally has a negative effect on the efficiency with which information systems execute. The two reasons for the decrease in efficiency of CASE-based applications are the:

- Lack of direct control over, and lack of ability to optimize, the source code that code generators produce.
- Increase in storage and data accesses required to implement business rules in terms of data instead of process.

Although the decrease in efficiency caused by CASE can be mitigated by automated optimization of the generated code and by expressing rules in terms of process, the increases would come at the expense of reliability—and often maintainability as well. Efficiency therefore represents an area in which different quality attributes can come into conflict. (See Fig. 13.6.)

### How CASE affects integrity

The use of ADW- or IEF-based CASE to develop information systems doesn't affect integrity in terms of increasing or reducing the ability of unauthorized persons to access a system, or a system's ability to withstand an attack by viruses. Security routines, which are an information system's first line of defense against unauthorized access, generally fall

| Effect on efficiency: DECREASE |
|---|

**Fig. 13.6** How CASE affects efficiency.

Effect on integrity: NONE

**Fig. 13.7** How CASE affects integrity.

outside of the portions of the application generated through CASE. Since neither ADW or IEF currently provide facilities to enhance system security, applications generated using these tools generally achieve integrity via calls to external routines, as do many traditionally developed systems. (See Fig. 13.7.)

### How CASE affects usability

The effects of CASE on information system usability are mixed. Applications generated using ADW or IEF afford their developers limited control over user interfaces compared with the control they would have if the systems were hand coded. When high productivity is achieved by developing systems from reusable components, or by using CASE tool features such as the IEF's implicit scrolling, even more control over the user interface is lost. Again we see the achievement of a quality attribute coming into conflict with another desirable attribute of CASE, this time the most sought-after CASE result—productivity.

Paradoxically, the same CASE results—object reuse and high productivity—can also increase usability. For instance, the use of screen templates, a common occurrence with ADW- and IEF-developed systems, can increase consistency, as can the reuse of certain objects, such as IEF Exit States. The high productivity with which CASE-developed systems can be maintained can also be used to regenerate systems with altered functionality that precisely meets new business requirements, eliminating the need for awkward workarounds—a common occurrence with traditionally developed systems, and a prime cause of poor usability. (See Fig. 13.8.)

### How CASE affects maintainability

The time and effort required to locate and correct objects that cause errors are substantially reduced by the logical and physical models from which ADW- and IEF-based systems are generated, CASE tool reports showing where analysis and design objects are used, and the high level of the action diagrams that drive ADW and IEF code generators. The same

Effect on usability: MIXED

**Fig. 13.8** How CASE affects usability.

Effect on maintainability: SIGNIFICANT COST REDUCTION

**Fig. 13.9** How CASE affects maintainability.

CASE facilities can be useful in identifying the impact of fixing an error on other parts of the system—a potentially costly problem when maintaining large-scale traditionally developed systems. Reaping this quality benefit, however, requires that the analysis and design models are kept strictly up to date. (See Fig. 13.9.)

## How CASE affects testability

Although neither ADW or IEF address testing directly by automating the testing process, the effort required to test a system can be reduced by these CASE tools, provided that testing begins early enough to take advantage of vertical CASE tool integration. Testing performed during an ADW or IEF analysis to ensure that the models are fully consistent with each other and that they faithfully reflect the business area's requirements and rules, can substantially reduce the amount of testing required during design and construction. The reduction in effort comes from testing analysis models and correcting model defects, which is many times less costly than the equivalent testing downstream, after the database and parts of the system have been generated. The problem here, and the reason why the reduction in effort required to test CASE-based systems is not always realized, is that insufficient attention is often given to testing during the protracted information engineering analysis.

In design and construction, testing effort can be reduced through a combination of:

- Action diagramming constructs and consistency checks that ensure that action diagrams are syntactically correct.
- Templates that can be used to leverage not only design approaches, but also test cases.

Due to the lack of attention to testing during analysis, and unrecognized design and construction testing leverage points, reduced testing effort remains a potential CASE benefit. (See Fig. 13.10.)

Effect on testability: POTENTIAL REDUCED EFFORT

**Fig. 13.10** How CASE affects testability.

Effect on flexibility: POTENTIAL REDUCED EFFORT

**Fig. 13.11** How CASE affects flexibility.

### How CASE affects flexibility

Flexibility costs, also referred to as perfective maintenance costs,[10] are reduced by CASE in two ways. The primary way in which CASE reduces flexibility costs is through the higher productivity with which it enables new functionality and features to be added to a system. The second way that CASE reduces flexibility costs is by providing a road map, in the form of analysis and design models, showing how and where the new functionality can be added with the least disruption and effort. These maintenance costs can, of course, only be reduced in this manner if the functionality and features being added fall within the CASE tool's capabilities and the analysis and design models are up to date so that they faithfully reflect the current state of the generated system. The reduction in effort required to modify CASE-developed systems is therefore a potential reduction that may not always be realized. (See Fig. 13.11.)

### How CASE affects portability

CASE can help reduce portability costs, or adaptive maintenance costs, by providing the means to regenerate CASE-based applications in new target technologies. Although database designs and user interfaces may have to be optimized to take full advantage of specific new technology features and quirks, substantial time and effort can often be saved. The catch is that regeneration of CASE-based systems into new target technologies only works when the technologies are supported by the CASE tool or by a third-party code generator that's fully compatible with the CASE tool. An important consideration when using third-party generators is that if the code generator interface doesn't support forward and reverse integration, the analysis and design models can lose their applicability over time, and with this loss, the ability of the CASE tool to reduce maintenance and flexibility costs. Portability is therefore a potential CASE benefit. (See Fig. 13.12.)

Effect on portability: POTENTIAL REDUCED EFFORT

**Fig. 13.12** How CASE affects portability.

---

[10]Roger Pressman, *Software Engineering: A Practitioner's Approach,* Third Edition, McGraw-Hill, 1992, Pages 663-665.

| Effect on interoperability: SIGNIFICANTLY REDUCED EFFORT |
|---|

**Fig. 13.13** How CASE affects reusability.

### How CASE affects reusability

Although reusability of system components is encouraged by information engineering, and enabled by ADW and IEF, this benefit remains elusive for many CASE users. The reason is that significant reuse can become a reality only when cultural and administrative barriers are addressed (see chapter 10). Reusability therefore remains a potential, rather than widely realized, quality benefit of CASE. (See Fig. 13.13.)

### How CASE affects interoperability

ADW and IEF, primarily through logical data models developed during planning and analysis, can substantially increase the ease with which programs and systems can be coupled. This benefit is a result of surfacing data inconsistencies early in the development process—ideally, during planning, before CASE-based application development begins—and expending the effort required to resolve inconsistencies. To the extent that planning tools and methodologies are used, this Upper CASE quality benefit can pay substantial dividends during and after development, as applications and their data are linked to provide needed information to the business. (See Fig. 13.14.)

### How CASE affects quality costs

Application development is universally affected by correctness and testability, and the use of ADW or IEF can significantly reduce quality costs in these key areas. For development environments in which target technologies are highly variable, portability quality costs can be significantly reduced as well, provided that the CASE tool code generator's capabilities and limitations are accounted for in the target technology selection process. While reusability can also serve to reduce application development quality costs, this represents an area of potential reduction since making reusability work is tricky and involves much more than CASE. Interoperability can also reduce application development quality costs,

| Effect on interoperability: SIGNIFICANTLY REDUCED EFFORT |
|---|

**Fig. 13.14** How CASE affects interoperability.

Application development quality costs: SIGNIFICANTLY REDUCED

**Fig. 13.15** How CASE affects application development quality costs.

Information technology quality costs: REDUCED

**Fig. 13.16** How CASE affects information technology quality costs.

especially for large organizations in which integration costs figure heavily into application development. (See Fig. 13.15.)

The information technology function may be the place in which ADW and IEF can be used to achieve the greatest reduction in quality costs. The reason for the high cost reduction in this area is that maintainability and flexibility costs account for 70% or more of many information technology budgets. When reductions in application development quality costs are added in, the potential for CASE-based quality increases to impact information technology costs can be significant. For most information technology organizations, this benefit is slightly reduced by the additional data center capacity costs required to offset the reduced efficiency with which CASE-based systems operate. (See Fig. 13.16.)

Company quality costs can be affected in three main ways by ADW- and IEF-based CASE. The first is that information technology quality cost reductions can add directly to the company's profitability or contribution. The combination of greater standardization and potentially reduced usability can have a more mixed effect on company quality costs, as the way these attributes affect costs depends on the way they impact business change management during application roll-out, and ultimately, business area productivity. The third main way in which ADW and IEF can affect quality costs at a company level is by the increased flexibility afforded by CASE being harnessed to provide information technology support for new business initiatives on a more timely basis, reducing the costs of lost opportunities. (See Fig. 13.17.)

## How CASE Can Influence Information Technology Business Effectiveness

In addition to providing productivity and quality improvements that, aside from impacting the company's bottom line, are largely information technol-

Company quality costs: POTENTIALLY REDUCED

**Fig. 13.17** How CASE affects company quality costs.

ogy related, ADW and IEF have the capacity to influence the ways in which information technology supports the business. CASE can increase the ability of information technology functions to support a business by:

- Helping to ensure that the business's strategic objectives are faithfully reflected in its information systems.
- Providing new and enhanced information systems on a more timely basis.
- Helping to ensure that the business's information is consistent, and that the information is available when needed.

When used to support the company's strategic information system planning process, CASE can not only help to document the company's strategic objectives, CSFs, critical assumptions, and information needs for its information technology function to see and understand, but can also help ensure that the company's data and applications support its strategic objectives. This support can be important since company objectives are not always obvious—or sometimes even known—to the individuals who make up its information technology function. Yet, taking strategic objectives, CSFs, critical assumptions, and information needs into account can potentially have a major impact on the company's ability to leverage its information and information technology assets for strategic advantage.

In addition to providing data and information systems that are strategically relevant, the capacity of ADW and IEF to increase the productivity and quality of the information systems delivery process can be harnessed to deliver applications to their business users much more quickly. In today's rapidly changing, information-intensive business environment, timing differences between early and late delivery of new information and processing capabilities can be used by a company to garner substantial competitive advantage or even to stay in business in the face of a poor economy and intense competition.

The combination of data consistency, a consequence of vertically and horizontally integrated logical data models at the enterprise and business area levels, and the increased interoperability afforded by CASE can add significantly to the accessibility and usability of a company's data—its information asset. For most companies, especially when they're large and geographically dispersed, consistent and integrated data is the basis upon which many meaningful information systems are built.

## Conclusions

CASE is becoming a mature and ubiquitous information technology and has the potential to solve many of the problems that have been experienced by companies engaged in large-scale information system development. When properly implemented and used, ADW and IEF can not only substantially increase application development productivity and quality, but also significantly decrease the time required to develop and maintain strategically relevant information systems.

But ADW and IEF represent more than just another new information technology. When used to support information-engineering-based integrated CASE, they represent an entirely new paradigm for application development—a reengineering of the way applications are conceived, developed, introduced, and maintained—a development paradigm that can affect the way the entire company interacts with its information technology resource, and a paradigm that can also be difficult and tricky to successfully implement.

For this new technology to be put to productive use, the technology, business, coordination, development project, and people-related risks that accompany CASE must be understood and managed. CASE tools such as ADW and IEF are complex and must be understood in terms of their metamodels, the techniques, methodologies, and target technologies that they can support, their vertical and horizontal integration capabilities, and value added consistency checks. The CASE-based methodology, an absolute requirement for success with ADW or IEF, must be carefully chosen for development features, CASE tool support, and cultural compatibility and impact. Information technology, business user, and management cultures, and the ways in which they interact with each other, can all be affected by CASE. CASE-related needs, expectations (which are almost universally inappropriate), skills, and appropriateness for each of these cultures must therefore be accounted for and carefully managed.

It's therefore neither a simplification nor an understatement to say that implementing ADW- or IEF-based CASE, so that a company can reap its broad array of benefits, can be difficult, and its implementation is accompanied by considerable risk. However large the problems and risks, my experience and firm belief are that successful implementation of CASE is achievable in most companies, provided that its problems and risks are acknowledged, understood, and properly managed.

I'm interested in learning about your experiences with and comments on implementation and use of ADW- and IEF-based CASE. You can reach me at:

Syberg Associates, Inc.
52 Vanderbilt Ave.
New York, New York 10017

# Index

## A



## B



## C

## P



## R



## S



## T

## U



## V



## W

# About the Author

John Stone is a recognized expert in strategic and tactical planning, business re-engineering, the practical application of Computer Aided Software Engineering (CASE), and developing and implementing information systems. His clients include such well-known companies as Mobil Oil, Procter & Gamble, *Reader's Digest*, Allied-Signal, Schering-Plough, and Met Life.

John Stone is a principal of Siberg Associates, a New York-based consulting firm that helps senior management formulate, design, and implement IT and business strategy so that the holistic process becomes part of their organization's culture.